100 Media Moments That Changed America

100 Media Moments That Changed America

Jim Willis

GREENWOOD PRESS

An Imprint of ABC-CLIO, LLC

A B C ⬤ C L I O

Santa Barbara, California • Denver, Colorado • Oxford, England

Library of Congress Cataloging-in-Publication Data

Willis, Jim.
  100 media moments that changed America / Jim Willis.
    p. cm.
  Includes bibliographical references and index.
    ISBN 978–0–313–35517–2 (hardcover : alk. paper) — ISBN 978–0–313–35518–9 (ebook)
1. Mass media—United States—History. I. Title. II. Title: One hundred media moments that
changed America.
P92.U5W525   2010
302.230973—dc22   2009042490

14 13 12 11 10   1 2 3 4 5

ISBN 978–0–313–35517–2   EISBN 978–0–313–35518–9
This book is also available on the World Wide Web as an eBook.
Visit www.abc-clio.com for details.

Greenwood Press
An Imprint of ABC-CLIO, LLC

ABC-CLIO, LLC
130 Cremona Drive, P.O. Box 1911
Santa Barbara, California 93116-1911

This book is printed on acid-free paper ∞

Manufactured in the United States of America

To Anne who provides a reason for it all

Contents

One Hundred Defining Moments: An Introduction to the Concept

Like any other institution, the media of newspapers, magazines, radio, television, and their online counterparts have been largely defined by many signature moments. These have been times of invention and reinvention, of developments both failed and successful, of overcoming some serious challenges, of breakthroughs, and of meshing well or poorly the frequently different goals of selling a product vs. selling a service. However, what is true of the media, which may not be so true of other institutions, is that many of these developments and victories have also produced changes in American society as a whole. A few examples might suffice to illustrate this point:

- When early American newspapers published *The Federalist* series in the late 18th century to promote ratification of the new Constitution, voters reacted by approving it, especially after the Bill of Rights was attached.

- When William Randolph Hearst promoted heavy coverage of the Cuban insurrection against Spain in the late 19th century, mostly for the purposes of beating Joseph Pulitzer in their newspaper circulation battles, America reacted by going to war with Spain. That deal seemed sealed after Hearst single-handedly declared the mysterious sinking of the U.S. battleship *Maine* to be the work of Spanish agents.

- When the nation's media presented nonstop coverage of the assassination and funeral of President John F. Kennedy in November 1963, the effect was a nation unified in its mourning and determined to move forward. The same effect was produced following the Oklahoma City bombing in April 1995, and the attacks on New York City's Twin Towers and Washington's Pentagon in September 2001.

- When 19-year-old Mark Zuckerberg developed a college posting site in 2004 called "Facebook," he opened up a social networking site that seemed to forever change the way people meet and communicate with each other, especially in the online universe. As these young people flocked to Facebook, many became addicted to it and all of them spent less time with the traditional media of television, radio, magazines, and newspapers.

- When Alan Funt developed the concept for a television show called *Candid Camera* in 1948, he launched a prime-time, reality-based entertainment program that has appeared on television in every decade since then as a regular series or special. Although designed as entertainment, *Candid Camera* depicted everyday people reacting naturally to some very funny staged provocations. The way these individuals did that showed a lot about human behavior. But Funt did far more by introducing American television audiences to "reality television" and opening the door for many more shows in years to come, including the popular *Survivor.*

There have been so many of these defining moments, in fact, that paring them down to 100 is no easy task. Keep in mind we are talking about a time span of more than 300 years. This is especially true when we are talking about not just the news media. This list also includes a few relevant representations of the entertainment media whose advertising revenue often makes it possible—especially in the case of television—to air an abundance of news programming. Even in cases where these are included, however, such as the entries on *Candid Camera* and MTV, these programs can also fall under the umbrella of news/public affairs shows for a number of reasons. *Candid Camera* is one example and the reason was just described for that. And MTV has become not only an important venue for music (changing the recording industry in the process), but the network has also developed nontraditional journalism that reaches younger Americans who might otherwise have tuned out of traditional news presentations.

It is important to note that the 100 entries (and 10 other vital moments appended later) *are not necessarily meant to be the most important* moments in media history, although most are. This is not a "Top 100" list, but it is an annotated list of 100 moments, some which took time in unfolding, which have been extremely important in the development of the media and—in most cases—the development of America and its culture as well. That makes the task somewhat easier because the author doesn't necessarily have to defend the inclusion of, say, the founding of NBC but not of ABC. In fact, NBC was the *first* network, and the line had to be drawn somewhere, given the parameters of 100 entries. Nevertheless, the list that is this book is certain to produce differences of opinion among readers. It might make things clearer to first list some key criteria that were used to decide the moments chosen for this particular list. These include:

- The event or person had an important significance in the development of American society. It had to change society—or at least a large portion of it—in some meaningful way.
- The event or person had important significance for the development of the media themselves. It had to change the media or journalism in some important way.
- The person and/or news medium gave a voice to those who needed a voice.

- The *way in which the moment was presented* by the media had to affect American society in some significant way.
- The development reflected an important change underway in society.
- The development or individual was just too unique not to be included.

Moments discussed in this book score high on more than one—and in some cases all six—of these criteria. They are not the only developments that might do so, but these were some of the most fascinating. As a journalist for more than a decade who has taught the history of journalism at universities for the past three decades, these are the moments that I have discussed most often in class. New ones are being added all the time. Some moments, like the Pearl Harbor attack in 1941, are vital to American History but didn't change the way media report the news. As a result, they are not included, although this event is discussed in a sidebar on p. 196.

A word about my operational definition of "moment" seems in order, too. Many of the entries in this book are, in fact, actual moments or times when an invention—such as Facebook—came into existence. In some cases, however, I use "moment" to define a process that took some time to develop. Such would be the case with the transition from television film reporting to electronic news gathering (ENG) and real-time reporting. A few of the "moments" are collective in nature because they track more than one individual who represented an overall trend in the media. Such is the case with the entry about fact or fiction in journalism and the trouble that the mistakes made by Janet Cooke, Stephen Glass, and Jayson Blair caused for media credibility.

The media has contributed mightily to the growth of America over the centuries, and vice versa. Any society is only as free as its media, and the media are only as free as their societal leaders allow them to be. America is extremely fortunate in having among its founding fathers, men who understood the importance of free speech and a free press to a democratic system of government. It was James Madison who saw the necessity of attaching safeguards of individual liberties to the Constitution. He realized the states would probably not ratify the document without such safeguards. Thus the Bill of Rights became those first 10 amendments and, after a bit of revision, the First Amendment emerged as the great safeguard of religious freedom alongside freedoms of speech and the press. Although as president he would later suffer the same frustrations as all presidents in dealing with the press, Thomas Jefferson is still remembered for uttering his famous belief that, were it left to him to decide between a free nation without a free press, or a free press without a free nation, he would not hesitate to choose the latter.

Part of the great American experiment is, in fact, this balancing of freedoms. For even in America, journalists are not absolutely free to say and write what they please without fear of consequence. The nation has gone through periods where some media voices have been silenced for a time, as in the early 20th Century under provisions of the Espionage Act and the Trading with the Enemy Act. Some provisions in these acts seemed directed at socialist media voices critical of American policy, especially with regard to the conduct of World War I. Those two acts no longer dog American journalists, yet still there are serious consequences when journalists stray too far across the line in damaging others' reputations. Laws regarding libel and invasion of privacy are still very much alive and can still cost the media mightily. Journalists have also realized that often the First Amendment freedom of the press has come into conflict with the Sixth and Fourteenth Amendments safeguarding individuals' rights to fair trials and due process of law. In those cases, the courts have had to intervene to decide which freedom should take precedence at that moment. Finally, the media also face economic pressures, at times, for being too far out of the mainstream in reporting and opinions. Often advertisers have dropped certain media, fearing they may be alienating audiences, afraid those audiences might associate the advertised product with the offending media outlet.

The best American journalists understand that the freedoms granted them under the revered First Amendment are not licenses to air or publish recklessly. Like all freedoms, they are to be used responsibly and, if they are not, the consequences may well kick in. The history of American journalism has had moments—some of the more shocking ones are outlined in this book—where media have gone too far in trying to build circulation or audience ratings. But there are so many more moments where journalistic freedoms have been used very responsibly and have contributed to the betterment of American society. It has been a rewarding experience in discussing these moments, and I hope the discussion of the moments of irresponsibility will act as a reminder that any freedoms can be misused or abused.

I decided to organize the book chronologically, starting in the colonial years of America and ending with January 2009, when my writing was finished. So the first section focuses on the new nation from 1690 to 1799, the second section covers the 19th century, the third covers the 20th century, and the fourth covers the 21st century up to 2009. Even a casual glance at the book will show the lion's share of entries fall within the 20th century which was, of course, the era in which most American institutions grew and flourished. It is also the era that produced two world wars and the time in which America began on horseback and ended up flying routine space shuttles. It was the century in which we began reading newspapers and wound up watching real-time, satellite-based television reporting of the Gulf War. Although there are fewer entries in the 17th, 18th, and 19th centuries, those entries are just as significant; in some cases, as with the creation of the First Amendment, even more important. As for the 21st century, well it is just beginning, isn't it? Yet already the developments have been amazing and have caused significant changes in the way we spend our time and in the ways we relate to each other.

At the end of the entries, I decided to append a section called "Stretching the List of 100" which could easily have made my initial list of entries—and which possibly should have . . . if I could have just decided which others to delete.

Any book is a compilation of ideas that come from a variety of sources. Certainly this book is no exception, and I am indebted to the many historians, researchers, industry observers, and writers who have explored these moments and many others in great depth. The sources are a mix of traditional print sources, credible online sources, and —in some cases—interviews which the author did in person or which were carried on television news and public affairs programs. A few sources stand out because they are used more than others. They include media historians Frank Luther Mott, Edwin and Michael Emery, Nancy Roberts, John Tebbel, William David Sloan, James G. Stovall, and James D. Startt, Louis L. Snyder, Richard Morris, and Eric Burns. The Museum of Broadcast Communication is a storehouse of information regarding the electronic media, as are the web sites for ABC, NBC, CBS, Fox, CNN, and PBS, each of which has discussions relevant to each company's history. Company web sites for print media were also useful in this regard. All of the photos used in this book came from AP Images.

Many other sources went into the research for this book as the notes section of the book will reveal. I wanted to let the narratives flow as unfettered as possible and tried not to overburden the text with citation numbers, and have saved them for either direct quotes and/or for facts and figures or points that may be controversial or seem opinionated.

On a personal level, I am indebted to several individuals who have made the research and writing of this book easier for me with their support and patience. These include my wife Anne and my sister, C. J., my faculty colleagues in the Department of Communication Studies at Azusa Pacific University, my dean David Weeks (who jogged my thinking in two conversations to include two important entries I had underestimated), and my ever-capable administrative assistant Debbie Cram.

Timeline of Media History

EUROPEAN ROOTS

1439 Johannes Gutenberg invents and uses movable type, enabling documents to be mass produced. This has a huge impact on the Reformation and Renaissance.

1455 Gutenberg publishes the Bible, which was the first major book to come off of a printing press. Some 180 copies were printed.

1644 Poet John Milton publishes the *Areopagitica* as an appeal to Parliament to rescind the Licensing Order of June 16, 1643. Milton's work stands as a classic defense of freedom of the press. It includes the notion, "He who kills a person kills a reasonable creature . . . but he who kills a book kills reason itself."

COLONIAL DEVELOPMENTS

1690 Postmaster Benjamin Harris publishes the first newspaper in the American colonies. It is *Publick Occurrences*, and it lasts only one issue before it is shut down by governing authorizes.

1704 Postmaster John Campbell publishes the *Boston Newsletter* which becomes America's first regularly published newspaper.

1719 The *Boston Gazette* is launched and is destined to become the leading newspaper of the American Revolution. Under editors Benjamin Edes and John Gill, it publishes letters and essays of the Sons of Liberty, fanning war flames. It is joined by another great Revolutionary War newspaper, *The Massachusetts Spy*.

1733 John Peter Zenger launches the *New York Weekly Journal* and defies the colonial governor in criticizing him. He is arrested in 1734 and tried in 1735 for seditious libel, but his attorney Andrew Hamilton pleads for "truth as a defense." The jury acquits Zenger, but the law stays the same for a half century, although Zenger is the last colonial publisher to be tried for seditious libel.

1732 Benjamin Franklin is known for making journalism respectable. He publishes *Poor Richard's Almanac* as a publisher in Pennsylvania after buying the *Pennsylvania Gazette*.

THE NEW NATION

1776 On January 10, writer and former corset-maker Thomas Paine anonymously publishes a monograph called *Common Sense* which calls for a declaration of American independence. Some 100,000 copies of it are sold throughout the colonies, igniting the spirit for independence and revolution. He follows this up with *The Crisis* pamphlet series in the early months of the war to strengthen the revolutionaries' resolve.

1787– Some 85 articles that have come to be called *The Federalist Papers* appear in
1788 the *New York Independent Journal* and other newspapers urging passage of the new Constitution and a strong central government.

1788 The states ratify the new Constitution, which now contains 10 amendments known as the Bill of Rights. The First Amendment to that Constitution specifically protects the freedom of the press.

1831 William Lloyd Garrison, a white journalist, launches *The Liberator* in Boston as an antislavery newspaper preaching abolitionism and igniting sectarian tempers which ultimately explode into civil war.

MODERN JOURNALISM BEGINS

1833 Benjamin Day publishes the *New York Sun* and is the first to sell his daily newspaper for one cent, launching the Penny Press era and ushering in the modern newspaper which features advertising and news as well as editorial content. News becomes a product as well as a service.

1835 James Gordon Bennett expands and solidifies the place of the modern daily newspaper, founding the *New York Morning Herald* and imbuing it with a great reporting staff which, among other things, invents the journalistic interview.

1841 Horace Greeley founds the *New York Tribune* which becomes the leading Whig newspaper in America. It gives a platform to the crusading and advocating voice of Greeley, whose eccentricities and varied causes are revealed to many happy readers in the pages of the *Tribune*. He also starts a weekly edition of the *Tribune* which is read nationwide and which pioneers take with them as they conquer the West.

1847 Frederick Douglass, a black journalist and the best-known black man in America at the time, launches the *North Star* as an ardent antislavery newspaper.

1848 New York publishers meet and create the Harbor News Association, which becomes the forerunner to the modern Associated Press wire service which doesn't take its modern form until 1900.

1851 Henry J. Raymond and George Jones launch the *New York Times* which is today the best known American newspaper in the world.

1878 Edward Wyllis Scripps starts the *Cleveland Penny Press* as the first link in the first chain of American newspapers. At the height of business, the Scripps chain will grow to include 32 fully-owned newspapers plus shares in 15 others.

1883 Joseph Pulitzer buys the *New York World* and builds it into the best-selling newspaper in America, launching the Yellow Journalism Era of highly-charged news reporting and sensationalism. Even so, his editorial page is a crusading giant, calling for reforms in government and society that benefit the common people.

1895 William Randolph Hearst comes to New York City to do battle with Pulitzer and buys the *New York Journal*, raising sensationalism to a new level as the two newspaper titans battle it out for subscribers and journalistic glory. Hearst's sensationalism seems to know no boundaries, and he is often credited with America's entry into the Spanish-American war with his coverage of problems in Spain.

1895 William Allen White buys the *Emporia Gazette* in Kansas for $3,000 and becomes the first man to gain fame as a small-town editor, eventually winning the Pulitzer Prize for editorial writing.

1896 Adolph Ochs buys the *New York Times* after its circulation had dropped to 9,000. He begins the process to turn it into the best daily newspaper in America.

20TH CENTURY DEVELOPMENTS

1901 Guglielmo Marconi, the "father of radio," transmits a wireless telegraph code across the Atlantic Ocean. The wireless era is born. Reginald Fessenden and Lee DeForest expand Marconi's work, sending voices over the air.

1912 The Radio Act of 1912 is passed by Congress after the *Titanic* goes down. It is learned hundreds of lives were lost because many ships in the area left their radio receivers unattended. This act set the future course for government regulation of broadcasting.

1920 A Westinghouse engineer named Frank Conrad broadcasts music from his Pittsburgh-area garage in 1920. Station 8XK is born as the first radio station and morphs into the giant KDKA, still on the air today.

1922 WEAF in New York City accepts the first radio advertising in 1922. "Toll broadcasting" becomes the means to finance broadcasting. The sale of advertising leads to establishing networks.

1926 RCA sets up a 24-station network and calls it the "National Broadcasting Company" (NBC).

1927 The Columbia Phonograph Company starts a competing radio network called the Columbia Broadcasting System, or CBS.

1927 The Radio Act of 1927 is passed after the 1912 act lapses. It is a time of chaos on the radio airwaves as competing stations often use the same frequency. The 1927 act assigns frequencies and licenses; broadcasters become "custodians" of the public's airwaves. The act morphs into the Communication Act of 1934, which regulates all of broadcasting and lasts most of the 20th Century until being revised in 1996.

1927 Bell Telephone labs and American Telephone and Telegraph (AT&T) give a public television demonstration in America over both wire and radio circuits. Pictures and sound are sent by wire from Washington, D.C. to New York City. A wireless demonstration also takes place from Whippany, New Jersey, to New York City. The age of television is born, albeit progress is delayed two decades by the development of radio and World War II.

1935 By now, radio has gained access to the news wires of the Associated Press and United Press International, and news finds a broadcast home. Reporters like William L. Shirer and Edward R. Murrow are destined to become legends.

1948 The first network television newscast premiers with anchor Douglas Edwards. The program is The *CBS-TV News*, later changed to *Douglas Edwards with the News*. NBC follows the next year with John Cameron Swayze's *Camel News Caravan*. Both programs are 15-minute shows.

1952 TV becomes a key force in the American political process during this year's presidential campaign between Dwight D. Eisenhower and Adlai Stevenson. For the first time, the public is exposed to political commercials, documentaries, and election-night specials.

1953 The FCC approves RCA's compatible color system for television. The first color program didn't come for another five years, however. It was *Bonanza*.

1953 Edward R. Murrow zeroes in on Sen. Joseph McCarthy and his witch hunt for communists in the government. Murrow uses his show, *See It Now*, to expose the junior senator from Wisconsin, much to the chagrin of CBS management, worried about alienating audiences.

1956 Videotaping system is invented and by 1960, most live programming gives way to taped programs.

1960 Some 70 million Americans gather around their TV sets to tune in the first televised debate between a Republican and Democratic nominee for president of the United States, and a new era of political coverage is born. The Republican is Vice President Richard M. Nixon, and his Democratic challenger is Senator John F. Kennedy.

1962 Walter Cronkite takes over as anchor for the *CBS Evening News*. He will anchor the newscast for two decades until 1982 and will become known as "the most trusted man in America." His show was the first half-hour network television newscast.

1963 Television shows its power to unite a nation in mourning as President John F. Kennedy is gunned down in the streets of Dallas, and television networks saturate the coverage and suspend all regularly-scheduled entertainment programming during a four-day period of national mourning.

1967 CBS producer Don Hewitt conceives of a news magazine show that will provide more time for stories addressing issues of importance to the American people. The show is called *60 Minutes*. It set the standard for TV newsmagazine programs, and more than four decades later, it is still a weekly ratings leader for CBS.

1969 The U.S. military creates a computer network called ARPAnet, which stands for Advanced Research Projects Agency Network. The Pentagon constructs it to link military contractors and universities doing research for the military. It is the beginning of the Internet.

1971 A secret study on the history of relations between the United States and Vietnam is leaked to the press. The *New York Times* and *The Washington Post* decide to publish the contents, which become known as the "Pentagon Papers." The administration of President Richard Nixon tries to block further publication of the documents, but the Supreme Court rules that the government cannot engage in prior restraint of information, referring to the First Amendment of the Constitution.

1972 Two young reporters for *The Washington Post* launch a series of investigations into illegal activities that will lead to the downfall of a U.S. president. The reporters are Bob Woodward and Carl Bernstein, the president is Richard Nixon, and the saga came to be known as "Watergate."

1975 Gerald Levin, a young executive at Time Inc., comes up with a new direction for television. He wants to create a network exclusively for existing local cable operators to supplement the broadcast networks. He decides to build the network on an existing time property called Home Box Office, or HBO. Its launch signals the beginning of cable television as a major force in the industry and is the start of cable networks as we know them today.

1976 On April 1, 1976, Steve Wozniak and Steve Jobs release the Apple I home computer and start Apple Computers. Although not the first home computer, Apple launches national interest in owning home computers, and the first Mac is just around the corner.

1980 Using an infrastructure he already has in place with his "Superstation" WTBS in Atlanta, Ted Turner launches the first 24-hour cable news network and changes the landscape of television news. The network is called CNN.

1982 The Gannett Company, under the leadership of Allen Neuharth, launches the nation's first comprehensive national daily newspaper and shakes up the newspaper world. The newspaper is called *USA Today*, and before long, nearly every newspaper in the country will be copying some of its unique features.

1984 Stanley Hubbard, owner of KSTP-TV in Minnesota, weds satellite communication with television and joins General Motors in offering a direct broadcast satellite service. Viewers can pick up TV signals from almost anywhere with home dishes about the size of large pizzas.

1993 CBS producer Lowell Bergman of *60 Minutes* teams up with Dr. Jeffrey Wigand, ousted head of research for Brown & Williamson Tobacco Co., to set the stage for exposing the process of "impact-boosting" of the addictive effects of cigarettes. CBS management delays the airing of the Wigand interview with newsman Mike Wallace, however, fearing a massive lawsuit. The incident spotlights the "chilling effect" that legal threats can have on reporting.

2003 War reporting regains the look of the Vietnam era where journalists are allowed to be embedded with frontline troops as Operation Iraqi Freedom, more commonly called the War with Iraq, begins. The graphic coverage of Vietnam had convinced the military to keep the press at arm's length in future wars, but the "embed" system returned and was updated for the long-running war in Iraq.

2006 NBC *Today Show* host Katie Couric breaks the glass ceiling for women in television news and becomes the first solo female anchor and managing editor for a nightly network evening newscast when CBS hires her to anchor the *CBS Evening News*.

THE AGE OF MEDIA CONVERGENCE

1991 British engineer Tim Berners-Lee creates an addressing system that can connect every computer in the world. He calls his creation the World Wide Web.

1993 Illinois graduate student Marc Andreessen develops a software program, Mosaic, to improve computer interconnections and allow scientists to browse each others' work. He and his colleagues tweak Mosaic into becoming Netscape, and it is the first Internet browser. Commercialization of the Internet moves into high gear.

1998 Larry Page and Sergey Brin create the search engine Google. Its genius is its massive database combined with "crawlers" that roam throughout the Web looking for new and existing sites, and then rates those sites in terms of relevant key works used. The age of media convergence has begun.

2004 A 19-year-old computer programming whiz and Harvard dropout named Mark Zuckerberg creates what will become the dominant social networking site of the early 21st century. It is called Facebook, and the idea spurs the creation of Twitter.

2005 On February 15, three men still in their early 20s start an Internet company out of their garage. The company is called YouTube, and it changes the way Americans search for, post, exchange, and process information.

Part I

The New Nation: 1690–1799

After several decades of hacking a series of colonies out of the wilderness of the New World, many early Americans set their sights to creating information systems from town hall bulletin boards, to discussions at taverns and coffee houses, to essays and pamphlets, and finally—in 1690—with the publication of the first American newspaper. That paper lasted only a single issue before a regular newspaper would begin publication 14 years later. The 18th century was America's century of revolutionary ideas which grew into a fever that fanned into a war, independence, and a new Constitution. Journalists were prime movers in all of this, and the following developments and individuals are indicative of how important this time was to the development of America and to the mass media.

I. AMERICA'S FIRST NEWSPAPER

While the first successful American colony was established in 1607 at Jamestown on a small river near the Chesapeake Bay, it would be followed three years later by the first New England settlement at New Plymouth, now the town of Plymouth, Massachusetts. With the development of the New England colonies, along with those further south along the Atlantic Coast, the American experiment was in full swing. However, it would not be until 1690 that the first American newspaper would appear, and then it would publish only one issue. That newspaper was *Publick Occurrences Both Foreign and Domestick*, and it was published by a colonial printer and bookseller named Benjamin Harris. The newspaper appeared in a single issue on September 25, 1690, and its stated purpose was that "the country shall be furnished once a month with an account of such considerable things as have arrived unto our notice."[1]

The newspaper was miniscule in size in comparison with later publications, but it was the breakthrough in public information the colonists had been looking for, and the people of Boston embraced it heartily. Here for the first time, a courageous London expatriate who had fled England after encountering trouble with British authorities over his writings there, risked legal trouble again by publishing information without authority of the Crown. Among the contents of that first and only issue were insinuations of incest in the French royal family.

The British authorities were less than amused over such a breach by a brash wildcat publisher and decided to thwart any other such attempts, thereby setting the standard for printing restrictions that would eventually help fan the flames for the Revolutionary War. On September 29, four days after the publication appeared on the streets of Boston, the Governor and Council of Massachusetts issued a broadside order banning the publication of "anything in Print without License first obtained from those that are or shall be appointed by the Government to grant the same."[2] The law seemed to work, and it was 14 years before the next serious newspaper appeared. That was *The Boston Newsletter*, published on April 24, 1704, by a Boston postmaster named John Campbell. Although it was only a small, single-sheet, double-sided publication, it had the distinction of being the first continuously published newspaper in America, appearing weekly until 1776 and having no competition for its first 15 years until the *Boston Gazette* appeared.

All three of these newspapers were primitive efforts by later newspaper standards, but the *Newsletter* provided colonists with much news from England, together with a smattering of local news, much of it shipping-related. The *Gazette* would become one of the leading revolutionary newspapers, helping to spur colonials on in their fight against the British. It is no accident that the first three American newspapers appeared in New England, and specifically Boston. Indeed, New England was the birthplace of newspapers because it held the largest concentration of colonists and because the educational levels were higher there than in the southern colonies. Also, since New Englanders were more concentrated in Boston and New York, they were more interconnected than their more southern counterparts. Finally—and this would become important later when newspapers turned to advertising as a means of financial support—New England was the commerce and shipping hub of the New World. Hence, that's where the money was.

2. JAMES FRANKLIN DEFIES AUTHORITY

In the era of colonial journalism, one is often drawn to the name of Benjamin Franklin, publisher of the *Pennsylvania Gazette* and a signer of the Declaration of Independence. However, it was Franklin's older brother James who first made an important mark in the history of press freedom on American shores. James was a risk-taking printer in Boston. He was approached by respectable but disgruntled colonials who had dubbed themselves the "Hell-Fire Club," and encouraged him to start a newspaper that was filled with livelier content. Many colonists wanted something more than official pronouncements of the colonial governor, shipping news, and news from England. Franklin accepted the challenge and launched *The New England Courant* in 1721. It was among the first four newspapers to be published in Boston.[3]

From the start, Franklin decided to publish without authority of the colonial government, defying the order that was still in place for publishers to first secure a license to print their newspapers. In addition, Franklin was the first colonial publisher to give readers what they wanted and needed rather than government-controlled and sanctioned information. Franklin, with the help of some members of the Hell-Fire Club, wrote essays and satirical letters similar to the ones found just a decade earlier in *The Spectator*, the popular English paper of Joseph Addison and Richard Steele. To have this kind of humor and satire published in the stronghold of Puritanism was shocking to some, but very welcome to others. Even Ben Franklin contributed to the satirical content, working as an apprentice to James. *The Cambridge History of English and American Literature* notes the following about Ben's contributions:

> The fourteen little essays from Silence Dogood to the editor are among the most readable and charming of Franklin's early imitations, clearly following *The Spectator* ... Silence rambles on amiably enough except for occasional slurs on the New England clergy, in regard to whom the *Courant* was always bitter, and often scurrilous. For the Hell-Fire Club never grasped the inner secret of Mr. Spectator, his urbane, imperturbable, impersonal kindliness of manner. Instead, they vented their hatred of dogmatism and intolerance in personalities so insolent as to become in themselves intolerant. Entertaining, however, the *Courant* is, from first to last, and full of a genuine humour and a shrewd satiric truth to life.[4]

On January 14, 1723, the *Courant* published an "Essay against Hypocrites," referring to (although not directly) Cotton Mather, probably the most well-known Puritan minister at the time and a man who would later be linked to the Salem witch trials. The issue at hand was smallpox inoculation, a new controversial health practice at the time which Mather promoted but which others—including Franklin and his followers—feared would spread smallpox rather than curb it. The essay had a mocking tone to parts of it, and the target was organized religion which was backing smallpox inoculation.

The colonial government took offense at the brashness of James Franklin in publishing without authority—especially publishing such "scurrilous" content. In its warning to Franklin to desist from such publication, the authorities said, "The tendency of the said Paper is to mock Religion, and bring it into Contempt, that the Holy Scriptures are therefore profanely abused, that the Reverend and faithful Ministers of the Gospel are injuriously Reflected on. His Majesty's Government affronted, and the pace and good Order of his Majesty's Subjects of this Province disturbed," the said *Courant*.[5] So James was arrested and taken to jail, to be tried for seditious libel and publishing without authority. While he was in jail, two things happened that became significant in the life of American journalism.

First, a large number of colonists protested his arrest, demanding his release on what were felt to be trumped-up charges. Indeed, Franklin and his newspaper had become an important institution to the colonists, and they couldn't understand why he had been arrested for simply printing entertaining insight and information. The colonial governor realized his administration needed a certain degree of goodwill from colonists in order to govern effectively, and Franklin was released after a few months and never had to face trial.

Second, while Franklin was in jail, his wife Ann continued to publish the *Courant*, although officially Ben Franklin was listed as its publisher before seeing his opportunity to flee his apprenticeship and moving to Pennsylvania. So Ann Franklin became the first woman newspaper publisher in the colonies.

James Franklin tried to keep the *Courant* going, despite the warnings of the colonial authorities that he was walking a thin legal line. But constant sparring with the Mathers and the Puritanical leadership of Boston eventually took its toll on him. After the 255th issue of the *Courant*, dated June 25, 1726, James Franklin folded the operation and moved to Rhode Island, hoping for a more tolerant and liberal environment. He died there in 1735. However, the courage and spunk that he showed in Boston would fuel other prerevolutionary publishers into publishing their newspapers without authority as well. In time, the licensing laws were rendered useless.

3. THE ZENGER CASE

One of the cornerstone freedoms of America is freedom of the press, often taken for granted except by many journalists who understand just how important it is. While it is hard to imagine an America without this basic freedom, Colonial America did not always have it and that is a big reason why it became a part of the First Amendment to the Constitution. It is interesting that a legal case which inspired press freedom in America was actually a case which had no legal effect at the time but which did advocate truth as a defense in libel cases. That case has commonly become known as the Zenger Trial, and it occurred in 1735. It was reported on by John Peter Zenger himself in his *New York Weekly Journal* on August 18, 1735, after his acquittal.

The background of the case is this: Zenger has started the *New York Weekly Journal* in response to an invitation by businessmen who wanted and needed more of a voice in the local government of the New York Colony so they could grow their businesses and prosper. Quickly, however, Zenger came into conflict with New York Governor William Cosby over what Zenger perceived as ineptitude, lax security measures, and manipulation of the colony's legal system to the advantage of a select few. These stories appeared in the *Journal* in 1734, prompting Cosby to have his prosecutor issue a warrant for Zenger's arrest on charges of criminal libel. Zenger wrote a story about that arrest in the November 24, 1734, edition of the *Journal*.

It is important to note that libel law at the time precluded anyone from offering a defense of the statement's truthfulness. It was sufficient for the plaintiff (prosecutor, in the case of criminal libel) to show that a statement was a criticism of the government and, therefore, of the government's authority. That was the law of Britain, and it carried over to the American colonies. Essentially, in fact, the British and colonial rule was, "The greater the truth, the greater the libel." It was reasoned that truth could well result in more harm than a lie since the latter could not be verified. Therefore it was seen that if Zenger admitted to publishing the criticism of Governor Cosby, the case would be over, de facto, and Zenger would be guilty.

It would be some nine months before the prosecution brought Zenger's case to trial. Zenger was kept in jail for this time, and his wife Anna continued to publish the newspaper in his absence, as Ann Franklin did for James. For his attorney, Zenger selected a noted New York lawyer named Andrew Hamilton who played an ace that no one saw coming. Early in the trial, Hamilton admitted that Zenger had written the statements under question, at which point the prosecutor asked Justice James Delancey to declare the trial over and order the jury to convict Zenger. Ignoring that, however, Hamilton surprised everyone by confronting the jury directly to argue the truth of the statements Zenger had published. To the apparent surprise of the prosecution, Delancey let Hamilton have his say, then let the jury retire and consider the verdict instead of declaring a mistrial on the spot. The only apparent reason that Delancey let this go without a mistrial was the popular support for Zenger which had arisen over the past few months among New York residents. In any event, the jury decided to disregard the judge's instructions to find Zenger guilty and instead returned a verdict of not guilty. At this point, Delancey could have overturned the jury's verdict since it went against British law on seditious libel, but he let that verdict stand, and Zenger was acquitted.[6]

One might think this case would have an immediate effect on changing libel law in New York and the other American colonies, but it did not. It was not until 1805—70 years later—that New York changed its libel law to allow truth as a defense. What did occur, however, was the realization that popular opinion was so important to governing officials that no other known charges of seditious libel were levied by the Crown against colonial newspaper publishers. The right to criticize government officials became a de facto right, and the road was paved for eventual press freedom in America.

4. THE *MASSACHUSETTS SPY* INCITES A REVOLUTION

The leaders of the Patriot movement were in trouble by the late 1760s. The colonies were not a tight-knit group in Massachusetts or elsewhere, and if colonists were to become aroused enough about the British occupation to do something serious about it, the Patriots had to be unified and reading from the same page. Enter Isaiah Thomas, a Boston printer with a zeal for getting the British off colonists' backs and the pen and wit to get others fired up. In 1770, Thomas began printing a newspaper that would be a backbone of the American Revolutionary movement in the wonderfully named *Massachusetts Spy*. The paper began as a three-day-a-week publication, although it later shifted to weekly status because of government attempts to suppress it and economic woes. Officially, the paper espoused the Whig doctrine of a set of economic freedoms for the American colonies which would give them control over their own affairs. As the colonies moved toward war with England, however, the *Spy* moved along with them.

Thomas had been an apprentice printer since the age of six and had learned to spell by setting type. A self-taught man, he became a scholar, owner of one of the best libraries in the country, and was the inaugural president of the learned Antiquarian Society.[7] He founded the *Spy* as a partnership with his former boss, Zehariah Fowle. The newspaper would actually wind up surviving, under different incarnations, until 1904. Soon. Thomas bought out Fowle, and the *Spy* became one of the best-read and most influential newspapers in the colonies. Adopting the Whig philosophy of reconciliation with England at the start, he saw this position was not going to work and soon became the Patriot voice of revolution in the colonies. He became enamored with the idea of using his newspaper as a propaganda tool for the Patriot cause and for the push for war. He was an eyewitness to the first battle of the Revolution, and an excerpt of the story he wrote about it is as follows:

> About ten o'clock on the night of the 18th of April, the troops in Boston were discovered to be on the move in a very secret manner, and it was found they were embarking in boats at the bottom of the Common; expresses set off immediately to alarm the country, that they might be on their guard . . . The body of troops in the meantime, under the command Lieutenant Colonel Smith, had crossed the river and landed at Phipp's Farm. They immediately, to the number of 1,000, proceeded to Lexington, six miles below Concord, with great silence. A company of militia of about eighty men, mustered near the meeting house; the troops came in sight of them just before sunrise . . . [8]

Both the *Spy* and the other main Patriot newspaper, the *Boston Gazette*, had to leave Boston as hostilities grew. The *Gazette* was moved to Watertown, while Thomas had his press smuggled out to Worcester where it remained through the war. And, by the end of the Revolutionary War, the *Spy* was recognized as the dominant publisher in Massachusetts. Altogether, Thomas had seven presses and some 150 staffers churning out his newspapers and some 400 books on medicine, science, agriculture, and law. Upon retiring from publishing in 1802, he wrote *The History of Printing in America*, a two-volume classic published in 1810.

5. THE COMMITTEES OF CORRESPONDENCE

In one sense, you could probably call the network that Patriot Samuel Adams put together the first newswire service in America. You could also call it the first—and one of the most successful—attempts at political propaganda in America. Either way, you'd be right when speaking of this pre-Revolutionary War effort to get colonists inflamed and to get the British off their backs. As journalistic historians Michael and Edwin Emery note, "As a propagandist, Adams was without peer."[9] He strongly believed that the colonists had a right to repudiate England, because England had turned its back on them in denying them basic rights of involvement in issues such as taxation. He looked at it the way a lawyer or judge might: if one party

Samuel Adams, political leader and revolutionary statesman, is shown in this undated painting. Adams was born in Boston, Massachusetts, in 1722 and died in 1803. [AP Photo]

breaks the contract (as, he said, England did), then the other party has the right to break it as well and consider the contract null and void. Adams not only was a brilliant writer and gatherer of facts that would bolster his cause, but in forming a network of like-minded colonists into what he called the "Committees of Correspondence," he magnified his voice. These "committees" would keep him abreast of news regarding English troops and alleged abuses by them, and he in turn would provide them with similar news. Each link in the chain would then tell others what they knew, much as member newspapers of today's Associated Press pass along information gleaned from other members.

Adams was born in Boston in 1722, putting him among the first generations of native-born, nonimmigrant colonists. He had no personal, firsthand ties to England and instead, supplanted that with his love of—and devotion to—early America. He was well educated, earning of master of arts from Harvard. He was also politically astute and was elected to the Massachusetts Assembly in 1765. A solid writer, Adams had a gift for exciting the passions of fellow colonists, and developed a cadre of friends in the printing business such as Benjamin Edes and John Gill, publishers of the *Boston Gazette*, and Isaiah Thomas, publisher of the *Massachusetts Spy*. He was one of the signers of the Declaration of Independence in 1776 and, following the Revolutionary War, served as governor of Massachusetts from 1794 to 1797. He was a cousin to another Patriot leader and second president of the United States, John Adams. Samuel Adams lived to see the new republic get a toehold, dying in 1803.

By May of 1764, Adams was calling for separation from England, and the Committees of Correspondence would later provide a megaphone for his call that all colonists would hear. The Committees were organized in 1772, and member "agents" kept Adams and others in the chain alerted to each and every important meeting. The utterances of the committees and their aligned publications such as the *Boston Gazette* painted the issue of separation from England—and ultimately the call to revolutionary arms—in stark terms of black and white. Adams became known as the "assassin of reputations" and the "master of the puppets." Here is how a journalistic historian describes Adams' method:

> He understood that to win the inevitable conflict, he and his cohorts must achieve five main objectives: they must justify the course they advocated; advertise the advantages of victory; arouse the masses—the real "shock troops"—by instilling hatred of the enemies; neutralize any logical and reasonable arguments proposed by the opposition, and finally phrase all the issues in black and white, so that the purposes might be clear even to the common laborer. Adams was able to do all this.[10]

If this propaganda technique sounds familiar, it should. It has been used down through the centuries by governments and movements wishing to make their position seem like the only patriotic and sensible one.

6. THOMAS PAINE WRITES OF "THE CRISIS"

As Colonial Americans plunged into war with England in 1775, most realized it was not going to be an easy fight and certainly not an easy victory. Local militias and a hastily organized Continental Army were going up against an experienced fighting force in British troops. Sometimes the only advantage it seemed that Gen. George Washington's troops had was the distance facing British reinforcements that had to come from England. Even so, the war's progress was uneven for the colonies, and the first few months seemed dark to many. It was in that atmosphere that a rebellious young Philadelphia writer named Thomas Paine stepped forward and penned an articulate defense for the war called *Common Sense*, which was his first call to arms that fanned the revolutionary flames for fellow colonials. That essay would be followed in that same year by probably the most famous essay of the Revolutionary War. That was the first of Paine's pamphlets called *The Crisis*, which was reproduced in revolutionary newspapers across the colonies and helped inspire their army in their fight for independence.

Paine was born in Thetford, England, on January 29, 1737 and emigrated to America in 1774 following philosophical differences with the Royals system in England. He arrived in Philadelphia in November 1774 and had a letter of recommendation from Benjamin Franklin, whom he had met in England. He used that to secure a position as managing editor of the *Pennsylvania Magazine*, contributing several essays and poems.

His essay *Common Sense* was put into pamphlet form and sold 100,000 copies in three months. Its popularity inspired the forthcoming essays of *The Crisis*. Paine had originally joined others like fellow Pennsylvania writer John Dickinson in advocating colonial reconciliation with England. But the Battles of Lexington and Concord in 1775 changed his thinking, and that is when he produced *Common Sense*.[11]

Paine had the uncanny ability to write as easily to intellectuals as to everyday colonial farmers. An ardent anti-Monarchist, he would later turn his attention to inspiring French revolutionaries. In *The Crisis*, he combined his grand vision for American society and a poetic style that produced the essay with the still-quoted phrase: "These are the times that try men's souls. The summer soldier and the sunshine patriot will, in this crisis, shrink from the service of their country; but he that stands by it now, deserves the love and thanks of man and woman. Tyranny, like hell, is not easily conquered."[12]

This was the first of what would be 13 essays, each called *The Crisis*, and it was written in the bleak days after George's Washington's forced retreat across the Delaware River in December 1776. Paine intended the essay to bolster the courage and spirit of the army and of the colonial population in general. Twelve more *Crisis* papers would follow, and each of them would be written to spur American resolve and keep them in the fight.

In 1777, a year in which four of these essays would be written, Paine was elected secretary of the Congressional Committee of Foreign Affairs. He eventually returned to Europe after the war in 1787, living in England and France.

7. BEN FRANKLIN PICKS UP A PEN

When colonial publisher James Franklin was arrested for contempt in publishing without authority of the governing British authorities, his younger brother Benjamin and James' wife Ann kept James' newspaper, *The New England Courant* running. But Ben, who had served as James' apprentice printer, also saw this as a chance for him to leave Boston and start out on his own in another colony. He had already discovered his talents as a writer in Boston, although he was prohibited by his brother to write under his own name. His opportunities to write for James' newspaper had been blunted by his brother, but that had not stopped him from contributing essays under the alias of "Silence Dogood."

Young Ben, still a teenager, had begun writing these Dogood essays in 1722 under the pseudonym of "Mrs. Silence Dogood." As a woman writer, he reasoned, the comments might even be perceived as more acerbic. And making her the wife of a country parson seemed to enhance the satire. The name was also a jab at Puritan leader Cotton Mather who adopted an always-serious tone commanding colonists to live upright lives and underscoring his ideals in his "Essays to do Good."[13] Both James and Ben were becoming critics of the rich and powerful—and sometimes hypocritical— influence of the Puritan community. These essays were a collection of funny and serious comments about New England life, often making barbed points about the

Puritan lifestyle. Franklin would write them and then slide them under the door of his brother's print shop at night. They became very popular among readers of the *Courant*, and they convinced Ben Franklin that he should become a writer.

When James was released from jail (he was never tried) Ben Franklin left Boston and headed to Philadelphia where he wrote the "Busy-Body Papers," a collection of satirical political essays which were run in the *American Mercury* magazine. He then purchased the *Pennsylvania Gazette*. Under Franklin's leadership, this newspaper would distinguish itself in several ways, among which would be to publish the first editorial cartoon in America. Ben produced it himself, and this, plus his commitment to well-written prose, made his newspaper the most popular in the colonies. He had a strong interest in politics, and his sharp wit, coupled with the reality of how far he could go without inviting government censorship, served him well with his provocative satire. He was a strong believer in free speech, which became a cornerstone of the American Revolution. He once noted, "If all printers were determined . . . not to offend anybody, there would be very little printed."[14]

As a publisher, however, Ben Franklin may be known best for his *Poor Richard's Almanack* which he began in Philadelphia in 1733. The almanac contained weather reports, recipes, predictions, short stories, political blurbs, and even homilies or sermons. It was second only to the Bible in popularity among New England readers.[15] It allowed Ben to deliver some of the wit he had accumulated, and it made famous many of his sayings such as, "A penny saved is a penny earned." Others were "Fish and visitors stink in three days," and "Half the truth is often a great lie," and of course, "Early to bed and early to rise, makes a man healthy, wealthy, and wise."[16]

Franklin became a man of many talents, from inventor, to politician and statesman, to writer and humorist. He was one of the signers of the Declaration of Independence and a leader in the Patriot cause for independence. As a newspaper publisher, however, he is probably best known for simply making journalism respectable: delivering news stories and commentary about significant issues, but doing so in an articulate, often wry and humorous manner.

8. THE *FEDERALIST PAPERS* STIR DEBATE

In September 1787, the newly written Constitution of the United States was sent to the states for ratification. However, it became apparent that selling a document like this to a people who had just gained their independence from a strong British central government might not be an easy matter. Therefore, the very next month on October 27, a series of articles began appearing in three New York City newspapers: the *Independent Journal*, the *New-York Packet*, and the *Daily Advertiser*. The articles appeared under the name "The Federalist," and the byline of "Publius." The first articles were actually written by Alexander Hamilton, who would eventually write 51 of them. James Madison would write 27, and John Jay would write five. The articles encouraged the ratification of the new Constitution. Historian Richard B. Morris has called them "an incomparable exposition of the Constitution, a classic in political science unsurpassed in both breadth and depth by the produce of any later American writer."[17]

An excerpt from the first essay, written by Hamilton, states the case for the Constitution right from the start:

> It has been frequently remarked that it seems to have been reserved to the people of this country, by their conduct and example, to decide the important question, whether societies of men are really capable or not of establishing good government from reflection and choice, or whether they are forever destined to depend for their political constitutions on accident and force. If there be any truth in the remark, the crisis at which we are arrived may with propriety be regarded as the era in which that decision is to be made.[18]

In many respects, the *Federalist Papers* became a well-engineered, sustained public relations campaign with the goal of America's adoption of the new Constitution. The centerpiece of the campaign was the series of articles which ran from October 27, 1787, to May 28, 1788. Many historians believe the most important of the series came with *Federalist No. 10*, written by James Madison, which argued directly for the ratification of the Constitution and appeared on November 22, 1987, a month after the *Independent Journal* began publishing the papers. In this essay, Madison tackled the issue of dealing with factions whose interests might by opposed to the individual liberties of others or the interests of the larger community. Madison reasoned that a nation which had a strong, large republic would be better suited to defend against internal opposition rather than several smaller republics—or states—would. Part of the genius of *The Federalist* series, however, was that many of them contained jewels that eloquently laid out the basis and road map for how a federal government should work for the benefit of its people.

The series appeared, however, in a highly-charged partisan press atmosphere where newspapers were routinely owned and/or influenced by political parties or factions. In the post-Revolutionary War days, the two main parties were the Federalists and Anti-Federalists, or those who opposed a strong central government and instead favored stronger states rights. So answering the *Federalist Papers* were writers like Samuel Bryan who published the first of his "Centinel" essays in Philadelphia's *Independent Gazetteer*. These essays, reprinted in other Anti-Federalist newspapers, warned against the dangers of investing too much power in a strong central government. In New York, the Constitution was assailed by a series of essays signed simply, "Cato." In fact, *The Federalist* series was actually a counterattack by Hamilton, Jay, and Madison, to these essays.

In the end, the Federalist movement emerged as more organized and determined while the anti-Federalists were less organized and had more localized interests. Nevertheless, the power of the Anti-Federalists may have been enough to deter ratification of the Constitution had it not been for the addition to the original document of a series of 10 amendments meant to protect individual rights from the federal government. These amendments, of course, became known as the Bill of Rights, and the Constitution was eventually ratified by all 13 states, starting with Delaware (on a unanimous vote on December 7, 1787) and ending with Rhode Island (in a close 34–32 vote) on May 29, 1790.

9. PRESS FREEDOM BECOMES THE LAW

Every journalism student soon learns about what journalists consider to be the most important protection offered by the United States Constitution, and that protection is found within the First Amendment and guards freedom of the press in America. It is part of the Bill of Rights—the first 10 amendments to the Constitution—which were introduced to the first Congress in 1789 by James Madison, and which became law in 1791 after the Constitution was ratified by the states. In fact, these 10 amendments were the reason the Constitution was ratified in the first place, as they were seen by the states as safeguards against a too-powerful central government.

The U.S. Constitution had been signed on September 17, 1787, but it contained no mention of essential freedoms now outlined in the Bill of Rights. Apparently the original framers did not see the need. However, as the ensuing debate between the Federalists and Anti-Federalists would show, there was indeed such a need. Madison was alert to that and thus proposed what were originally 12 amendments.

The First Amendment reads, "Congress shall make no law respecting an establishment of religion, or prohibiting the free exercise thereof; or abridging the freedom of speech, or of the press; or the right of the people peaceably to assemble, and to petition the government for a redress of grievances."

Over the centuries, that one partial phrase in which "press" appears has proved to be a bulwark for journalistic freedom unlike other countries whose constitutions detail for several pages a "freedom of the press" clause. As part of the Soviet Union, for example, Russia's press freedom clause ran 15 pages, and this was a country which definitely did not have a free press. When a "freedom" needs 15 pages for detailing, the truth of the statement, "The devil is in the detail," becomes obvious. So although the mention of the press in the U.S. Constitution is fleeting, it is there and unmistakable that America was to be a country with a free press. It is not only the foundation on which the American news media is built, but many believe that the openness for discussion and criticism it offers is essential to the American Democracy itself. Its genius may well be in its simplicity and lack of detailed explanation.

The fact that this amendment appears first in the Constitution has caused many members of the clergy and many members of the media to opine that these concerns were foremost in the minds of the founding fathers. While certainly there is truth to that—after all, America was a place of refuge for dissidents from England—many constitutional scholars say we shouldn't read too much into the actual placement of the amendment in the Constitution. For example, Dr. David Weeks, professor of history and political science at Azusa Pacific University, notes, "Actually, the First Amendment was not really the first originally proposed amendment. It was really third. Two other amendments came before it but were disapproved. So freedom of religion, speech and the press were not necessarily first in the minds of the founding fathers."[19]

For example, the originally proposed First Amendment dealt with apportionment of elected representatives, proposing a somewhat complicated formula for the number of representatives per thousands of constituents. The original Second Amendment dealt with congressional pay raises and required intervention by the senators and representatives before any changes to their salaries could take effect. (Actually, however, this article would be ratified much later in 1992 as the Twenty-seventh Amendment.)

The First Amendment has time and again been the deciding factor in Supreme Court decisions affecting how American journalists can or cannot do their business. In the landmark 1964 case of *New York Times v. Sullivan*, Justice William Brennan wrote the First Amendment provides that "debate on public issues . . . [should be] . . . uninhibited, robust, and wide-open."[20] And this was the decision that gave journalists an extra measure of freedom in writing about public officials, requiring libel plaintiffs to prove not only inaccuracy but "actual malice" in the way the stories were written. And seven years later, in the *New York Times Co. v. United States*, the Supreme Court would cite the First Amendment as the foundation for the "no prior restraint" rule that forbids preventing news media from publishing or airing stories in advance.

Debate has continued to swirl over the years about whether the First Amendment protects the right of journalists to keep their sources confidential. Some judges believe it does, because if sources can't be guaranteed confidentiality, then they wouldn't talk to reporters in the first place. Hence, the press would be prevented from writing important stories informing the public of problems. Other judges don't perceive the First Amendment as offering that absolute protection, especially in cases where an individual may be on trial for a felony and whose defense may depend on subpoenaing that source to testify at trial. In that case, a conflict arises between perceived protections granted by the First Amendment and those granted by the Sixth and Fourteenth Amendments, which allow individuals to examine witnesses and to avail themselves of due process to the law. That debate is an ongoing one.

NOTES

1. The Massachusetts Historical Society, as retrieved on www.masshist.org/objects/2004april.cfm.

2. Ibid.

3. Frank Luther Mott. *The History of American Journalism*. New York: Harcourt, 1964.

4. *The Cambridge History of English and American Literature in 18 Volumes* (1907–21). Volume XV: *Colonial and Revolutionary Literature*.

5. "The Electric Ben Franklin: The New England Courant," as retrieved on www.ushistory.org/franklin/courant/story.htm.

6. Michael Emery, Edwin Emery, Nancy L. Roberts. *The Press and America: An Interpretive History of the Mass Media*, 9th ed. Boston: Allyn & Bacon, 2000, p. 40.

7. Ibid.

8. Ibid., p. 53

9. Ibid.

10. Ibid., p. 49.

11. *The American Revolution*, as retrieved on http://americanrevwar.homestead
.com/files/Paine.htm.

12. Thomas Paine. *The Crisis*, December 23, 1776, as retrieved on www.ushistory
.org/PAINE/crisis/index.htm.

13. "Silence Dogood," as retrieved on http://library.thinkquest.org/22254/
dogood.htm.

14. Stuart A. Kallen. *Benjamin Franklin*. Edina, Minn: ABDO Publishing,
2001, p. 18.

15. Steve Potts. *Benjamin Franklin*. Mankato: Bridgestone Books, 1996, p. 13.

16. Kallen, *Benjamin Franklin*, pp. 13–18.

17. Richard B. Morris. *The Forging of the Union: 1781–1789*. New York: Harper
& Rowe, 1987, p. 309.

18. Alexander Hamilton. *The Federalist Papers No. 1: General Introduction*.
From *The Independent Journal*, October 27, 1787, as retrieved on http://
xroads.virginia.edu.

19. David Weeks, in an interview at Azusa Pacific University, December 10,
2008.

20. Brian J. Buchanan. "About the First Amendment," First Amendment Center,
as retrieved on www.firstamendmentcenter.org.

Part II

The 19th Century: The Pioneering Spirit Abounds

The 19th century was the era when America grew and expanded from the Atlantic to the Pacific and fought a war that redesigned the southern border with Mexico. It was a century of pioneering spirit which carried over from land exploration and conquest, to the many inventions and developments in industry and in the nation's institutions. Developments in the media were in the forefront of these moments as this section reveals. From the decade of the 1830s that gave us the birth of the modern mass-circulation daily newspaper, to the end of the century that gave us the era of Yellow Journalism and the first inventions in radio, this was quite a century.

10. FOUNDING THE *NEW YORK SUN*

In 1833, Benjamin Day ushered in the so-called Era of the Penny Press. He dropped the price of his *New York Sun* to one cent (while other papers were selling with limited success for six to 10 cents), began stocking it with news of and for the common man and woman, solicited advertisers, and launched the day of the mass-circulation daily newspaper. Day's experiment, soon to be replicated by competitors in New York, provided a clear demarcation from the era of the specialized, partisan newspapers of the post-Revolutionary War time and what would become the age of the modern newspaper.

The older newspapers were more expensive, which put them beyond the range of most Americans of the day, and they were financed by that high subscription price and often by political parties or movements. Their pages were filled with news of politics and business and were, for the most part, pretty boring reads for the common man and woman of the early 19th century. With the launching of Day's *New York Sun*, the modern newspaper would sell for a penny, with the lion's share of the operating revenue and profit coming from advertising. The new pricing scheme, plus the different kind of news that filled its pages, put the daily newspaper into the hands of the common people, and they relished it. Circulations boomed, which lured in more advertisers who paid well to reach tens of thousands (soon to be hundreds of thousands) of readers each day. Fueling the public's interest was news that connected with the average American: startling crime news, stories of sexual escapades, government and business corruption, editorial crusades pushing the interest of the common American, human-interest features, personality profiles, and a dose of science fiction for good measure.

It wasn't long before Day was joined by other publishers touting—and expanding—his new idea of news. These other media barons included James Gordon Bennett (Sr. and Jr.), Horace Greeley, Robert McCormick, and decades later, Joseph Pulitzer and William Randolph Hearst. The news that was fashioned by Day and later perfected by Bennett Sr., Pulitzer, and Hearst, came to be known as "sensationalism," in that it targeted the emotional senses of readers who obviously liked being jolted. Historian Michael Emery, however, notes the following about sensationalism:

> Whenever a mass of people have been neglected too long by the established organs of communication, agencies have eventually been devised to supply that want. Invariably this press of the masses is greeted with scorn . . . because the content . . . is likely to be elemental and emotional. Such scorn is not always deserved.[1]

This Penny Press Era unleashed journalism from the restraints that kept it from reaching and focusing on common people. In that sense, it was much more egalitarian and had a greater democratizing effect on America than that which came before. Much of the tradition of literary journalism was given birth in the age of the Penny Press. Journalists were not only fact-gatherers but also storytellers who understood the importance of making their stories lively to reach readers, many of whom might not otherwise be interested in stories of government or business corruption. The element of humor was also added to stories and headlines, not only making it easier to read the news of the day but also adding a sometimes-welcome relief valve to the tensions created by such heavy tidings. Some of the writers who started out as journalists in the 19th century included Mark Twain and Richard Harding Davis.

11. GREELEY LAUNCHES THE *NEW YORK TRIBUNE*

Growing up on a poor New England farm in the early 19th century, Horace Greeley attended school irregularly despite showing a deep interest in acquiring more knowledge. His education would come in a nontraditional way. He was hired as an apprentice to a Vermont newspaper editor and then worked as a printer in New York and Pennsylvania. In 1831 he gathered his meager resources and moved to New York City where he would found the *New Yorker*, a weekly journal of literature and news. The journal gained prominence among educated New Yorkers, but it never made much money. Greeley continued to contribute articles to it but set about launching another publication in 1841 which would become one of the most popular newspapers in 19th century America: the*New York Tribune*. The paper seemed as eclectic as Greeley himself, and he used it to promote a variety of causes and devoted space to politics, social reform, news, literary and intellectual issues.

Critiques of Greeley were that he was more an idealist than a realist, and more of a socialist than a capitalist. He promoted and explained the communitarian thinking of Fourier and went so far as to invest in a kind of utopian community at Red Bank,

WHAT IS SENSATIONALISM?

The American news media are built upon a simple equation: More readers or viewers equal more advertisers and higher ad rates. That revenue then drives the news operation's ability to gather information and process it for consumers. The theory is that the news media which are financially successful are those which can remain independent from special interests. The problem becomes what some publishers or news directors feel they must do to attract that large audience. At various cycles in history, that has meant resorting to sensationalism. It occurred in 1833, in the 1890s, the 1920s, and is flourishing today in tabloid papers, TV shows, and on the Web.

Sensationalism is journalism that intentionally goes for the emotional jugular. It is often reporting that takes an event that is dramatic in and of itself, and then heaps added "pseudo-drama" onto that reality. In short, sensationalism is reporting that hypes reality, hoping to jerk a tear from the eye of the reader or viewer or make them stand up and cheer. Sensationalism relies on the overuse of descriptive adjectives, may dwell on graphic violence or sex, and—in the case of television—makes abundant use of slow-motion video and heart-wrenching music.

During the 1890s, this sensationalism became known as "yellow journalism," named for a popular comic strip character called the Yellow Kid which first appeared in Joseph Pulitzer's *New York World* and then William Randolph Hearst's *New York Journal*. Most historians believe sensationalism reached its zenith—or depths—in the circulation battles between these two newspaper giants.

America seemed to tire of yellow journalism as the 20th century began, and the revamped *New York Times* began setting a more serious standard for American journalism. But many newspapers lapsed back into sensationalism in the 1920s when it became known as "jazz journalism." It arose in New York City, just as yellow journalism had three decades earlier. Tabloid-size papers were illustrated richly with graphic photographs and large, scary headlines. The era fit the "roaring twenties," which was the time of ebullience felt by the nation following the dark days of World War I. Tabloid journalism, or jazz journalism, emphasized Hollywood celebrities, gangsters and prohibition, and graphically violent photographs. Leading the charge were tabloids like the *New York Daily News*. One famous front page featured a full-size picture of Ruth Snyder as she was being electrocuted at Sing Sing Prison in 1928. The photographer for the *Daily News* shot the photograph with a camera strapped to his leg. At the moment of electrocution, he jerked his pants leg up and clicked the shutter.

Modern versions of sensationalism are found most readily in the supermarket tabloids like *The National Enquirer* and on tabloid TV shows like *Inside Edition* and celebrity-oriented shows like *Showbiz Tonight*. Online, sites like TMZ.com perform the same tabloid function in about the same way.

New Jersey, founded on communitarian principles. The communitarian philosophy emphasizes the importance of the collective group over the individual, and the idea of individuals working and living together as a commune was a centerpiece to this thinking. At one point, Greeley even had a young Karl Marx on his payroll, espousing the benefits of the collective over the individual.

The *Tribune* found favor among two seemingly disparate groups: eastern intellectuals and the more daring easterners who would become the pioneers of the westward movement. Communitarian principles were often put into action as small groups of settlers stopped along the way west to form communities and towns, many of which would grow into cities. While the westward movement was known for individualism, these individual families of settlers realized they needed to bond with other settlers for safety and success. Greeley, in fact, promoted the principle of homesteading whereby government would distribute free land to settlers. The *Tribune* espoused this principle and issued the famous charge to "Go West, young man!" Many easterners took Greeley up on his charge, and they took the *Tribune*—and its cousin the *Weekly Tribune*—along with them. Many of these settlers felt they came to know Greeley personally through reading his thoughts in the *Tribune*, and the publisher became known as "Uncle Horace" to many.

Horace Greeley, newspaper editor of the New York Tribune, *is shown, date unknown.* [AP Photo]

The *Tribune*, under Greeley, saw itself as a kind of moral compass for America, opposing issues like monopolies, child labor, and capital punishment. The *Tribune* also opposed the Mexican-American War and opposed slavery on both moral and economic grounds. Although Greeley and his newspaper were admired, the publisher was also perceived as being very eccentric in his multifaceted reform ideas. Since this was the era of "personal journalism" where a newspaper often became a visible extension of the owner's personality, the *Tribune* was tarred with the same critiques. In terms of popularity, it was an important paper but did not match the popularity of rivals such as James Gordon Bennett's *New York Herald*. Part of the reason was Greeley's refusal to engage in the kind of popular sensational journalism that Bennett did.

Greeley had a strong interest in politics and was even nominated by the Liberal Republicans to oppose U.S. Grant in seeking the 1872 presidential nomination. But his image as an eccentric and curmudgeon would spell defeat for him. The era of personal editorship was coming to a close (to be resurrected briefly by Pulitzer and Hearst in the 1990s), and the paper passed on to other editorial leadership. Greeley died in 1872 and, ironically, the high-minded *Tribune* would be merged in later years with Bennett's sensational *Herald* to become the *New York Herald Tribune*, and would last nearly 100 years to 1967.

12. THE GREAT MOON HOAX

How important is it for Americans to know that an entertaining article, book, television program, or movie is as true as it claims to be? When it comes to inspiration and entertainment, is truth really all that important to most people? Moments in history captured elsewhere in this book such as the journalistic hoaxes of Stephen Glass and Janet Cooke or the rigged quiz shows of television history have explored this question. Probably the first major journalistic hoax perpetrated on American newspaper readers, however, came in 1835 with a series of six reports in the *New York Sun* which purported to describe what life was like on the moon. In history, it became known as "The Great Moon Hoax."

The first part in Richard Adams Locke's series appeared on August 25, 1835, under the headline, "Celestial Discoveries." An excerpt of the brief story read, "We have just learnt (sic) from an eminent publisher in this city that Sir John Herschel at the Cape of Good Hope, has made some astronomical discoveries of the most wonderful description, by means of an immense telescope of an entirely new principle."[2] The news about Herschel going to South Africa in 1834 to set up an observatory was true, but a large portion of the story about Herschel's alleged discoveries and credited to a current *Edinburgh Journal of Science*, a publication, were untrue. The journal had, in fact, been out of business for some time and contained no such reports as described in the *Sun* series.

Nevertheless, that didn't stop the *Sun* from running four columns describing what Herschel had seen of the moon through his powerful telescope. R. J. Brown, editor-in-chief of Historybuff.com, writes this about Locke's series: "So fascinating were the descriptions of trees and vegetation, oceans and beaches, bison and goats, cranes and pelicans that the whole town was talking even before the fourth installment appeared on August 28, 1835, with the master revelation of all: the discovery of furry, winged men resembling bats."[3]

Locke's story about Herschel noted, "We counted three parties of these creatures . . . walking erect towards a small wood . . . Certainly they were like human beings, for their wings had now disappeared and their attitude in walking was both erect and dignified . . . About half of the first party had passed beyond our canvas; but of all the others we had perfectly distinct and deliberate view. They averaged four feet in height, were covered, except on the face, with short and glossy copper-colored hair, and had wings composed of a thin membrane . . . "[4]

Readers were magnetized by this purportedly true series of descriptions of these moon creatures, and the circulation of the *Sun* soared to the highest level achieved by any newspaper in the world at the time: 19,360. Of course, competitors in the newspaper business were beside themselves, wanting to get similar reports for their readers. A group of scientists from Yale University went to New York to view the original journal article, but they were basically sandbagged by *Sun* editors who moved them from office to office before they gave up and returned to New Haven. But when one of the *Sun*'s newspaper competitors, the *Journal of Commerce* asked permission to reprint the *Sun*'s series as a pamphlet, Locke stepped forward and admitted he had authored the descriptions of moon life. The publication had caused such a stir that even writer Edgar Allen Poe admitted to stopping work on a novel because he felt depressed over being outdone by the *Sun*. After the series was revealed as a hoax, Poe still wrote of his admiration for Locke's stunt. In the book, *The Sun and the Moon*, Matthew Goodman wrote:

> Poe's finely tuned sense of literary competitiveness caused him to disparage Locke's most celebrated work as shoddily constructed, if elegantly delivered, but he also could not help but admire what he saw as Locke's consummate skill as a hoaxer; his calm, his audaciousness, his ingenuity. Sometimes one of those feelings was ascendant in Poe, and sometimes the other—as in his 1841 Autography series, when he extolled Locke . . . as "one among the few men of unquestionable genius whom the country possesses."[5]

Did readers care that Locke's series was a fabrication and that the descriptions of moon creatures were made up out of whole cloth? Many seemed not to care and continued to devour stories in the *Sun* in the following months and years. Others decried the use of fiction in a journal ostensibly purporting only facts. In the end, this was the first of the great journalistic hoaxes, but it would definitely not be the last. Latter-day examples such as author James Frey's mixing of fact and fancy in his best-selling *A Million Little Pieces* showed the same mixed results among readers: Some felt betrayed, but many didn't seem to care. They still found inspiration and entertainment from the stories told, true or not.

13. STANLEY FINDS LIVINGSTONE

One of the most flamboyant newspaper publishers in history was James Gordon Bennett, Jr., publisher of the *New York Herald*. Learning about the value of mixing entertainment with actual news from his father, Bennett commissioned an expedition led by his popular reporter Henry Morton Stanley to go to Africa and locate a missing Scottish missionary named David Livingstone. Of course Stanley would send back reports to the *Herald*'s readers of his derring-do adventures in finding the good doctor, and it would all lead up to a presumed rescue, splashed across the front pages of Bennett's newspapers as readers looked on in awe. That was the plan, anyway, and the fact that Bennett hatched it shows how far back the idea goes of staging news and/or mixing news and entertainment to sell more media product to consumers.

Surprisingly, the plan played out as intended, although it took quite a bit longer than Bennett had envisioned. This is how it all happened:

In March of 1866, a year after the Civil War ended, a Scottish explorer-cum-missionary named David Livingstone journeyed to East Africa and found himself near the mouth of the Ruvuma River. Friends and family knew about this much of his adventure, but from that point forward, his whereabouts were unknown as the African bush country seemed to engulf him and he apparently disappeared. News of Livingstone's disappearance reached Bennett, and he saw a story in the event. Some three years had already passed since the last known sighting of Livingstone, and many were wondering what had become of him. Was he dead? Had he been captured by African tribes? Had he gone mad? Bennett resolved to find out and sell some newspapers in the process. To do this, he summoned reporter Stanley to his quarters in a Paris hotel (why Bennett had migrated to Paris was a story in itself), and gave him his charge: Go and find the missing Livingstone. Money is no object, and you can start by drawing 1,000 pounds now to start your journey. When you are done with that, draw another thousand, and another until you find him. And by the way, don't forget to send back dramatic stories of your progress.

Not one to skimp on an expense account or to miss out on enjoying the journey, Stanley took his time getting to Africa and then finding Dr. Livingstone. Altogether the search took two years and is described this way by Louis Snyder and Richard Morris:

> Stanley's expedition from Zanzibar into the interior of Africa was an epoch in African exploration. The meeting of reporter and explorer at Ujiji on November 10, 1871, made one of the most famous newspaper stories of all time. The first news that Stanley's expedition had been crowned with success came in a dispatch from the London correspondent to the Herald, published on July 2, 1872, which read: "It is with the deepest emotions of pride and pleasure that I announce the arrival this day of letters from Mr. Stanley, chief of the Herald Exploring Expedition to Central Africa ... I hasten to telegraph a summary of the Herald's explorer's letters, which are full of the most romantic interest, while affirming, emphatically, the safety of Dr. Livingstone."[6]

A FLAMBOYANT LIFE

Perhaps it was a given that James Gordon Bennett, Jr., would not live an ordinary life. After all, his father had created one of the best-read daily newspapers in New York (the *Herald*) built largely on a steady diet of sensationalism. Bennett Jr. would become heir to that newspaper and the fortune his father created, and he would expand the newspaper's juiciness by imbuing it with his own personal flamboyance.

Although born in New York City in 1841, Bennett was raised by his mother in Europe to avoid the antisocialite stigma attached to his father's sensational newspaper. In 1866, after several years given over almost completely to various enjoyments of the young and rich including yacht racing and polo, Bennett was given control of the *Herald*'s editorial department by his father and almost immediately launched the *Evening Telegram* which exploited sensationalism as much—or more—as did the *Herald*. But the young Bennett also showed his interest in newsgathering, and his scoop on the massacre of Gen. George Armstrong Custer in 1876 was an example of that. His journalistic schemes for the newspapers spared no expense, as witnessed by the 1869 charge he gave to reporter Henry M. Stanley to find Dr. David Livingstone—the presumably lost medical missionary—in Africa.

But it was Bennett's personal escapades that would send him back to living in Paris as something of a social exile from New York City. Bennett became engaged to a New York socialite named Caroline May after living the life of a wealthy playboy and carousing with various showgirls in the city. When he showed up at an engagement party at May's New York condo, Bennett was drunk and proceeded to bob and weave among the city's upper crust who had been invited to the gala. Embarrassing May and her family, Bennett reportedly felt nature's call and—perhaps remembering his time as a volunteer fireman—staggered over to a large fireplace in the parlor, dropped his pants and urinated into the flames in front of a crowded room of guests. May was aghast, her brother Frederick was infuriated and, according to a story in *The Perry Chief* "publicly horse-whipped" Bennett to teach him a lesson. Other accounts have the two men meeting for a duel the next day where both fired and missed the other. Whatever actually occurred between the two antagonists, Bennett's marriage to Caroline May never materialized. In fact, Bennett would not marry until he was 73 years old. After his self-imposed exile in Paris where he began *The Paris Herald*, the forerunner of the *International Herald Tribune*, Bennett returned to New York and organized the first polo match in America and helped found the Westchester Polo Club in 1876, the first of its kind in the United States. But from 1877 to his death in 1918, Bennett lived in Europe, continuing to run the *New York Herald* from his $600,000, 314-foot yacht, the Lysistrata.

The antics of Bennett and his father gave rise to the old but then-often-used expletive "Gordon Bennett!" which was a kind of minced oath and a version of *God blind me.*

—"Gordon Bennett!" by Gary Martin, *The Phrase Finder*, www.phrases.org/meanings/gordon-bennett.html.

Stanley's own long account of the search ends with this excerpt and a line that has gone down in history:

There is a group of the most respectable Arabs, and as I come nearer I see the white face of an old man among them. He has a cap with a gold band around it, his dress is a short jacket of red blanket cloth, and his pants—well, I didn't observe.

I am shaking hands with him. We raise our hats, and I say: "Dr. Livingstone,
I presume?" And he says, "Yes."[7]

Still on a bottomless vat of company expenses, Stanley found himself uneager to leave
Africa, so he stayed on for another four months. He tried to coax Livingstone into returning
as well, but the explorer said he had found the life he was seeking and was still searching for
what brought him to Africa in the first place: the ancient fountains of Herodotus, thought to
be the source of the great Nile River. Livingstone would never find the fountains as death
would overtake him in his continued search. However, he remained a staunch opponent
of the African slave trade and even wrote in a letter to the *Herald* before he died, "All I
can say in my solitude is, may Heaven's rich blessing come down on everyone—American,
English, Turk—who will help to heal this open sore of the world."[8]

14. THE FIRST ADVERTISING AGENCY

When Volney B. Palmer became America's first advertising agent in Philadelphia in
1841, he helped to underscore the importance of advertising as the primary revenue
source for the news media which, at the time, were limited to newspapers and magazines. Advertising had been around since the beginnings of newspapers when John
Campbell published the country's first regular newspaper with *The Boston Newsletter*
in 1704. But until the advertising "brokers" like Palmer began appearing in the mid-
1800s, businesses placed ads in a piecemeal fashion with little thought given to advertising campaigns or how the system of advertising could work to their benefit. On the
media side, the creation of the advertising agency meant a much steadier and predict-
able stream of advertising volume. It also helped newspaper publishers and advertising
managers in their annual budgeting processes and in allowing them to deal one-on-one
with a third-party professional instead of the sometimes emotional advertiser who was
probably not too knowledgeable about the advertising process.

But Palmer also did his part in expanding capitalism in America by helping make
consumers aware of the many goods and services available to buy and in knowing
how to encourage advertisers to spend money to promote their goods and services.
Palmer's idea was to insert an experienced and knowledgeable agent between the
advertiser and the news media. His feeling was that many businesses did not understand the dynamics of advertising enough to develop effective ad campaigns, and that
newspapers were more interested in gaining ad revenue from businesses than in the
specific needs of each business. So Palmer set about contracting with newspapers for
large chunks of ad space at discounted rates. He would then counsel advertising clients
about their ad needs and resell the space he bought to the advertisers at a higher rate.
His commission would be the difference between the two rates.

Nearly three decades later, in 1869, Palmer's agency was bought by Francis Ayer who
founded N. W. Ayer & Son, which still exists as a leading advertising agency today. Ayer
took Palmer's ideas a step or two further. For example, whereas advertisers created their
own ads under Palmer's system, Ayer had his agency create the ads themselves following

market research his firm did. Ayer also changed the billing system by giving clients the same rates that he paid for the ads, plus an agreed-upon agency commission.[9]

Advertising agencies have made it easier for both clients and the media to transact business, and they have inserted a professional middle person into the process, helping to ensure the needs of both are met.[10]

15. DOUGLASS LAUNCHES THE *NORTH STAR*

As sectionalism grew in America and the issue of slavery in the South fueled a growing abolitionist movement in the North, individuals stepped forward to plead the cause of the black man. At first these courageous publishers were white men, the most important of whom was William Lloyd Garrison, whose newspaper *The Liberator* began in Boston in 1831, preached an end to slavery, and championed equality for blacks. Garrison was not the first to publish an abolitionist newspaper, however. That honor fell to Charles Osborn who, in 1817, launched *The Philanthropist* in Ohio. He was followed by Benjamin Lundy, who began *The Genius of Universal Emancipation* in 1821 in Boston and made it the most influential of the early abolitionist papers until *The Liberator* was launched a decade later. But Osborn, Lundy, and Garrison were all white publishers, and the blacks were still waiting for someone from their own race to step forward and plead their case.

This is a photo of a daguerreotype of abolitionist Frederick Douglass. [AP Photo]

That man would be Frederick Douglass, a black journalist who began publishing the *North Star* in 1847 in Rochester, New York. This newspaper was an ardent antislavery paper published by the best-known black man in America in the pre-Civil War days, himself an escaped slave. After enduring a series of beatings in working on a Maryland plantation, one of which came for a failed escape attempt, a 20-year-old Douglass managed to hop a train north to Philadelphia in 1838 disguised as a free black sailor, and then on to New York City. Douglass had a sharp mind and, while in Baltimore, often engaged in discussion with freed, educated blacks. He was a brilliant orator who captivated many audiences with his strong rhetoric.

His search for work took him to New Bedford, Massachusetts. After living there a short time, he began reading Garrison's paper, *The Liberator*. Douglass found the inspiration he was looking for and as he would write in his autobiography, "The paper became my meat and drink. My soul was set all on fire."[11] Douglass later moved to New York, and it was in Rochester, a hotbed of abolitionism, that members of the American Anti-Slavery Society prevailed upon him to conduct a lecture tour, and that catapulted him to fame in the North as an articulate and zealous opponent of slavery. He would win greater fame in 1845 with the publication of his autobiography.

Two years later, Douglass launched the *North Star*. It was named for the star at the head of the Big Dipper which runaway slaves followed to find their way into the free territories of the northern states. Douglass became a leader in the abolitionist movement, and for the first time blacks realized they had one of their own race speaking for them, and that infused them with even greater pride and resolve. His newspaper, which was published until 1851 when it was merged with the *Liberty Party* paper published by Gent Smith, reached a circulation of more than 4,000 readers in America, Europe, and the Caribbean. But many of those readers were movers and shakers who influenced public opinion.[12]

The slogan of the *North Star* was, "Right is of no Sex—Truth is of no Color—God is the Father of us all, and we are all brethren." Although at heart it was an abolitionist newspaper fighting for the rights of blacks, the newspaper also supported the feminist movement of the 19th century as well as rights for other suppressed groups.

Douglass would also serve as an adviser to President Abraham Lincoln during the Civil War, and he was a leader in the fight to adopt constitutional amendments guaranteeing that blacks would have the same civil liberties—including voting rights—as white America.

16. FOUNDING THE ASSOCIATED PRESS

Like many of the "moments" discussed in this book, the founding of the world's premier news agency cannot be traced back to an actual single moment in time. Instead, the Associated Press and its concept grew out of the need by various newspapers, geographically dispersed from the center of action at any one time, to have eyes and ears present at the event and to be able to send those reports back to member newspapers.

Today, the result of these attempts to meet that need has resulted in the Associated Press, which has some 8,000 members/subscribers in 243 bureaus around the world.[13] Virtually every daily newspaper and most broadcast stations in America are members of the Associated Press, which holds a near monopoly among Western print news agencies. Only Reuters comes close to the size of the Associated Press, but this European news agency has come to be known more for its financial news services than for AP's general-interest news offerings.

The AP, however, is unique because it is a cooperative, or consortium, of individual newspapers and broadcast stations. Hence the name "Associated" Press, which connotes the association involved. Unlike United Press International, another American news service which challenged the AP during the second half of the 20th century, the AP is not a stand-alone business that gathers and sells news to clients. A news medium joins the AP rather than subscribes to its services. Upon joining, there is an expectation that any stories which members produce may wind up as Associated Press stories as well. While the AP has a stand-alone news staff, many AP stories are done by reporters who work for member news organizations.

The AP actually grew out of an agreement of New York City's leading newspapers in 1849 to establish a cooperative news agency that became the Associated Press of New York. Soon, other regional APs were sprouting up in other parts of the country to service their areas.[14] The job of uniting these various regional APs was not easy, and it was not until 1900 that the incorporation papers of the AP were written. They were broad enough to ensure that the association was obligated to service all newspapers wanting it. Soon, however, the AP leadership found a way out of that non-exclusive arrangement and a new AP was founded as a nonprofit membership association under New York State law. Melville E. Stone became its first general manager.[15]

In addition to being a cooperative news service with each member supplying news from its region, it was decided the cost of running the AP would be shared by all members as well. That cost would include building a separate AP staff, supervised by a general manager who answered to a board of directors elected by the AP's membership. The new bylaws also forbade members from subscribing to other wire services, although that restriction was later dropped, as was one giving "protest rights" to any member newspaper wanting to keep a competing newspaper from securing AP membership. The AP collected domestic and international news, setting up foreign bureaus and working with European media to open up the possibility of sale of its news to foreign newspapers as well.

Under Kent Cooper, who became general manager in 1925, the AP flourished. Some of Cooper's significant contributions to the wire service were the following:

- The AP grew its number of bureaus and staffs at home and around the world.
- The AP expanded its services at the state level for local newspapers.
- He established the AP Wirephoto Service, which has become one of the best known and most reliable sources for news photos around the world.
- He formed the AP Radio-TV Association to provide news services to broadcast media.

- He launched automatic news printers, called teletypes, that replaced telegraph systems and operators.
- He developed more human-interest news, although not as much as the AP's rival, UPI.

One of the significant effects of the Associated Press has been creating in editors across America a more uniform sense of what national and international news stories are important. A casual glance at the front pages of American newspapers over the years, for any given day, will show that influence of uniformity which the AP has had. In fact, over the years, many editors have challenged their reporters, "Okay, if this is such a big story, then why doesn't the AP have it?" And it is largely because of the AP that critics in other parts of the world have complained long and loud about so much of the flow of international news coming from one western news agency. But the ability of the AP to put stories from far-flung places into the hands of editors for any hometown newspaper that wants it—but can't afford to chase it themselves—has been a remarkable positive achievement unmatched by any other invention of the news industry before network television and the Internet. Even with these latter two inventions, it is often overlooked that much of the information found in these media platforms originated with AP reporters.

Although the AP was challenged in the first half of the 20th century by United Press, a newsgathering service founded by Edward Scripps, and in the second half by the UP's evolution to UPI when it joined with the smaller International News Service, the AP flourished and UPI did not. Most industry observers attribute the AP's genius to its cooperative membership model instead of a stand-alone business that supplied news and information to paying clients.

17. OPENING THE CIVIL WAR

Probably the ultimate scoop for any American newspaper would be eyewitness reporting of the first major battle of a major war involving the United States. So it was that a reporter for the *Richmond Dispatch* recorded the opening moments of America's Civil War when, on July 20, 1861, Union troops met Confederate troops on the battlefield of Manassas Junction, Virginia, some 25 miles southwest of Washington, D.C. It must have been a surreal scene to await a battle that everyone in the area knew was coming. Carriages carrying congressmen, senators, and other government leaders—along with many wives bearing picnic lunches—followed Union troops south from Washington to watch an expected Rebel defeat at a place near Manassas known as Bull Run (or Bull's Run as some Virginians called it). As the battle unfolded, this civilian cheering section spread out their lunches on a nearby hill to watch what they believed would be victory for the Army of the Potomac.

As often happens, however, battles often take on a course of their own, and expected victors are not always the actual winners. In the case of the Manassas fight, this is exactly what happened when Confederate General Thomas J. "Stonewall"

Jackson was reinforced by the troops of Gen. Kirby Smith, sending the Union forces running on their heels back to the Potomac River. Under the headline of, "The Fight at Manassas! Brilliant Victory!" the *Richmond Dispatch* reported in part:

> MANASSAS JUNCTION, July 18—Victory perches upon our banners. The army of the Potomac, under the command of General Pierre G. T. Beauregard, gave battle to the enemy today at Bull's Run, four miles from Manassas Junction, in a Northwest direction, and three miles to the left of the Alexandria Rail-Road. The enemy attempted to cross the ford at several points in great numbers, but were repulsed by our brave and determined troops three times, with heavy loss on the enemy's side. The enemy retreated about five o'clock in the afternoon in confusion, two of our regiments pursuing them. A large number of them have been taken prisoners. On our side, the casualties are few.[16]

The reporting shows two things that would become common in Civil War reporting from both sides. One is the general format of the *summary lead* which attempts to answer—albeit briefly—the key questions the reader might have within the first paragraph. The second shows the favoritism and allegiance of the newspaper doing the story. Southern newspapers obviously favored the Confederate side and vice versa. In the case of this story on Bull Run, the reporter had no real way of knowing he was witnessing the opening battle of what would be a four-year war between the North and the South. Indeed, both sides thought the war (called the "Civil War" by the North and the "War Between the States" by the South) would be a relatively short one. Ultimately, there would be thousands of more newspaper stories published before the bloody campaign came to an end. Northern history has called this the First Battle of Bull Run, while many southerners still refer to it as the Battle of Manassas since the South often named their battles for the nearest town.

18. CREATING THE INVERTED PYRAMID

What does a war have to do with the structure a reporter uses to write his or her story? To a large degree, that question was answered by the American Civil War, a conflict which many journalism historians believe served as the mother of invention for a classic news writing style.

When the fighting began, many northern correspondents found themselves in southern states trying to send back their dispatches over telegraph wires. In so doing, they were competing with military field commanders needing to use the transmission systems at the same time. Even more problematic, the correspondents knew that Confederate military commanders were intent on preventing communiques from Union soldiers from getting through. One of the favored means of such prevention was simply cutting the telegraph wires. For the northern war correspondents, however, that also meant their dispatches would not get back to their editors in the North.

The correspondents knew that was a constant threat, so they devised a system of pumping a summary of the key facts into the opening portion of each story, and that story section became known as the lead. The name eventually given to formats using this opening summary was the "inverted pyramid," employing the metaphor of an upside down triangle with the broad portion at the top and the narrowed portion at the bottom. To a correspondent, that translated as summarizing the key facts of the story in the first couple of paragraphs and waiting until later for the details which would be told in their perceived order of importance. Should Confederate troops be in the midst of cutting wires while a story was being sent, at least the summary of that story might get through. The new story structure worked, and journalists came to realize there were longer-lasting benefits of the inverted pyramid as well. The main advantage of summarizing the story in the opening paragraph or two was it served as an attention-getter for busy readers who otherwise might pass by an important story were they first have to slog through details rather than an overview of the event.

An example of how the inverted pyramid was used for the story of President Abraham Lincoln's assassination is often cited by writing coaches such as Chip Scanlan of the Poynter Institute for Media Studies. That story, appearing in the *New York Herald* on April 15, 1865, reads in part:

> This evening at about 9:30 p.m. at Ford's Theatre, the President, while sitting in his private box with Mrs. Lincoln, Mrs. Harris and Major Rathburn, was shot by an assassin, who suddenly entered the box and approached behind the President.
>
> The assassin then leaped upon the stage, brandishing a large dagger or knife, and made his escape in the rear of the theatre.
>
> The pistol ball entered the back of the President's head and penetrated nearly through the head. The wound is mortal.
>
> The President has been insensible ever since it was inflicted, and is now dying.
>
> About the same hour an assassin, whether the same or not, entered Mr. Seward's apartment and under pretense of having a prescription was shown to the Secretary's sick chamber. The assassin immediately rushed to the bed and inflicted two or three stabs on the chest and two on the face. It is hoped the wounds may not be mortal. My apprehension is that they will prove fatal.
>
> The nurse alarmed Mr. Frederick Seward, who was in an adjoining room, and he hastened to the door of his father's room, when he met the assassin, who inflicted upon him one or more dangerous wounds. The recovery of Frederick Seward is doubtful.
>
> It is not probable that the President will live through the night.
>
> General Grant and his wife were advertised to be at the theatre ... [17]

The main testament to the value of the inverted pyramid story format is that it has endured to this day as a favored means of telling a breaking or "spot" news story. It is the classic story style and, as this example shows, it is built around the answers to six often-heard one-word questions and a seventh two-word question added later. Those questions addressed in a summary lead are *who, what, when, where, how, why,* and *so what?* The *why* often takes longer to answer and is sometimes relegated to later in the story but, essentially, these are the questions that form the focus of a summary lead which is the key feature of an inverted pyramid format. Once past the lead, the story segues into a section amplifying the points just summarized, and the remainder of the story is given to specific details and quotes.

The inverted pyramid certainly has had its challengers from other formats which hearken to more literary and narrative writing styles, but reporters realize the inverted pyramid is the favored means of telling an important, breaking news story that readers or viewers have not heard about. Newspapers use the format less frequently than before, simply because television—and now the Internet—have taken away most of the ability for newspaper reporters to write stories their readers are not already familiar with. Live television reports and constantly-updated Web news wreaks havoc on a print system which requires hours in lead time from reporting to publication and distribution of the news to readers. The fact, however, that all daily newspapers now have Web editions has returned much of that ability for newspaper reporters to break stories, albeit on the Internet and not in their hard-copy newspapers. So, for print editions, the inverted pyramid has largely given way to more *narrative* formats, or a return to the righting of the pyramid where readers enter the story through an interesting extended anecdote or individual profile before the story fans out to the larger story. That is also a format which lends itself well to television, although even TV reporters will often still use the inverted pyramid for important breaking news stories.

Given the nature of the inverted pyramid—and the fact that the story was meant to dwindle in importance as it went along and had no formal conclusion, the format was found to be very helpful by editors. For many years, stories written in this format were often just cut from the bottom if they wouldn't fit in the newspaper space reserved for them. It was not always the best way of editing a story, however, because a reporter might save a good quote or anecdote as a conclusion to their story. Or the space for the story might be so tight in the first place that the story was written very short and tight to start with, and there were no extraneous details. So this kind of "bottoms-up" editing often caused arguments between reporters and editors, and still does today.

Finally, some writing coaches have recently come to question what they refer to as the "idiot logic" of the inverted pyramid, or the fact that readers are not stupid and know that if a story is written with all the important facts on top, there is scant reason to read further into the story. So, the argument goes, reporters who use the inverted pyramid are actually signaling the readers they can, if they so choose, stop reading after the first couple of paragraphs because they will have digested the most important facts by then.

19. THE FIRST NEWSPAPER CHAIN

By the mid-19th century, cities were growing by leaps and bounds all across the United States. The Industrial Revolution was in full swing, and that was drawing more and more people into the nation's urban areas not just in the East, but also the Midwest, South, and West. More jobs led to higher incomes and more educational opportunities for the country's population. The industrial revolution also led to improved technologies which allowed businesses to ratchet up their production schedules and make products and services available nationwide. The newspaper industry was no exception, and newspaper barons began buying up more newspapers and forming chains as the former era of personal journalism gave way to corporate journalism. Relatively small, locally-based and family-run newspapers began evolving into large, geographically dispersed, vertically-integrated businesses. Into this picture stepped a young Illinois journalist, Edward Wyllis Scripps, who began the first of the nation's chains of newspapers.

In 1873, E. W. Scripps' older brother James founded the *Detroit Evening News*. E. W. began working on the paper, first as a copy boy, then reporter and took over as city editor in 1875. He believed in the idea of "personal journalism" or crusading for worthy causes and exposing frauds perpetrated on the common citizens by the rich and powerful. Scripps' enthusiasm for personal journalism grew rapidly, and he also came to see it made good business sense as well. His dreams of a kind of "Roman Kingdom" as he called it, grew. By 1878 he decided to start building that empire, and he began the *Cleveland Penny Press* as the first link in that chain. He would go on to launch or buy some 32 newspapers, with shares in 15 others, that became America's first (of many) newspaper chains and which would form the cornerstone of the E. W. Scripps Co.

As a publisher and businessman, Scripps distrusted both socialism as well as capitalism, a paradox that made him a lifelong protestor of the status quo. His personal motto became, "Whatever is, is wrong," and that only fueled his newspapers' crusading spirits. To underscore his belief that a newspaper should serve to enlighten and educate its readers, he adopted a graphic lighthouse as the company's logo with the charge, "Give light and the people will find their own way."

But Scripps also understood business, and his growing empire prospered. His methodology for building that newspaper chain was to choose a small, promising town, start a newspaper, hire a young and ambitious editor, then give that editor time to expand the paper's success or shut it down if it didn't grow. His mandate to his editors was, "Make money and serve the poor and working classes." Scripps newspapers would come to reflect independence, enlightenment, protest, and human interest. Other than Detroit, Cleveland and Cincinnati, big newspapers in the chain came to include the *Rocky Mountain News* in Denver, *The Commercial-Appeal* in Memphis, the *Daily Camera* in Boulder, Colorado, and the *Knoxville News Sentinel* in Knoxville, Tennessee. While these papers remained the cornerstone of the empire, some larger Scripps dailies were acquired by other media companies in the newspaper buying frenzy of the 1970s and 1980s.

Scripps also founded the only viable American-based alternative to the Associated Press wire service when he began the United Press wire service, which became United Press International. For decades, nearly every major newspaper in America subscribed to both the AP and UPI, with many editors favoring the more colorful writing style of UPI.

In the early 1920s, Scripps added "Howard" to the company's operating name, which became Scripps-Howard, to reflect and recognize the great contribution of Roy W. Howard, an aggressive young newsman who rose to become president and chairman of the board of the company. Years later, the company's name would revert simply to the E. W. Scripps Company.

By 2008, the company held interests in cable networks, newspaper publishing, broadcast television stations, electronic commerce, interactive media, and licensing and syndication. Scripps operates daily and community newspapers in 18 markets, 10 broadcast TV stations, five cable and satellite television programming networks, a television retailing network, and online search and comparison shopping services.

Time magazine said the following about Scripps in 1962, at the height of the Scripps company's popularity:

> Scripps-Howard is the most viable and most successful newspaper chain in the U.S. It has endured for 84 years, longer than any other group, including the venerable Hearst papers. Unlike Hearst, which loses money despite a circulation larger than Scripps-Howard's 3,074,150, Scripps-Howard has consistently made money from birth . . . Whatever the reasons, the Scripps-Howard system indisputably works.[18]

Time added that a key reason for the Scripps' success was the management philosophy which prevented meddling from the top and a conviction that local editors know best how to run their local newspapers. Essentially, Scripps began the formula of hiring good people, then getting out of their way to let them do the job they were hired for.

When Scripps retired, he and his half-sister Ellen were principal donors to the founding of the Scripps Institute of Oceanography, located in San Diego. Today the Ohio University School of Journalism carries the name of the E. W. Scripps School of Journalism.

20. LAUNCHING *GODEY'S LADY'S BOOK*

Within the magazine industry, the women's magazine is a big seller. In 2008, five of the top ten circulating magazines in America were women's magazines: *Better Homes and Gardens*, *Good Housekeeping*, *Family Circle*, *Ladies' Home Journal*, and *Woman's Day*.[19] One of the earliest, and certainly most popular women's magazine was *Godey's Lady's Book*, launched in 1830 by Louis A. Godey, who owned it for almost 50 years, most of those under the editorship of Sarah Josepha Hale. Godey envisioned a magazine that would appeal to women and pick up on the popularity of gift books of the day. The magazine featured original American articles and essays written by both men and women, as well as patterns for home sewing projects and sheet music for pianists. The magazine contained some of the best writers of the day, including Edgar Allen Poe, Nathaniel Hawthorne, and Washington Irving. Hale featured three special issues that included articles written only by female writers. Despite the high price of the magazine, it was one of the most popular magazines of the day, vying for popularity with the venerable *Saturday Evening Post*. With Hale at the helm as editor, *Godey's Lady's Book* had some 150,000 subscribers at its height.[20]

In writing her 1931 history of *Godey's*, author Ruth E. Finley noted of the magazine's significance, "Here almost a century ago were the beginnings of the various departments—cookery, beauty, health, architecture, gardening, interior decoration—so highly developed in today's home magazines. All was handled very differently, yet with an amazingly modern touch."[21] Finley also noted, "But soon it was evident . . . Somebody was putting up a good fight for children and women, and was especially concerned for the latter's intellectual and economic freedom."[22]

Under Hale's editorship, the magazine flourished. But the magazine was only one of this woman's many accomplishments. Indeed, Hale seems one of history's truly unsung heroes. Born Sarah J. Buell on a New Hampshire farm in 1788, Hale was a 34-year-old mother of four in 1822 when she and her sister started a millinery business following her husband's death. She launched her literary career with a book of poems called *The Genius of Oblivion and Other Original Poems*, and that led to the publication of a novel, *Northwood*, which was well-received by the public and critics alike. It dealt with the issue of slavery. Her notoriety led to her being named editor of a new magazine devoted to women readers. She moved to Boston to edit *Ladies Magazine and Literary Gazette*, a name changed to *American Ladies Magazine* in 1834. Now 36 and the mother of five, Hale had launched a magazine editing career that would last until 1877, most of which would be spent working for Louis Godey, who was so impressed with her work that he bought the magazine she was editing, moved it to Philadelphia and called it *Godey's Lady's Book*. As editor, she worked

This is a November 26, 1996, photo of a painting of Sarah Josepha Hale which was created by James Reid Lambdin in the early 1800s and now hangs in Newport, New Hampshire. Hale was a women's rights advocate born in Newport, New Hampshire in 1788, and among her many achievements was persuading President Abraham Lincoln to proclaim a national Thanksgiving Day in 1863. [AP Photo/Jim Cole]

for the advancement of women, was a leader in raising funds to preserve Mount Vernon, and crusaded for the economic independence of women. Hale is also known for encouraging President Abraham Lincoln to create a national Thanksgiving Holiday, and she is also credited with writing the classic children's poem, "Mary Had a Little Lamb."

21. JOSEPH PULITZER BUYS THE *NEW YORK WORLD*

With the country's population growing and focusing around the cities, the interest in news grew wider and wider. Along with it came more advertising. News became an even bigger product than it had been in the era of the penny press. One of the greatest newspapers of this latter era was the *New York World*.

The *World* had been launched in 1860 but, in a little more than a decade, it was losing about $40,000 annually (and was down to 15,000 subscribers) when a St. Louis newspaper publisher named Joseph Pulitzer bought it for $346,000. Pulitzer had already made a name for himself in Missouri, building the *St. Louis Post-Dispatch*. Pulitzer was a man of many contradictions. He grew mighty in stature, yet he was a weak physical specimen of a man. He exuded idealism on his editorial page, yet he was a zealous opportunist in building his newspaper into the most popular in the country. He had begun his adult life as a Republican but became a Democrat, championing the cause of the common man. His news pages reeked of sensationalism, yet his editorial pages exuded reformism. He was a recruiter of top journalistic talent, yet he remained a man distrustful of anyone who would work for him. He was involved in one of the most intense businesses imaginable and was often irritable, yet in his later years he needed total tranquility for his health and lived inside a padded home which some called "the vault" to keep away from noises.[23]

Perhaps his major contradiction was that, while insisting on accuracy in reporting, he built a newspaper bathed in what became known as "yellow" journalism, named for "The Yellow Kid" comic strip that Richard Outcault created for him. It was said of Pulitzer that he had the articulate voice of Horace Greeley but the dirty hands of sensationalist publisher James Gordon Bennett, Sr.

To many, what Pulitzer had was the total newspaper in the *New York World*. In saving it from bankruptcy and recreating it, he would draw upon the pattern set originally by Benjamin Day and Bennett to turn his *World* into the most popular daily of its day, filling it with human-interest news, a crusading spirit for the common man, international news, financial reporting, advertising, and sensationalism. The latter attribute was not confined to news stories, either, but found its way into headlines such as "Baptized in Blood," and "Mangled by Mongrels." And he would also infuse it with humor, which even found its way into obituary notices such as one for inventor Cyrus McCormick which noted, "Cyrus McCormick invented a great reaper, but the Grim Reaper cut him down, and now he is no mower."[24]

In lighting a journalistic fire, Pulitzer advanced the cause of egalitarian, everyday journalism that would take journalism to a greater height of popularity and prosperity than ever before. Before long, Pulitzer's success would inspire another young publisher—William Randolph Hearst—to move to New York from San Francisco and purchase the *New York Journal*, launching the well-known era of Yellow Journalism. Hearst was the son of a wealthy westerner who had made his money in silver mines. He became enraptured with what Pulitzer was doing in New York and tried to copy it in San Francisco by having his father buy him the *San Francisco Examiner*. He practiced Pulitzer's editorial formula there, then brought it to New York where he purchased the *Morning Journal* in 1895, renaming it the *New York Journal* and building its circulation to some 500,000 subscribers. One of the means he used to do this was by buying away most of Pulitzer's newsroom stars including cartoonist Outcault.

Pulitzer justified his brand of journalism by saying there is no way to expose sin and corruption in business and government unless reporters write about it in a way that makes people want to read it. His editorial equation was one that has been used by many successful newspaper publishers over the decades: Circulation = Advertising = Independence. He eventually grew tired of the yellow journalism war with Hearst and, in the late 1890s began rising above sensationalism and casting himself as the "conscience" of journalism. He endowed Columbia University with a grant to create a school of journalism which today is the Columbia Graduate School of Journalism, and insisted on making ethics its cornerstone.

By the time of Pulitzer's death in 1911, *The World* had more than 300,000 subscribers. It was in much better financial condition than Hearst's *Journal*, however, because

Joseph Pulitzer, the publisher of the New York World *and the* St. Louis Post-Dispatch, *was considered one of America's outstanding journalists at the time of his death in 1911. He left $2,500,000 for the founding of the Pulitzer School of Journalism at Columbia University and the annual Pulitzer prizes for outstanding work in journalism and letters. This is an undated file photo. [AP Photo/ files]*

Pulitzer always put money back into building a better newspaper, whereas Hearst lacked such business sense and simply loved to spend huge sums of the money he earned.

22. THE ADVENTURES OF NELLIE BLY

Elizabeth Cochrane was a trailblazer for women in daily journalism and a key link in the history of investigative reporting in America. She also added a strong dash of entertainment to the journalistic profession that was evolving in the late 19th century. In fact, her very pen name of Nellie Bly was adapted from the Stephen Foster song of the same name. And before latching onto that name, she had the nickname "Pink," given by her mother who christened Cochrane in a pink christening gown.

Bly was born in 1864 and made her name in newspaper journalism at a time when the newsroom was a male domain. Women, if hired at all, were usually relegated to society news. But Bly, who grew up in Pennsylvania, dreamed of becoming a general news reporter and began her career by writing a letter to the editor of the *Pittsburgh Dispatch*, responding to the newspaper's advice column called "Women's Sphere." The aspiring writer signed her letter, "Little Orphan Girl." Editor George Madden was impressed and published an open letter asking for "Little Orphan Girl" to write and provide him her real name and address. Cochrane had just turned 18. Showing her spunk, she decided to go in person to the newspaper instead of sending her name and address, and talked the editor into hiring her as a writer for the *Dispatch*. She did not envision herself as a writer of society news and instead began reporting on social issues dealing with working women, conditions in factories, and proposals for reforming divorce laws that would give women divorcees more equal treatment. One of her most famous assignments came later in an undercover stint to report on conditions in a women's insane asylum.[25]

The editors were impressed, but persisted in seeing a woman writer as better suited to doing women's stories on gardening, fashion, and cultural issues. As much as she loved writing for the newspaper, Cochrane—who had by now taken the pen name of Nellie Bly—became frustrated with the editors' wishes and decided instead to quit the *Dispatch*. Soon after, however, she agreed to return to the paper to carry out an assignment reporting from Mexico. She then spent half a year in that country, sending back stories published under the headline of "Nellie in Mexico." The series focused on poverty and corruption by political officials in Mexico. Her reporting was a hit with readers, and Cochrane loved her role as a foreign correspondent, but the Mexican government found her too troublesome and evicted her from the country.[26] At home, however, a star was born.

Many journalistic historians refer to Nellie Bly as the inventor of investigative reporting. She was certainly proficient at going undercover to get stories. Among her disguises was posing as a poor sweatshop worker to expose the cruel conditions which factory work posed for women.

When she returned to the United States from Mexico, Bly decided to move to New York City and work for a larger newspaper. Her persuasive talents won her a good reporting job at the *New York World*, owned by the famous Joseph Pulitzer. Her very first assignment at that paper became one of her most famous. She would be "committed" to the Women's Lunatic Asylum on Blackwell's Island to report on the horrible conditions for women patients there.

Bly's most famous adventure, however, came in the fall of 1888 when the *World*'s editors decided to send man around the world in less than 80 days, to beat the time of the fictional Jules Verne character in his book, *Around the World in 80 Days*. Bly, however, persuaded her editors to send her on the journey instead of a man. She threatened to quit and do it for another newspaper if they disagreed. She got the assignment, and the next November she began her journey. Her travel adventures were published daily by the *World* and became an essential part of their readers' days. In the end, not only did Bly beat the 80–day mark but she beat it by nearly eight days. When she arrived home in New York, she was greeted with brass bands, parades, and fireworks.

The name Nellie Bly was now a household name in America, and many young women aspired to become a newspaper reporter just like her. Bly returned to crusading in the news pages for social reforms and equal treatment for women until marrying and retiring from journalism in 1895.

23. THE *MAINE* GOES DOWN

America has had its share of wars which have left large segments of the population wondering why they were necessary. Among those questionable engagements was the Spanish-American War in the late 19th century. Many give credit—or blame—to the start of this war in Cuba to eccentric and flamboyant newspaper publisher William Randolph Hearst and how he ordered his newspapers to interpret the sinking of the USS *Maine*, an American battleship that sunk under mysterious circumstances in Havana Harbor on February 15, 1898. Hearst's newspaper, the *New York Journal*, proclaimed the sinking the work of the Spanish government and he called Americans to war with Spain.

The trouble in Cuba had begun in 1895 when native insurrections began rebelling against Spanish rule. Many Cubans fled when fighting broke out, and many of them landed in New York and Florida. They spent time trying to build support among Americans for the cause of the Cuban rebels, and their story spelled controversy, compassion, and street sales to Hearst and Joseph Pulitzer, who were locked in a pitched circulation battle between their newspapers the *Journal* and the *New York World*. Conditions for Cubans worsened in 1896 when the Spanish government installed Captain-General Valeriano Weyler as their leader in Cuba to enforce Spanish polices. These policies grew more repressive, as the Spanish herded many Cubans into small camps where more than 100,000 of them died. Weyler, named "the butcher," was blamed for these deaths, and stories about Spanish atrocities—both real and made-up —laced the pages of the New York City newspapers and interested many readers. Competition for news became fierce between Pulitzer and Hearst, and Hearst sent

The explosion which tore the U.S. battleship Maine *apart in the harbor at Havana, Cuba, February 15, 1898, was dramatically portrayed in this sketch by an American magazine artist of the time. Of a complement of 326 men, 266 were lost. An American board of inquiry made an extensive examination of the wreckage and reported to the Navy Department that the explosion was caused by an exterior mine. A month later, the war between Spain and the United States was on. [AP Photo/fls]*

reporters James Creelman and Richard Harding Davis to Cuba to report on the trouble, and artist/illustrator Frederick Remington to illustrate the conflict.[27]

Events would reach a head with a *Journal* exclusive on February 9 when the paper published a private letter from the Spanish ambassador to the United States to a newspaper editor from Spain who was visiting Havana. The ambassador referred to U.S. President William McKinley as "weak and catering to the rabble." That infuriated U.S. readers. Then, on the night of February 15, an explosion occurred aboard the American battleship *Maine*, docked in Havana Harbor. Some 266 Americans perished in this explosion which sunk the ship. Although the cause of the explosion was never really known, Hearst's *Journal* interpreted it his own way, and in no uncertain terms. On the morning of February 17, the front page of the Journal was devoted to the sinking of the *Maine* under the headline, "Destruction of the War Ship Maine as the Work of an Enemy." Another headline on Page One read, "Naval Officers Think the Maine Was Destroyed by a Spanish Mine." On the same page, the *Journal* offered a $50,000 reward for information leading to finding the perpetrators.[28]

For his part, Pulitzer ordered his editor to be a little more cautious in attaching blame, but the large, dramatic illustration of the ship being blown apart did its part in rallying Americans to battle.

PISTOL-PACKING HEARST

Not only did William Randolph Hearst exert a huge influence in whipping up sentiment for the U.S. war with Spain by sending reporters and artists to document—if not embellish—the alleged Spanish atrocities against the Cubans; he also got involved in the actual war coverage himself. Hearst found himself impatient waiting for the stories of his star reporter James Creelman, and he also found himself craving the action Creelman and other journalists were experiencing reporting the war in Cuba. So Hearst boarded his lavish yacht, *The Vamoose*, and sailed to the island to find Creelman and help him report the war.

Caught up in the adrenalin of the fight, Creelman offered to lead a bayonet charge on the small fort at which the Spaniard troops were dug in at the top of the hill. "This was hardly the business of a correspondent," Creelman wrote later, "but whatever of patriotism or excitement was stirring others in that place of carnage had got into my blood, too . . . I began to realize that I had ceased to be a journalist and was now—foolishly or wisely, recklessly, meddlesomely, or patriotically—a part of the army, a soldier without warrant to kill." He was wounded by a bullet in the process and found himself lying on the ground looking up into a set of familiar eyes belonging to his boss, William Randolph Hearst. Creelman recalled the experience this way:

> Some one knelt in the grass beside me and put his hand on my fevered head. Opening my eyes, I saw Mr. Hearst, the proprietor of the *New York Journal*, a straw hat with a bright ribbon on his head, a revolver at his belt, and a pencil and notebook in his hand. The man who had provoked the war had come to see the result with his own eyes and, finding one of his correspondents prostrate, was doing the work himself. Slowly he took down my story of the fight. Again and again the ting-ing of Mauser bullets interrupted. But he seemed unmoved. The battle had to be reported somehow. "I'm sorry you're hurt, but"—and his face was radiant with enthusiasm—"wasn't it a splendid fight? We must beat every paper in the world." After doing what he could to make me comfortable, Mr. Hearst mounted his horse and dashed away for the seacoast, where a fast steamer was waiting to carry him across the sea to a cable station.

—James Creelman. *On the Great Highway: The Wanderings and Adventures of a Special Correspondent.* Boston: Lothrop Publishing Co., 1901, Chapter 8, http://www.cardinalbook.com/creelman/highway/iso8859/index.htm

Soon, this kind of constant, graphic reporting turned American public opinion toward going to war with Spain and aiding the suffering Cubans. Military units sprang up, including the famous Rough Riders, led by future President Theodore Roosevelt, and Congress passed a $50 million defense bill for war. While Pulitzer's *World* urged caution before springing into war, Hearst's *Journal* let his horses run and urged the country to go to war. When war did come, Hearst not only had his best reporters like Creelman in the field covering battles, but he even went himself, brightly dressed with a large straw hat and pistol in his sash, lending whatever support he could to his staffers.

Historians often refer to the Spanish-American War as "Mr. Hearst's War," and many believe the publisher fostered the spirit for war to beat Pulitzer in their highly-pitched circulation battles in New York City.

24. ADOLPH OCHS BUYS THE *NEW YORK TIMES*

It is hard to imagine a time in the United States when the *New York Times* was not seen as the most important and respected newspaper in the country, the true "newspaper of record." Yet, although the *Times* has been in existence since 1851, it was not until 1896 that the newspaper began to become the giant it proved to be in the industry and such a huge influence on the United States and its government. It didn't appear it would be that way when the *Times* was founded in 1851 by Henry Jarvis Raymond, a journalist and politician, and his partner George Jones, an ex-banker. Not that the newspaper didn't have influence. During the mayoral reign of Boss Tweed, the *Times* published a series of revealing articles (in 1870–1871) that would lead to the end of the Tweed era and his domination of New York City government. That series and its impact caused the influence of the *Times* to grow, although it was only a harbinger of what would be coming when Adolph Ochs acquired the newspaper in 1896.[29]

Adolph S. Ochs, publisher of the New York Times, *is shown, date and location unknown.* [AP Photo]

Ochs was publisher of the *Chattanooga Times* when he decided to move to New York and take on Joseph Pulitzer and William Randolph Hearst, publishers of the *New York World* and the *New York Journal* who were taking journalistic sensationalism to new heights—or depths. He determined that the public's taste for yellow journalism had ebbed and that the time and city were right for a newspaper that would look at news more seriously. The year after he took over the newspaper, he created the *Times*' slogan of "All the News That's Fit to Print." Under the leadership of Ochs and his heirs in years to come, the *Times* grew in stature to become one of the leading newspapers in the world. Among its many achievements have been:

- Winning some 100 Pulitzer Prizes, the highest professional honor a journalist and publication can achieve, by 2008.

- Becoming the first newspaper to receive a real-time wireless transmission from a naval battle in the 1904 Russo-Japanese War.

- Becoming a national newspaper by delivering its daily product to every state in America.

- Becoming an international newspaper, first by launching an international edition in 1946, and then converting it to joint publication of the *New York Herald Tribune* and *The Washington Post* and launching it in Paris as the *International Herald Tribune* in 1967.

- Becoming the centerpiece of a 1964 landmark libel case (*New York Times Co. v. Sullivan*) which wound up in the Supreme Court and established the "actual malice" rule for media stories involving public figures. In that decision, the Court said journalists must be allowed some latitude in reporting and commenting on public figures, and that they shouldn't be held liable for mistake unless they engaged in reckless disregard for the truth.

- Publishing the full text of one of the most revealing studies in American history when, in 1971, it published the so-called "Pentagon Papers." These was a classified Department of Defense history of America's involvement in the Vietnam War from 1945 to 1971. The study had been leaked to *Times* reporter Neil Sheehan by Daniel Ellsberg, a former State Department official. The documents were published over several days and, after the first of the reports appeared, President Richard Nixon ordered Attorney General John Mitchell to get a federal court injunction ordering the *Times* to stop publishing the series. The case went to the Supreme Court after *The Washington Post* began publishing the same papers. Three weeks after the first documents were published by the *Times*, the Court held 6–3 in *New York Times Co. v. United States* that the injunctions were not constitutional under the no-prior restraint interpretation of the First Amendment. It was an extremely important decision in the history of press freedom in America.

- Publishing the most highly respected book review section in the world.

- Rising to the top of newspaper circulation leaders in America and by 2008, trailed only *USA Today* and *The Wall Street Journal* in circulation with more than 1.1 million copies circulated on weekdays and 1.6 million on Sundays.[30]

The *New York Times* has been published by the Ochs-Sulzberger family (Arthur Hays Sulzberger was an early *Times* publisher), which like Chicago's McCormick-Patterson family, is one of the country's greatest newspaper dynasties. Although the *New York Times* became a publicly traded company in the 1960s, the family continued to control it via ownership of most of the Class B voting shares, giving them the right to vote on all matters. Arthur Ochs Sulzberger, Jr., became publisher of the *Times* in 1992 and chairman of the board of The New York Times Co. in 1997, succeeding his father, Arthur Ochs Sulzberger.[31]

25. MARCONI (OR FESSENDEN) LAUNCHES RADIO

In 1896, a 22-year-old Italian physicist named Guglielmo Marconi sent and received a coded telegraph message over a distance of two miles. Three years later, he was transmitting the same kind of messages between France and England over the English Channel, and by 1901 he was sending messages across the Atlantic Ocean. With these inventions in telegraphy, the wireless era was born, and that opened the door to the medium we know today as radio.

Marconi took his invention to England where he received the world's first patent for a system of wireless telegraphy. In 1897 he created The Wireless Telegraph & Signal Company which was renamed Marconi's Wireless Telegraph Company Limited three years later. After the successful English Channel transmissions, Marconi built four permanent wireless stations in England and France. He was granted another important patent in 1900 (Patent No. 7777) for "tuned or syntonic telegraphy" and in December, 1991, he defied then-current logic that wireless waves were affected by the earth's curvature. To do that, he had to send wireless signals across the Atlantic—some 2,100 miles between England the Newfoundland—and his attempt was successful. Marconi received numerous honors for his inventions, topped off by being awarded the Nobel Prize in Physics in 1909.[32]

Do his inventions make Marconi the "father of radio" as many contend? Not if we're talking about the transmission of voices. That kind of wireless transmission was first done by Reginald Fessenden, a Canadian inventor who began working in 1886 for Thomas Edison and made advances in audio signal receiver equipment. Later, while working for the United States Weather Bureau, he developed the heterodyne principle, or the combination of two signals producing a third audible signal or tone. He also developed a high-frequency transmitter and was the first to transmit speech effectively over the distance of one mile in 1900. So, in terms of voice transmission, that was actually history's first known radio transmission. Six years later, with the help of outside funding—some of it from the young General Electric Company—to further his developments, he used his newly developed alternator-transmitter to send an entire short audio program on Christmas Eve, 1906, from Brant Rock, Massachusetts. Among the program offerings was his own live violin version of *O Holy Night*. Since there were few—if any—publicly owned radio receivers at the time, the audience consisted of shipboard radio operators on the Atlantic coast. Fessenden never really

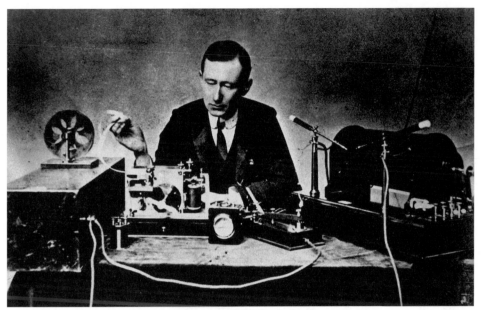

Italian physicist Guglielmo Marconi, who claimed he invented radio, reads signals on a tape recorder, left, with a 10-inch spark coil used for ship-to-shore radio tests in this 1901 photo. [AP Photo]

profited from his inventions, however, and his patents were sold in 1921 to the Radio Corporation of America (RCA).

In a real sense, both Marconi and Fessenden can be called fathers of radio because each supplied a key part of the medium's development: Marconi for sending wireless telegraphy signals in the first place and Fessenden for wireless voice transmission.

NOTES

1. Michael Emery, Edwin Emery, Nancy L. Roberts. *The Press and America: An Interpretive History of the Mass Media*, 9th ed. Boston: Allyn & Bacon, 2000, p. 97.

2. Richard Adams Locke. "Celestial Discoveries," The *New York Sun*, August 25, 1835, as retrieved on August 8, 2008 on http://www.historybuff.com/library/refmoon.html.

3. Ibid.

4. Ibid.

5. Matthew Goodman. *The Sun and the Moon.* New York: Basic Books, 2008, p. 246.

6. Louis L. Snyder and Richard B. Morris. *A Treasury of Golden Reporting.* New York: Simon & Schuster, 1962, p. 191.

7. Ibid, p. 196.

8. Ibid.

9. Ralph M. Hower. *The History of an Advertising Agency: N.W. Ayer & Son at Work, 1869–1939.* Cambridge: Harvard University Press, 1939.

10. Donald R. Holland. "Volney B. Palmer, 1799–1864: The Nation's First Advertising Agency Man," *Journalism Monographs*, Association of Journalism and Mass Communication Education, May 1976.

11. William David Sloan, James G. Stovall, James D. Startt. *The Media in America: A History*. Worthington, Ohio: Publishing Horizons, 1998, p. 150.

12. Ibid.

13. "About Us," www.ap.org.

14. Emery, Emery, and Roberts. *Press and America*, 244.

15. Ibid.

16. *Richmond Dispatch*, July 18, 1861, p. 1, as reprinted in *American Datelines*, Ed Cray, Jonathan Kotler, and Miles Belle (eds.), New York: Facts on File, 1990, pp. 52–53.

17. Chip Scanlan. "An Examination of the Inverted Pyramid." Poynter Institute, June 6, 2003, as retrieved on August 10, 2008, on www.poynter.org.

18. *Time* magazine, October 19, 1962.

19. "Average Circulation for Top 100 ABC Magazines," Magazine Publishers of America, as retrieved on August 10, 2008, on www.magazine.org.

20. Fred Lewis Pattee. *The First Century of American Literature: 1770–1870*. New York: Cooper Square Publishers, 1966, p. 392.

21. Ruth E. Finley. *The Lady of Godey's: Sarah Josepha Hale*. London: J.B. Lippincott Co., 1931.

22. Ibid.

23. Frank Luther Mott. *The History of American Journalism*. New York: Harcourt, 1964.

24. Ibid.

25. SloanStovall, Startt. *Media in America*, p. 229.

26. Ibid.

27. Emery, Emery, Roberts. *Press and America*, pp. 201–205.

28. Ibid.

29. Mott. *History of American Journalism*.

30. Jennifer Saba. "New FAS-FAX: Steep Decline at NYT while WASJ Gains," *Editor & Publisher*, as retrieved on August 10, 2008, on www.editorand publisher.com.

31. "New York Times Timeline." The New York Times Company, as retrieved on August 11, 2008, on www.newyorktimes.com.

32. Retrieved on August 13, 2008, on http://nobelprize.org/nobel_prizes/physics/laureates/1909/marconi-bio.html.

Part III

The 20th Century: Growth and Tragedies Define America

By far, the 20th century provided most of the moments contained in this book's cataloguing of important media developments. After the 19th century provided the modern-day model of the American media—mass-circulation publications with news and entertainment for everyone, supported mainly by advertising revenue—the 20th century refined and expanded this model in a number of ways. For one thing, in the opening years of this century, the media expanded beyond print publications to radio, then later television, and finally into the new frontier of the Internet. The nature and process of journalism also grew up in this era, as the concept of objective journalism and the separation of fact and opinion became bulwarks of the American press. Toward the end of the century, however, those two concepts would once again merge in some media, most notably several cable television news shows.

26. *THE SHAME OF THE CITIES*

Among the annals of investigative reporters in America, the name of Lincoln Steffens is unrivaled in many ways. And the series of reports that made Steffens a household name in many of the cities he worked came to be known collectively as "The Shame of the Cities" series which appeared in *McClure*'s magazine. The publication of *The Shame of the Cities* into book form in 1904 brought together six of these articles that exposed the corruption of governments in Chicago, Minneapolis, Pittsburgh, St. Louis, Philadelphia, and New York.

Steffens was a leading investigative reporter—or "muckraker" as President Theodore Roosevelt tagged them—who had worked as a reporter covering crime for the

45

New York Evening Post in the freewheeling "yellow" journalism era of the 1890s. Steffens majored in depth more than sensationalism, however, and focused more on uncovering police and local government corruption than anything else. Steffens held a working theory that almost every city had two governments. One was a textbook government, publicized by the city but nonexistent in reality, and the other was the real government, characterized by rampant political corruption. Steffens worried about men and groups who had power, because he felt power was too alluring and would tempt men to misuse it. He once noted that, "Power is what men seek, and any group that gets it will abuse it."[1] That pretty much summed up his motivation for doing the "Shame" series.

As a police reporter in New York, Steffens' work in exposing police corruption in New York helped to defeat the Tammany machine's candidate for mayor in 1894 and elect a reform candidate, William Strong. It was Strong who then created the Board of Police Commissioners which would be run by Theodore Roosevelt in his pre-White House days.

When Steffens left the Post and went to work for *McClure*'s magazine, he took his working theory of corrupt city government with him and tried it out in each of six cities, starting with St. Louis, which had become the fourth largest city in America by then. Steffens felt it was one of the worst-governed cities in the country, along with Philadelphia, and he set out to prove it with his first "Shame of St. Louis" article. Later in his *Shame of the Cities* book, Steffens commented on the level of corruption in St. Louis:

> The blackest years were 1898, 1899, and 1900. Foreign corporations came into the city to share in its despoliation, and home industries were driven out by blackmail. Franchises worth millions were granted without one cent of cash to the city, and with provision for only the smallest future payment; several companies which refused to pay blackmail had to leave; citizens were robbed more and more boldly; payrolls were padded with the names of non-existent persons; work on public improvements was neglected, while money for them went to the boodlers. Some of the newspapers protested, disinterested citizens were alarmed, and the shrewder men gave warnings, but none dared make an effective stand.[2]

After exposing St. Louis in *McClure*'s, Steffens took on the other five cities on his list: Chicago, Minneapolis, Pittsburgh, Philadelphia, and New York. Each became that edition's focus of the "Shame" series, and each followed the same general model as the first installment in the series. Each also generated a lot of heat for the local governments in the cities Steffens set his sights on. As a result of this kind of investigative reporting and the success it generated for the magazine, more hard-hitting probes would follow from other newspapers and magazines. Governments and industries became the target of investigative reporters, and two of these industries were meat packing and the oil companies. Roosevelt had borrowed the term "muckraking" from John Bunyan who used it in *Pilgrim's Progress* to describe a stable hand too busy staring at the muck to look up. He had intended it, when applying it to reporters, to be derisive. After Steffens' exposes', however, "muckraking" became a term of pride to most American journalists of the day.

As for Steffens, he became disillusioned with the United States and left for Europe and spent the latter years of his life in Italy. He published his famous book, *The Autobiography of Lincoln Steffens* in 1931, which charted the journey of a liberal intellectual, to a reformer, to a revolutionary, and finally to a disillusioned cynic.

27. THE BEGINNING OF PUBLIC RELATIONS

One might wonder how the development of public relations changed the news media. In fact, there may have been no single institution that has changed journalism as much as public relations. Most of the stories the media run have had their origins in a news release or a contact from a public relations practitioner. Public relations has become a staple of the supply side of journalism. And the institution of public relations can be traced back to a Princeton graduate and former business reporter for Joseph Pulitzer's *New York World*. Ivy Lee became a publicist after leaving the *World*, and then found a way to enlarge that role into America's first public relations counsel.

What Lee did was to elevate public relations from mere press agentry. He was the first to develop a set of principles that he believed all public relations practitioners should follow. Lee stressed delivering accurate and truthful information instead of the hype and exaggerations common among press agents of the day. He wanted to separate public information from the P.T. Barnums of the day. Among his pronouncements about PR was the following: "This is not a secret press bureau. All our work is done in the open. We aim to supply news . . . In brief, our plan is, frankly and openly, in behalf of business concerns and public institutions, to supply to the press and the public of the United States prompt and accurate information concerning subjects which is of value and interest to the public."[3]

Lee became the nation's first public relations counsel when he was hired by Pennsylvania Railroad in 1906 to be a conduit to newspapers and the public about the railroad's progress. He brought his journalistic approach to the job and he understood the demands and needs of the press and worked hard to accommodate them in telling the railroad's story. He developed his theory of openness into daily practice. When there were accidents involving his client's trains, he supplied ample information for the press and set up facilities for them to help journalists report their stories. He realized that improving relations with the press was only half his job; the other half was convincing traditional business executives of the railroad that it was in their interest to be open with the media instead of keeping secrets. The management learned to buy into Lee's approach, and the principle of public relations as a management function was born.

Lee's reputation spread and other companies began asking him to be their PR counsel as well. One of the toughest challenges he faced was as public relations counsel for the Colorado Fuel and Iron Company, which was owned by the John D. Rockefeller, Jr., family. The company became mired in a widely publicized labor dispute which erupted into violence in the infamous co-called "Ludlow Massacre" at the Colorado plant. Lee was curious as to why newspapers seemed to emphasize labor's side of the dispute while little was being said about management's side. Essentially he discovered that labor leaders were doing a much better job getting their story out to the press. He set about to level the playing field by starting a campaign of informational leaflets that were not just targeted at the media, but at people his research identified as opinion leaders both within the state and around the country.

Lee is remembered not only as the nation's first public relations counsel but also as the man who laid down some principles of PR that have endured until today, although unevenly practiced by companies and PR firms. Nevertheless, in switching the focus of PR from press agentry to advising businesses to align themselves with the public interest, Lee made a great contribution. And in maintaining open communication with the press, he made the job of reporters easier in producing accurate news accounts.

28. THE SINKING OF THE *TITANIC*

The sinking of the luxury liner *Titanic* just after midnight on April 15, 1912, was a huge story for the news media, and it was also the first major event in which the infant medium of radio played a role. The *Titanic* was the pride of the White Star Line, and this was its maiden voyage when it left Southampton, England, on April 10 bound for New York City. Aboard were 2,200 passengers and crew, and the ship was heralded as the safest and most luxurious of passenger vessel ever put to sea. The *Titanic* was seen as so safe, in fact, that it had a mere 20 lifeboats which—should a tragedy occur—could hold only half of the passengers and crew aboard. In hindsight, the safety provisions appear laughable, but that is how confident the management of White Star Line was that this ship was virtually unsinkable.

The story has been told often and in many forms, but four days out of Southampton, the *Titanic* struck an iceberg at 11:40 p.m. and disappeared from the face of the ocean before 12:30 a.m. At first, the damage seemed slight, but as water gushed in, it became obvious that first impressions were wrong. The ship, and all souls aboard were in mortal danger. Over half of the passengers and crew would find no safety in the lifeboats and would have to go down with the ship or take their chances in open waters until rescue arrived. But the North Atlantic was icy, and anyone going into the water could hope to survive only a short time.

Passenger John Thayer witnessed the sinking from a lifeboat and observed, "We could see groups of the almost fifteen hundred people still aboard, clinging in clusters or bunches, like swarming bees; only to fall in masses, pairs, or singly, as the great after part of the ship, two hundred and fifty feet of it, rose into the sky, till it reached a sixty-five or seventy degree angle."[4]

The ocean liner RMS *Carpathia* was the closest ship to the *Titanic*, but the news of the ship's trouble was late in being received because no one was manning the *Carpathia*'s radio receiver when the *Titanic* radio operator was sending out SOS calls over his wireless. So it wasn't until the next morning that the *Carpathia* made it to the site and rescued only 705 survivors. A total of 1,527 others perished in or shortly after the

40 minutes it took for the *Titanic* to go under. Ironically, the *Carpathia* itself would sink some six years later after being struck by a German submarine's torpedo.

The first person to report news of the *Titanic*'s sinking was a young radio buff who held one of the many licenses available during a mostly unregulated fledgling radio era in America. His name was David Sarnoff, a man whose genius who would later build radio into an empire of the air. But for now, Sarnoff was working as an operator at the John Wanamaker store in New York while pursuing a degree in engineering at the Pratt Institute. Wanamaker had seen the potential in the infant radio industry and had outfitted his store with powerful commercial wireless equipment.[5] Sarnoff was at the controls on a quiet mid-April afternoon when he picked up signals in his earphones stating, "Titanic struck an iceberg. Sinking fast." Unfortunately, there were no details, nor was there any identification of the message sender. Nevertheless, Sarnoff conveyed this information to newspapers in the city and remained glued to his set listening for further information and tapping out alerts to all ships at sea near the *Titanic* that this ship was in trouble. He received a wireless message from one of those ships, the *Olympic*, and the radio operator signaled that the *Titanic* had indeed sunk and that the *Carpathia* was steaming to New York with rescued survivors. The intrepid Sarnoff then contacted the *Carpathia* to get survivors' names.

Then, over a 72-hour period sitting at his wireless key, Sarnoff provided the world the first and only story of the sinking. Hearing of this, President Taft issued an order for all other wireless stations in America to shut down, giving Sarnoff the best chance to get his messages out with minimal interference. Outside Wanamaker's, thousands of New Yorkers gathered in the streets, and among them were many who were expecting their loved ones to arrive on *Titanic*'s maiden voyage in a few days. They were given the details as Sarnoff received them and also the names of the survivors. Sarnoff did not leave his wireless post until the last of the 705 survivors was identified.

Following this tragedy, an investigation revealed the *Carpathia* should have arrived on the rescue scene hours earlier but had not done so because its radio operator was asleep in bed, having abandoned his wireless key. Congress felt great pressure to pass a law requiring all ships carrying more than 50 people to carry wireless equipment and operators. The act also mandated 24-hour radio watches, with two operators, and ordered an ongoing system of maintenance for the radio equipment. Within a year, more than 500 American ships were carrying radio equipment and wireless operators.

29. THE PRESIDENT MEETS THE PRESS

It is unlikely that the 28th president of the United States, Woodrow Wilson, knew the historic feat he undertook when he began the formal institution of the presidential press conference. Nevertheless, before that moment, there existed no formal, regular means for the nation's media to interact with the president of the United States. It seems odd that some 124 years passed in a democracy before such formal interaction would begin, but such was the case. And even Wilson didn't use the press conference very long after becoming angered over reporters prying into his family's personal affairs. He was also spending more and more of his time focusing attention on the coming war with Europe. It came to be ironic, in fact, that the president who had originated the press conference and then abandoned it, wound up mounting the greatest public relations movement with the media that the country has ever seen when he created the Committee on Public Information (CPI) and enlisted a willing media's support in going to war with Germany.

The formal presidential press conference was taken off the shelf and renewed by Wilson's successor, Warren G. Harding, and it has been a fixture in the White House ever since with greater or lesser degrees of use. Today it offers an opportunity for journalists to fire questions at the nation's chief executive and have those answers beamed live into the living rooms of America. Some presidents have used the press conference a lot; some have used it very little. Presidential historian James Pollard notes many believe that Calvin Coolidge held more news conferences that any other president.[6] Others cite Franklin D. Roosevelt as the president who used it even more, however. Although Roosevelt was the only president to spend three terms in the White House, he still used the press conference more than 1,000 times, averaging about two press conferences a week.[7] That is a record unmatched by any president; certainly recent ones.

Presidents who used the press conference much less frequently were Richard M. Nixon, whose disdain for the press was well known and well documented, and George W. Bush, who used the press conference less and less after he became the object of so much national criticism for his war policies regarding Iraq and his administration's mishandling of Hurricane Katrina rescue efforts. But presidents who have exuded charm, grace, and charisma in front of the cameras have used the press conference opportunities well. Ronald Reagan, Bill Clinton, and Barack Obama have been three such presidents.

The media have a more routine way of getting news about the president via the daily White House press briefing, carried out by the president's press secretary. Unlike the more formal presidential press conference where reporters exhibit respect, decorum, and follow rules laid down by the White House, these daily press briefings are more of a free-for-all, more akin to the give-and-take atmosphere in the British Parliament when the prime minister appears for questions and interaction. These briefings often show what a seemingly impossible position the press secretary is in, having to placate reporters looking for the truth and adept at spotting lies, and being the chief public relations practitioner for the president. Under Clinton's press spokesman, Mike McCurry, these daily briefings went live to the public, a decision McCurry regretted making. "It was a huge error on my part," McCurry told the *New York Times*. "It has turned into a theater of the absurd."[8]

Like the presidential news conference itself, these live briefings offer advantages for both the White House and the Washington press corps. For the journalists, they offer an opportunity to hold the White House accountable on live (usually C-Span) briefings. And, as Katharine Seelye added, they help get the reporters more on-air exposure. For the White House, the briefings allow the president's chief spokesperson to deliver a message directly to the public without being reinterpreted by a journalist.[9] In any event, as the briefings have shown time and again, a certain level of mutual mistrust exists between journalists and the White House. It also shows the Catch-22 situation reporters find themselves in, should they decide to show aggression and frustration instead of respect at these briefings. If they are polite and respectful, they are often treated in a condescending manner and aren't provided real answers to their questions. If they grow more belligerent, especially on camera, then they are derided for lack of respect and are vulnerable to attacks by the public.

30. WITNESSING THE DAWN OF WORLD WAR I

While America's entry into World War I didn't begin until 1917, the war in Europe had been raging since 1914, following the realignment of the European balance of power with a unified Germany. The French were upset with Germany for losing territories in the 19th century, and England had become a staunch military and economic competitor with Germany. Add to all this the desire of Germany to secure a status more becoming an advanced European nation, and the fuse was lit for trouble. Like many such fuses that ignite in far-off places, however, many Americans kept themselves relatively uniformed, since there was so much to deal with in their daily lives in the United States. It was reporting by journalists such as Richard Harding Davis which would eventually open American eyes to the dangers rising abroad, and one of those early stories was Davis' account of German troops goose-stepping through Belgium in August, 1914.

Davis was every journalist's dream of a foreign correspondent and war reporter in the late 19th and early 20th centuries. He had covered the Spanish-American War for Hearst and was there for the opening of the War in Europe in 1914. The highest-paid reporter of his time, Davis was also a playwright, a male model for clothing ads, and an international celebrity. It is said that Davis could identify with anyone he met, and he immersed himself in many of the events he covered.

Davis positioned himself in Europe to get a good look at the launching of the German offensive to stake its claim and make its name in Europe in 1914. Germany had invaded Belgium with the ultimate purpose of swinging in a wide circle on France. The outclassed Belgium army tried, but offered little resistance to what became a two-week campaign. By end of that time, German troops were marching through the streets of Brussels. Davis, an Errol Flynn-style foreign correspondent for William Randolph Hearst's newspaper empire, was on hand to witness the event. He was known by many as the "glamour boy of war correspondents."[10] Davis filed a riveting account of the German march. Realizing he himself was now in occupied territory, Davis struck a deal with an English messenger to spirit his news story back to London for publication. The story got out, but Davis was threatened with execution by the Germans, who first believed him to be a British spy before letting him go. His story appeared in *The News Chronicle* of London on August 23, 1914, and reads in part as follows:

> The entrance of the German army into Brussels has lost the human quality. It was lost as soon as the three soldiers who led the army bicycled into the Boulevard du

Regent and asked the way to the Gare du Nord. When they passed, the human note passed with them.

What came after them, and twenty-four hours later is still coming, is not men marching, but a force of nature like a tidal Wave, an avalanche or a river flooding its banks. And at this minute, it is rolling through Brussels as the swollen waters of the Conemaugh Valley swept through Johnstown.

At the sight of the first few regiments of the enemy, we were thrilled with interest. After three hours they had passed in one unbroken steel-gray column, we were bored. But when hour after hour passed and there was no halt, no breathing time, no open spaces in the ranks, the thing became uncanny, inhuman. You returned to watch it fascinated. It held the mystery and menace of fog rolling toward you across the sea.[11]

There are many great examples of war reporting, but this was certainly one of the best, both in reporting and writing as well as in impact. It was this kind of reporting that caused American readers to put down their morning coffee cup and say across the table that this was a problem that may involve America one day soon. Arno Dosch-Fleurot called this story "a picture of imperialism itself coming down the road."[12]

31. WILSON DRAFTS GEORGE CREEL

America declared war on Germany on April 6, 1917, over the objections of many Americans and several influential newspapers including the *Chicago Tribune, The Washington Post, Los Angeles Times, San Francisco Chronicle*, and *Cleveland Plain Dealer*.[13] These newspapers still preached isolationism and anti-interventionism and warned of the dangers of becoming involved in someone else's war. But their voices were drowned out by most other newspapers in the country as Americans felt they saw the handwriting on the wall in the dangers of German domination of Europe.

To help cement this resolve, the Wilson Administration created the United States Committee on Public Information (CPI) just one week after the war declaration. Brought in to chair the committee was a respected newsman in George Creel. This journalist had already made quite a name for himself as an investigative journalist working for the *Kansas City World*, the *Denver Post*, and the *Rocky Mountain News*. President Wilson believed it was vital to get the news media on his side for entering the war because he realized the tremendous influence newspapers had on public opinion. So his decision to draft a well-respected journalist to lead the war propaganda effort was no accident, but a calculated move which proved very effective. Before he was through, Creel eventually mobilized some 150,000 Americans to help him carry out the wide-ranging mission of the CPI, which included disseminating facts about the war effort and coordinating the American government's propaganda efforts. Included in these civilian propaganda troops were 75,000 public speakers who he dubbed the "Four Minute Men," mobilized to give short speeches across America promoting the war effort. As Emery notes of Creel's efforts:

The opportunity Wilson gave to Creel was a greater one than any other person had enjoyed in the propaganda arena . . . Creel first opened up government news channels to the Washington correspondents and insisted that only news of troop movements, ship sailings, and other events of strictly military character should be withheld. He issued a brief explanatory code calling on the newspapers to censor such news themselves voluntarily. Throughout the war, newspaper editors generally went beyond Creel's minimum requests in their desire to aid the war effort. In May 1917, the CPI began publishing an official bulletin in which releases were reprinted in newspaper form. Before the war was over, this publication reached a daily circulation of 118,000.[14]

To a large degree, World War I was characterized by a press that did not need reminding of its patriotic duty by the American government, because most journalists evidenced that spirit voluntarily, offering censoring of their own reports beyond the official censorship guidelines. Nevertheless, by any account, Creel's committee was successful in aiding the war effort and uniting public opinion. In fact, writing about it in his classic book *Public Opinion*, journalist Walter Lippmann called it the single greatest example of creating one unified public opinion ever achieved.[15]

Not only did the CPI serve well as a propaganda tool, it is also remarkable that most of its 6,000 press releases were deemed accurate by the journalists using them, and few were called into question according to researcher Walton E. Bean, who wrote in 1941: "It may be doubted that the CPI's record for honesty will ever be equaled in the official war news of a major power."[16] Emery notes, however, this assessment does not take into account sins of omission or concealment by the government of facts relating to the war.[17]

A part of Creel's mission was to encourage editors to use common sense in censoring their own newspapers. He asked editors to first clear any doubtful articles with his office. This request was backed up by the weight of the Espionage Act, so editors had cause to pay attention. Creel was himself vested with no official censorship authority, but he could ask the U.S. Post Office or the Justice Department to enforce provisions of the act if he discovered violations among editors.[18] It turns out that fears of newspapers violating security provisions were largely unfounded as most of the nation's press chose to join the nation's war effort, rather than risk breaching security that could deter from victory overseas.

After the war, Creel wrote about his experience with the CPI in a book called *How We Advertised America*. Before he was through, he would write more than a dozen other books. He described America propaganda by saying, "Our effort was educational and informative throughout, for we had such confidence in our case as to feel that no other argument was needed than the simple, straightforward presentation of facts."[19] Creel later became chairman of he National Advisory Board of the Works Progress Administration in 1935, was an ardent Democrat, and ran against writer Upton Sinclair for Governor of California. Neither candidate was successful in his bid.

32. STATION 8XK GOES ON THE AIR

Regular radio broadcasts began when a Westinghouse engineer named Frank Conrad began airing music over his primitive garage station 8XK in the Pittsburgh suburb of Wilkinsburg in 1916. That station would receive the first official broadcasting license in 1920 with the call sign KDKA, which is still on the air as one of the premier radio stations in the country. On November 2, 1920, the country would hear the first U.S. presidential election returns over that station. With the launching of Station 8XK, the era of broadcasting began and changed the world forever. As a medium, radio was envisioned from its inception and through its first two decades as a point-to-point medium. Its developers and marketers saw its application primarily in two areas and two areas only: (1) As a means of ship-to-ship and ship-to-shore communication on the high seas with high strategic value to the U.S. military during World War I, and (2) As a means for individual amateur ("ham") radio operators to communicate with each other. In popular films like *Frequency* (2000), the use of radio as point-to-point communications is seen graphically—albeit in this sense in a story with sci-fi elements—as a son and his deceased father communicate to each other across time.

The phenomenon of radio in the early 20th century was similar to that of computers in the latter two decades of that century: In each case, the technology ran ahead of market awareness and understanding. Inventors and developers had assembled the needed technical puzzle pieces of radio and computer communication long before the market knew what to do with these media. The technology was there, but the "killer application" was missing. How would people use these new media, and why would they find them essential to their lives? In market terms, that question morphed into, "How can we make money off this technology?"

In the case of radio, it was—ironically—an engineer who answered the marketing question by firing up station 8XK from his Pennsylvania garage and playing phonograph records over it to whatever ham radio operators might have their headsets attached. As it turns out, a lot of them did, and point-to-point radio evolved almost overnight into broadcasting. So were Conrad and 8XK the first broadcasters in America? In one sense, yes, because it was the first station to be granted a commercial license by the U.S. Department of Commerce. In another sense, no, according to broadcast journalist and freelance broadcast historian Elizabeth McLeod.[20] She points out that Conrad, after receiving his license in 1916 as 8XK, went on the air with experimental voice and music broadcasts right through World War I. Since Westinghouse, for whom he worked, held a major defense contract, the government protected his radio license during the war when they were suspending every other company's license. The Wilson administration felt it best to focus radio development on war applications, and it didn't want the new developments to fall into enemy hands. So radio's commercial development came to a standstill during the war, although the interest picked up shortly after the war ended. Other media companies, like the Detroit News, received radio licenses during 1919–1920. That company's station 8MK began an ambitious schedule of programming during the summer of 1920 and became station WWJ.

As for Conrad and his 8XK, its early promise convinced Westinghouse to invest heavily in the station and apply for a commercial broadcasting license, as opposed to the amateur class license that all radio stations received up to this point. That license was granted on October 27, 1920, and the government assigned the station the call letters of KDKA. Programming under this new license began November 2 with the coverage of the Warren Harding/James Cox presidential election.

So, officially, Station 8XK/KDKA was the first commercially licensed broadcast company, although there were other fledgling efforts at broadcasting going on at the same time, and a few of them actually preceded Conrad's successful effort. Today, however, KDKA claims the mantel of the first radio station as can be seen from this excerpt from its promotional material which also provides an interesting anecdote about Conrad's initial motivation:

> At 6:00 pm, on Tuesday, November 2, 1920, a few men in a shack changed the course of history. Four pioneers, announcer Leo Rosenberg, engineer William Thomas, telephone line operator John Frazier and standby R. S. McClelland, made their way to a makeshift studio—actually a shack atop the Westinghouse "K" Building in East Pittsburgh—flipped a switch and began reporting election returns in the Harding vs. Cox Presidential race. At that moment, KDKA became the pioneer broadcasting station of the world. The events that led to KDKA Radio date back before 1920. Dr. Frank Conrad, Assistant Chief Engineer of Pittsburgh's Westinghouse Electric Company, first became interested in radio in 1912. In order to settle a $5.00 bet with a co-worker on the accuracy of his $12.00 watch, Conrad built a small receiver to hear time signals from the Naval Observatory in Arlington, VA. (Conrad won the bet). Fascinated with this new hobby, Conrad turned next to construction of a transmitter, which he housed on the second floor of his garage in Wilkinsburg. The first official record of thisstation, licensed 8XK, appears in the August 1, 1916 edition of the Radio Service Bulletin.[21]

33. THE FOUNDING OF RCA

In 1921, the Radio Corporation of America (RCA) came into existence, ironically at the encouragement of the U.S. Navy Department, and from this corporation came the landmark maker of home electronics equipment and the first radio and television network of NBC. When America entered World War I, the radio industry was in its infancy. All commercial development of radio came to a standstill, and the government took over developments with an eye toward using radio as a war communication tool to help achieve victory. The transAtlantic radio telegraph station at New Brunswick, N.J., was taken over by the U.S. Navy. Owned by the Marconi Wireless Telegraph Co. of America, the station had a powerful 50,000-watt transmitter that the Navy replaced with a 200,000-watt version, built and installed by General Electric (GE). GE paid for the transmitter and its installation, and it became the only reliable transoceanic communication facilitator for the Navy from 1918 to 1920, when it was returned to its owner.

British Marconi, which owned its American counterpart company, began negotiations in March, 1919, to buy two dozen of these transmitters and purchase exclusive rights to their use. But the Navy Department worried about a sale that would transfer to England a monopoly on worldwide communications for an unspecified period. Instead, the Navy proposed that GE organize an American radio operating company that would be controlled entirely by Americans. That group would then have more control over international communications. So on October 17, 1919, GE took the lead in organizing the RCA and made U.S. citizenship a requirement for membership to its board of directors. American Marconi was merged with RCA and ceased to operate as a communications company. The chief companies which were cross-licensed to operate as RCA were GE, AT&T, Western Electric, and Westinghouse Electric and Manufacturing Co. The final agreement was formalized in 1921, and an American communications giant came into existence.[22]

In 1926, RCA purchased two radio stations, WEAF in New York and WCAP, renamed WJZ, in Washington, paying $1 million for both and announcing later that year the launching of a new division called the National Broadcasting Company or, as it came to be known, NBC. The new subsidiary would be divided among RCA, which would own 50 percent, General Electric (30 percent), and Westinghouse (20 percent). NBC officially began on November 15, 1926. WEAF and WJZ would be the flagship stations of the network which, in 1927, were divided into the Red Network and the Blue Network. The Red Network would air commercial entertainment, while the Blue network would offer news, public affairs, and cultural programming, without commercial sponsorship. In 1939, the Federal Communications Commission (FCC) ordered RCA to divest itself of one of the two networks, and after several court fights, the Blue Network became ABC in 1945. But in the so-called "golden age" of radio networks (1930–1950), NBC set the standard for quality and commercial success in entertainment programming, virtually beginning the serial format for radio—and later—TV shows.[23]

RCA remained in existence as a communications company until 1986, and its brand remains on home electronics products today. Among the achievements of RCA was its 1929 purchase of the Victor Talking Machine Co., which was the largest maker of phonographs in the world at the time. This new division became RCA-Victor, and it began selling the first electronic turntable in 1930 and released the first 331/3 rpm records to the public. RCA was also the first company to demonstrate an all-electronic television system at the New York World's Fair in 1939. When the FCC introduced the National Television Systems Committee (NTSC) television operating standard, commercial television transmission was authorized in 1941, and RCA took the lead in selling TV sets immediately after World War II ended. Its NBC radio network developed its counterpart television network which today still maintains a strong market share in the competitive world of broadcast and cable television.

34. WILLIAM ALLEN WHITE'S "MARY WHITE"

American journalism is filled with many examples of fine prose which, had they not been published in newspapers, might surely have been published in other literary venues. One such example of journalistic prose came in 1921 in the pages of a small-town daily newspaper in Kansas, and it was entitled simply, "Mary White." It was written by a unique American journalist named William Allen White who defied tradition in the way he built his career and made his influence known around the nation.

White was one of the greatest American journalists of all time, and also one of the few who left big-city journalism to focus on small-town journalism and make his impact felt from America's heartland. Starting his career in 1892, as an editorial writer for the *Kansas City Star*, he used his innovative style to connect with readers and became a leading voice for progressivism in the state of Kansas. His influence was felt far beyond Kansas, however, and he ultimately became a candidate for the U.S. presidency.

The son of a small-town doctor, White left Kansas City and returned to his native Emporia, Kansas, with a loan of $3,000 which he used to buy *The Emporia Gazette*. A big problem faced by White was the fact he was a Republican in a state that was strongly reform-minded. He solved that problem by calling for changes in the state, crusading for the environment, working men's compensation, and the abolition of child labor. In Emporia, White crafted some of the finest American prose in the form

William Allen White, shown in this Walker family collection photo, was to be known later in life as the "Sage of Emporia," but first gained national recognition for his August 15, 1896 editorial, "What's the matter with Kansas?" White bought the Emporia Gazette *in 1895 and was its publisher for nearly 50 years. White's granddaughter, Barbara Walker, is now editor of the* Gazette. *[AP Photo/Walker Family Collection, ho]*

of editorials, two of the most notable were his sarcastic "What's the Matter with Kansas?" and his searing personal tribute to his fallen daughter which he simply called, "Mary White." In the case of the former editorial, which lashed out at the state's Democratic leaders, White placed the blame for Kansas' problems on "shabby, wild-eyed, rattle-brained fanatic" populists who were "spending the state into the poor house." He wrote the editorial in a moment of anger, set it aside, and decided not to publish it. However, the piece found its way to national Republican leaders who reprinted it and sent it to various newspapers around the country where it was printed. It made White famous across America. But the editorial White did publish about the death of his daughter Mary was the one that drilled its way into the heart of many Americans.

White and his wife Sallie lost their 16-year-old daughter Mary in 1921 when she was out riding a horse, struck a low-hanging branch from a tree, fell to the ground and died. The grief the family felt was put into words by White in the pages of the *Emporia Gazette* and resonated with all readers who had ever lost loved ones, or feared losing them. Published on May 17, 1921, it read in part:

> The Associated Press reports carrying the news of Mary White's death declared that it came as the result of a fall from a horse. How she would have hooted at that! She never fell from a horse in her life. Horses have fallen on her and with her—"I'm always trying to hold 'em in my lap," she used to say. But she was proud of few things, and one was that she could ride anything that had four legs and hair. Her death resulted not from a fall, but from a blow on the head, which fractured her skull, and the blow came from the limb of an overhanging tree on the parking ... She loved to rollick, persiflage was her natural expression at home. Her humor was a continual bubble of joy. She seemed to think in hyperbole and metaphor ... No angel was Mary White, but an easy girl to live with, for she never nursed a grouch five minutes in her life ... A rift in the clouds in a gray day threw a shaft of sunlight upon her coffin as her nervous, energetic little body sank to its last sleep. But the soul of her, the glowing gorgeous, fervent soul of her, surely was flaming in eager joy upon some other dawn.[24]

Over the years, "Mary White" and others of White's editorials have been reproduced around the world and are part of the official collection of the Kansas Historical Society. They moved countless numbers of readers and helped advance the tradition of personal, literary journalism in America. As for William Allen White, his legacy of excellent journalism continued throughout his life and beyond as the University of Kansas School of Journalism, one of the best in the nation, carries his name. Ironically, the University of Kansas was the school White attended but left before graduation to purchase the *Emporia Gazette*.

In his lifetime, White became a powerful voice of Midwestern progressivism. Although tempted, he never left Emporia to take his journalism to the big cities. But he also had national clout, was a friend of Theodore Roosevelt and supported President Wilson's League of Nations. White's journalistic legacy was huge. He never lost hope and refused to be defeated. He cared passionately about Kansas, covered and served his town well, and adopted the philosophy "You do your most important work in your own backyard." He brought great literary style into his writing. At one point, using a metaphor that his fallen daughter would appreciate, he said, "Language lives and strains to gallop; give it a light rein."

35. HENRY LUCE LAUNCHES *TIME*

When Henry Luce and his friend Briton Hadden conceived of a national news maga-zine in 1922, they could not have known the publishing empire that would grow out of it, or that one day, an average of one in five Americans would be regularly reading a Luce publication. Nevertheless, that would be the case as the publishing empire now known as Time, Inc., covers the globe with its magazines and books. The empire began with the launching of *Time* magazine March 3, 1923, the publication that would be the first weekly newsmagazine in America and which would give rise to stalwart competitors in *Newsweek* and *U.S. News and World Report.*

Luce came to journalism in a unique way. He was born in China, the son of a poor missionary couple from the Presbyterian church. Luce learned Chinese before he learned English. He spent the first 13 years of his life in China, traveling to Europe for the first time when he was 14 and winning a scholarship for studies in America the next year. There he was a student at Hotchkiss School in Lakeville, Connecticut. He loved his studies and did well, keeping himself busy away from the classroom by editing the school's publication, the *Hotchkiss Literary Monthly.* It was there that Luce met Briton Hadden, and the two formed a personal and professional symbiotic rela-tionship that would serve them well in life. After graduation, both enrolled in Yale, and both would take leadership positions on the *Yale Daily News* where Hadden was chairman and Luce was managing editor.

In doing a military stint together following college, the two friends dreamed of beginning a new kind of newspaper that would give people more depth and under-standing of the world around them. Possibly because of his missionary upbringing and time spent in China, Luce had also developed a passion for people around the world and found a way to combine that compassion with his literary interest. Luce is known for making the statement that, "I became a journalist to come as close as possible to the heart of the world."[25]

The conversations and dreaming quickly turned to reality as the two men managed to raise almost $90,000 and, with Luce as business manager and Hadden as editor-in-chief, *Time* was launched in 1923. The magazine became a success, although Hadden died just six years after its launch. His grieving friend and partner, Luce assumed both leadership titles at the magazine and the enterprise soared as *Time* became the first national news magazine. The venture was helped in part by the decision of the com-pany to start a radio program called "The March of Time" in 1931 to provide people with in-depth news broadcasts that would parallel what the magazine was doing. This cross-platform exposure gained the magazine even more attention and boosted its readership, as well as provided an innovative weekly news broadcasts to Americans.

Luce would follow his *Time* success with another groundbreaking publication in 1930 when he launched *Fortune*, a newsmagazine focused on the business community. That would be followed six years later with a magazine that—along with *National Geographic*—would set the standard for magazine photojournalism. That magazine was *Life*, launched in 1936. Luce would turn his attention to the family domestic front with *House and Home* in 1952, and would publish a magazine that set the standard for sports journalism with *Sports Illustrated* in 1954. Luce would remain editor-in-chief of all his publications until 1964, and was also a lifelong Republican supporting many conservative and philanthropic causes in America and around the world. He died in 1967. Today, his company is called Time, Inc., and is owned by Time Warner, a giant media conglomerate which publishes more than 120 magazines around the world.[26] As of 2008, *Time* had 3.4 million subscribers in the United States.

36. NBC LAUNCHES A NETWORK

The National Broadcasting Company (NBC) was founded in 1926 as early industry pioneers realized that joining forces would be the best way to grow the industry and provide profits for companies each specializing in different aspects of the home appliance and electronics industry. So it was that General Electric, RCA, and Westinghouse came together to found the company which became the first broadcast network in America. Six years after its inception, RCA would emerge as the sole owner of the company and would remain so for more than five decades until it was purchased by General Electric, which owns and operates NBC as a subsidiary today.

What the three companies put in motion was a system which would become the so-called "two-tiered" system of broadcasting in the United States, consisting of broadcast networks at the macro level, and local broadcast stations at the micro level. But the two levels were intertwined, and the fortunes of a network could help or hurt the fortunes of local affiliated stations, and vice versa. The network structure also allowed for a well-financed source of broadcast programming that was out of reach of many local stations, and that programming would help to create a common ground—both in news and entertainment programming—for all Americans. Media theorists would say it paved the way for what media scholar Marshall McLuhan would later call the "global village."

NBC became the home of many early-day entertainers, and among its earliest hit programs was the comedy show *Amos 'n' Andy*, which would later try to transition to television but would be found too racist by many American viewers. Nevertheless, the show created a standard for almost all serial programs in the early days of radio. Among the many stars who would be featured on NBC in the early days were Al Jolson, Bob Hope, Jack Benny, George Burns, and Gracie Allen. The network had popular shows like *Fibber McGee and Molly*, *The Great Gildersleeve*— which was probably the first spin-off show in history—and *Death Valley Days*.

All of these programs and stars would make the transition to television versions of these shows.

NBC was founded in a different way than the Columbia Broadcasting System (CBS), which would launch in 1927. Whereas CBS was founded as an independent company, NBC was the product of the three-company consortium whose primary goal was to produce programming as a way of marketing and selling home radio receivers. After all, RCA, General Electric, and Westinghouse were all in the infant home appliance industry but needed enticement to move these new radio sets. So the future of NBC was tied to the future of RCA which, as mentioned earlier, emerged as its sole owner. In turn, the growing popularity of NBC programming aided RCA as it fought for improved technical standards in broadcasting.[27]

What NBC did, under RCA leadership, was to institute what was at first called "chain broadcasting," taking control of a number of high-power radio stations and inviting other radio stations around the country to affiliate with NBC and receive its programming. Chain broadcasting came to be known as "network broadcasting." NBC decided actually to set up two networks, a Red and a Blue network, and used two large stations as their flagships. WEAF in New York City would be the lead station for the Red Network and would feature advertiser-sponsored entertainment and music broadcast programs. WJZ in Washington, D.C., would be the flagship station for the Blue Network, which focused on providing news and cultural programming free of advertiser sponsorship. The FCC eventually became concerned about RCA's dominance in broadcasting and later ordered it to sell one of the two networks. So the Blue network was sold to Edward Noble in 1943 and soon became the current American Broadcasting Company, or ABC.[28]

When television captured the hearts and minds of Americans following World War II, the broadcast network structure was already in place since both NBC and CBS had strong radio networks. So it was a simple matter to expand those programming services out to television stations which chose to affiliate with the television counterparts of the radio networks. The influence and breadth of NBC has grown and the company has become an international media enterprise offering cable networks such as CNBC and MSNBC, as well as the second largest Spanish-language television network, Telemundo, which it purchased in 2002. Altogether, NBC employs more than 7,000 people around the world and produces hundreds of hours of weekly programming for viewers in more than 100 countries.[29]

37. BILL PALEY BUILDS CBS

William S. Paley did not found the Columbia Broadcasting System (CBS) radio and television network, but his guiding genius made it the influential empire it became.

CBS was originally named United Independent Broadcasters, Inc., on January 27, 1927. In April 1927, just four months after United organized, the Columbia Phonograph Broadcasting System was formed to act as the sales agent for United. The idea was that United would pay each of 16 member stations $500 per week for 10 hours of radio time. But Columbia found it could not sell enough time, and the young United network faced collapse within a few months. When the Columbia Phonograph Company backed out of the venture, United bought the stock and it was then that the network was named the Columbia Broadcasting System. William S. Paley and his family entered the picture then and bought most of the CBS stock. Before long, under Paley's leadership, the network began to grow.[30] The 16 original CBS network stations included ones representing both large and small markets from the East Coast to the Midwest. Among them were WNAC (Boston), WEAN (Providence), WMAQ (Chicago), KMOX (St. Louis), WJAS (Pittsburgh), WKRS (Cincinnati), and WCAO (Baltimore). The first broadcast over the new network was launched on Sunday, September 18, 1927, and the originating station was WOR in Newark, where the first control room was also the men's restroom.

Paley's genius and his leadership talents became obvious early in CBS history. Says the Museum of Broadcast Communications, " 'A 20th-century visionary with the ambitions of a 19th-century robber baron,' as the *New York Times* described him, Paley took over a tiny failing network with only 16 affiliate stations and developed it into a world-class communications empire. Delegating management details to others, he had a seemingly unfailing sense of popular taste and a resultant flair for programming."[31]

Paley believed that the original idea of paying affiliates to carry network programming wasn't as feasible as simply getting them to agree to running network-sustaining programming for free. They would receive payments from CBS for commercially supported programs, however. At the time, stations ran both sponsor-free as well as sponsored programming. In some ways, Paley followed the model created by William Randolph Hearst, at least in his recruiting methods. Just as Hearst hired away some of the best and brightest staffers from arch-rival Joseph Pulitzer and his *New York World*, so Paley raided NBC, luring top talent away to CBS. And also like Hearst, Paley realized the importance news reporting would play in the success of a network. So he urged development of a CBS News division before World War II, and sent correspondents such as William L. Shirer and Edward R. Murrow to Europe to report on the run-up to war and the war itself. Soon the entire news division would be headed by Murrow, who became known in the industry as the "conscience" of television journalism. In seeing the potential in news and public affairs programming, Paley allowed CBS to stake its claim as a pioneer in these areas, while NBC was developing mostly entertainment programming.

Among other contributions, Paley is known in the broadcast industry for bringing together a great team of managers, on-air talent and behind-the-scenes genius that earned CBS the industry moniker of the "Tiffany Network" for a period of several decades. CBS led the program ratings many of those years, although its image as the premier news network would ebb and flow. In one disturbing moment, Paley disagreed with Murrow over the newsman's passion for exposing Sen. Joseph McCarthy and refused to pay for advertising promoting the program where Murrow challenged McCarthy head-on. He allowed the program to air, but Murrow and producer Fred Friendly paid for the *New York Times* ad themselves. Following the episode,

THE BUSH-RATHER INTERVIEW

When George Herbert Walker Bush assumed the mantle of presidency following President Ronald Reagan, he walked into a media storm created in part by controversy surrounding his role in what was known as "Irangate." The issue was how much did Bush know about the deal to trade arms to the Iranians for the lives of American hostages who were freed when Ronald Reagan entered the White House? The arms-for-hostages story was late in breaking and Bush, as former head of the CIA and vice-president under Reagan, was believed by many to have been a part of the arms deal or at least to have known about it. These were charges he vehemently denied, and that denial reached its zenith during a famous 1988 interview with Dan Rather, anchor of *CBS Evening News*. In that interview, done during the heat of Bush's campaign, Rather broached the subject of what Bush knew of the arms-for-hostages plan, and when he knew it. Rather zeroed in on a meeting at which others said Bush was present; it was a meeting in which the arms-for-hostages deal was discussed, and Secretary of State George Schultz was also there. The infamous portion of that January 25, 1988, televised interview went this way, in part:

RATHER: You weren't in the meeting?

BUSH: I'm not suggesting. I'm just saying I don't remember it.

RATHER: I don't want to be argumentative, Mr. Vice President.

BUSH: You do, Dan.

RATHER: No . . . no, sir, I don't.

BUSH: This is not a great night, because I want to talk about why I want to be president, why those 41 percent of the people are supporting me. And I don't think it's fair . . .

RATHER: And Mr. Vice President, if these questions are—

BUSH: . . . to judge my whole career by a rehash on Iran. How would you like it if I judged your career by those seven minutes when you walked off the set in New York? [Note: In reality, Rather was in Miami and he was off the set for six minutes, when CBS let the NFL game of the week run into the time slot reserved for Rather's newscast.]

RATHER: Well, Mister . . .

BUSH: . . . Would you like that?

RATHER: Mr. Vice President . . .

BUSH: I have respect for you, but I don't have respect for what you're doing here to-night.

RATHER: Mr. Vice President, I think you'll agree that your qualification for President and what kind of leadership you'd bring to the country, what kind of government you'd have, what kind of people you have around you . . . .

BUSH: Exactly.

RATHER: . . . is much more important that what you just referred to. I'd be happy to . . .

BUSH: Well, I want to be judged on the whole record, and you're not giving an opportunity.

RATHER: And I'm trying to set the record straight, Mr. Vice President.

A media firestorm ensued over this interview, and the next night it was Dan Rather who was the focus of it as other network reporters tried to interview him on whether he thought he went too far in trying to get the vice president to address the issue of Iran-Contra. Rather responded that he was not the story; that the story was still what Bush knew about the arms deal, when he knew it, and whether he was being forthright about it to the American people.

—CBS Transcript of January 25, 1988 interview by Dan Rather of Vice President Gorge H. W. Bush, as contained in, "When Dan Rather Tried to Hold a Bush Accountable," by David Corn, published on March 11, 2005 on www.commondreams.org and accessed through that Web site. Full transcript also available at www.tvnews.vanderbilt.edu.

Paley decided to dramatically reduce the number of probing news programs Murrow could do, insisting he do more celebrity interviews. Murrow left CBS with a warning to other broadcasters that television had become an unfriendly medium for news. The network would regain its reputation for comprehensive news coverage, however, especially during the 20-year tenure of newsman Walter Cronkite's anchoring of the *CBS Evening News* that began in 1961 and lasted until 1981 when he was replaced with Dan Rather.

38. CISSY PATTERSON SHAKES UP WASHINGTON

One of the greatest publishing dynasties in American journalistic history produced one of the most flamboyant editors—and the first female editor—of a metropolitan city daily. That editor was Elinor "Cissy" Patterson, and William Randolph Hearst appointed her as editor of his *Washington Herald* in 1930. What began as a lark by the mercurial Hearst became one of his better decisions, however, as Cissy Patterson shook up not only Washington, D.C., but also the Herald and the newspaper world at large.

Cissy Patterson came from the family tree of the famed Joseph Medill who built the *Chicago Tribune* into the dominant newspaper of the Midwest and one of the best newspapers in the country. Medill, a tough frontier journalist who was big on Lincoln and the Republican Party, created a publishing dynasty that spanned Chicago, New York, and—with Cissy Patterson—Washington, D.C. He was a mix of brute virility, Godlike authority, and arch-conservatism, and at least the first two of those traits were part of Cissy's makeup as well.

When Medill died in 1899, he left the *Chicago Tribune* to daughters Katharine McCormick and Elinor Patterson. McCormick's son Robert ran it, although a great rivalry began with his cousin Joseph Medill Patterson when the two were given equal control over the *Tribune*'s newsroom. Trouble arose because Patterson was a liberal and McCormick was very conservative. At the end of World War I, the two decided that McCormick would stay in Chicago as the sole publisher of the *Tribune* and that Patterson would leave and move to New York City where he would launch the *New York Daily News* as a tabloid newspaper. Cissy Patterson was Joseph Medill

Patterson's sister, and his daughter was Alicia Patterson, who would found New York's *Newsday* newspaper.

Young Elinor Patterson did not seem to initially share the family's enthusiasm for journalism. Born in Chicago, the daughter of Elinor and Robert Patterson and granddaughter of Joseph Medill, she would always be known as "Cissy," the name her brother gave her in childhood. She later changed the spelling of Elinor to Eleanor, and some biographers believed she did this out of admiration for first lady Eleanor Roosevelt. This admiration, however, did not prevent the editor from opposing Franklin Roosevelt's international policies as president.

Cissy was educated at the elite Miss Porter's School in Farmington, Connecticut, and moved with her uncle Robert S. McCormick and his wife to Austria when he was appointed ambassador there. In her young adult years, Cissy was drawn into the life of a wealth celebrity family, falling in love with an Austrian Count, Joseph Gizycki and marrying him in 1904 in a socialite's wedding in Washington, D.C. Things went bad with the marriage, however, he left her and took their daughter with him as he returned to Austria. Cissy crusaded to have her daughter returned and, under political pressure from Austria, the count was ordered to return the countess. Cissy and her daughter then moved to Wyoming where Cissy became a rancher, then wrote two novels, worked briefly for her brother Joesph Patterson at his newly founded *New York Daily News*, then worked for Hearst who thought it would be interesting and fun to appoint a woman as editor of his *Washington Herald*.[32]

Cissy began work at the *Herald* on August 1, 1930 and immediately set out making the paper popular with all levels of Washington society, doubling its circulation and putting her woman's imprint on the newspaper. She was a hands-on editor who insisted on the best of everything from writing and layout, to typography, graphics, and even comics. She encouraged society reporting and development of a strong and vibrant woman's page, and she bucked newspaper tradition in hiring many women as reporters. In demeanor, she might have appeared similar to the 2006 character of Miranda Priestly, played by actress Meryl Streep in the film, *The Devil Wears Prada*. Cissy would appear at work in expensive clothing, often with a pet dog in tow, creating a personal contrast with her editorial desire to connect the newspaper with working women. While brother Joe Patterson was succeeding at the *New York Daily News* with his focus on the common man as espoused in his slogan, "Tell it to Sweeney!," Cissy's slogan was, "Tell it to MRS. Sweeney!" She wound up buying the *Herald* from Hearst, and she merged it with the *Washington Times* to form the *Washington Times-Herald* in 1939.[33]

Commenting on Cissy, her brother and cousin and their unique imprint on American newspapers, journalistic historian John Tebbel has noted:

> The personal, individual element disappeared from chain journalism with the passing of Hearst and Scripps, just as it did in the case of single papers with the demise of men like Col. Robert R. McCormick and his cousins Joseph Patterson and Eleanor "Cissy" Patterson, all of them cast in the nineteenth-century mold of powerful eccentricity ... Cissy Patterson's paper, the *Washington*

Times-Herald, has long since disappeared, with its publisher, but it is still remembered for its own particular brand of insanity.[34]

Among her editorial decisions were to oppose U.S. entry into World War II, carrying on the isolationist tradition of cousin Robert McCormick in Chicago and her brother Joe in New York.[35]

39. THE COMMUNICATIONS ACT OF 1934

The Communications Act of 1934, passed on June 19 of that year, set the legal standards that radio and television broadcasters were required to follow for six decades until the act was rewritten in the late 1990s. As with much legislation, this act did not come into existence quickly, and in fact grew out of earlier congressional legislation that covered a period of two decades.

A curiosity to some in America is why the government chooses to regulate some media platforms yet leaves others unregulated, unless one counts laws involving libel, invasion of privacy, and the distribution of pornography to minors, which apply all media. The answer is that the federal government doesn't so much regulate the media themselves as the public airwaves which some of them use, most notably the broadcast media. Federal regulation of the broadcast media goes back to the earliest days of radio. After the *Titanic* went down in 1912 and some 1,500 passengers and crew lost their lives, it was learned that help did not arrive in time for many would-be survivors because the closest ship in the area had an unattended radio set when the *Titanic* radio operator was sending out SOS signals. To prevent that from happening again, Congress passed the Radio Act of 1912 that required all ships to have manned radio stations and required those wireless operators to be licensed by the federal government and keep those licenses current. The act also set "spheres of authority" for federal and state government regarding radio operator regulation, provided for giving and removing radio licenses, and set fines for violators. The act also assigned frequencies for radio stations. The Radio Act of 1912 thus became the first federal regulation covering the infant radio industry in America. It would be followed by other acts as the radio industry grew from point-to-point communication to broadcasting. Before stepping ahead with more regulation, however, the federal government would take a step back when radio station owners rebelled, pressuring President Calvin Coolidge to order the government out of the broadcast regulation business.

Not surprisingly, chaos ensued on the airwaves. With no licenses that assigned specific frequencies on the radio dial to the many radio stations that were emerging, several radio signals would vie for attention on the same frequencies with those signals overlapping and producing a kind of radio babble for listeners. Order would be restored, but not for 15 years until Congress passed the Radio Act of 1927. With this act, order was restored on the airwaves and the industry actually prospered under its provisions. More importantly, this act let radio transmitters only use the channels, or airwaves, assigned them; the public was deemed the rightful owners, and the broadcasters were only the "custodians" of these airwaves. Thus, the Radio Act of 1927 set the underlying philosophy for all future broadcast regulation: A limited number of broadcast airwaves existed, the public owned them, and stations would be assigned the right to use assigned airwaves, with those rights subject to review at various time intervals and for various reasons. Further, the act stated that when a license is awarded, the standard of evaluation for a station to keep that license would be the "public interest, convenience, or necessity." The Federal Radio Commission (FRC) was set up to enforce this "trustee model" of regulation.

The Communications Act of 1934 was a natural extension of the 1927 radio act, as it contained provisions to include television and replaced the FRC with the FCC, which still exists today as the regulating body for the broadcast industry. The 1934 act also transferred regulation from the Interstate Commerce Commission to the new Federal Communications Commission (FCC). The act would remain intact, despite several attempts to revise it, until January 3, 1996, when Congress would replace it with the new Telecommunications Act of 1996, repealing some of its provisions limiting station ownership and reflecting the deregulatory philosophy of that time.

Orson Welles, center, explains to reporters on October 31, 1938, his radio dramatization of H. G. Wells' "War of the Worlds." Meanwhile, Columbia Broadcasting System made public the transcript of the dramatization, which was aired the night of October 30 and caused thousands of listeners to panic because of the realistic broadcast of an imaginative invasion of men and machines from Mars. [AP Photo]

40. *THE WAR OF THE WORLDS* BROADCAST

The merger of news and entertainment (once coined as "infotainment") has been a part of the American news media almost from the start. From Benjamin Franklin's satirical "Silence Dogood Essays," to the stunts staged by press barons such as James Gordon Bennett, to the high-point of yellow journalism in the Pulitzer-Hearst battles of the late 19th century, on through to today's television newscasts, entertainment has been a part of the news. At no point in history, however, have Americans mistaken pure entertainment for news as much as they did the night of October 30, 1938, when a young radio personality named Orson Welles delivered what has become known as the "War of the Worlds Broadcast." Welles was narrator and director of a regular CBS radio program called Mercury Theater on the Air. For a special Halloween broadcast, Welles decided to present a live radio drama adapted from H. G. Wells' book, *War of the Worlds*, about an alien invasion of the planet Earth.

Helping convince audiences that this was the real thing, the first half of the 60-minute program was comprised of a series of "news bulletins" and "flashes" ostensibly reporting that Martians were invading earth. Helping the illusion of reality was the fact that Mercury Theater had no sponsors, hence no commercial interruptions. It was what CBS called a sustaining show, and the ad-free atmosphere lent itself to uninterrupted "news" stories about the invasion. Mass hysteria erupted, especially in New York and New Jersey since Grover's Mill, New Jersey, was the alleged ground zero of the invasion. Many people fled their homes in panic, others huddled terrified within their walls.

The program actually began as a routine show originating from the CBS studios in New York City and featuring music being played by the CBS orchestra. Soon, however, the music was interrupted by a series of news flashes which grew more and more frequent during the first half-hour. There was the report of a "meteorite" crashing in New Jersey that turned out to be something more ominous when reporter "Carl Phillips" described the landing of a rocket capsule from Mars. The drama peaked as Phillips told horror stories of the Martians incinerating local residents with "heat rays." The first landing was followed by many others throughout the United States as the aliens set about wreaking havoc on America. The first half of the program concluded with a "news reporter" played by actor Ray Collins broadcasting from the top floor of the CBS building. Collins described how Martians were invading New York City and pouring poisonous gas out on the residents below. Occasionally, Welles would enter the drama as a famous astronomer named Professor Richard Pierson who would comment on the invasion. The drama ended in the same way that H. G. Wells ended his novel: the Martians could not withstand the earth's bacteria and all died.

When the play ended, Welles reentered the show as himself and reminded listeners about something he had said briefly at the top of the show: this was an adaptation of the H. G. Wells novel and not the real thing. But many Americans missed the opening moment of the show, did not hear that, and wound up believing they were under attack. Many studies were done on the impact of the show, and one found that some six million Americans had heard the broadcast, 1.7 million believed it all to be true, and 1.2 million actually were terrified.[36] In the angry public reaction that followed the show, many called for laws that would prevent radio from airing fictional shows as news programs. However, CBS reminded the public that it had already issued disclaimers within the program itself. Nevertheless, the network agreed it would never again use the phrase, "we interrupt this program" for entertainment purposes.

41. ADOLF HITLER STEPS INTO HISTORY

The entry of Adolf Hitler into infamy predated by at least five years his entry into the average American consciousness. The reason is largely attributable to the nations' media managers who were more focused on what the American public wanted than what they needed to know about a very real European threat. It was 1938 before Hitler started becoming a household name in most American homes, although he actually burst onto the scene in Western Europe in 1933. Some media did report on what this enigmatic and charismatic politician was up to, but most did not. Americans were tired of bad news, having just come through the Depression, and most were young enough to have served themselves in the first World War or whose friends and relatives did. The unwanted memories of fighting Germans and losing sons were still too fresh to worry again about what that country as up to. And the fact that this former enemy nation might be falling under the spell of a dictator was not something that evoked sympathy from many Americans.

So it was that most of this country's media were looking the other way when Hitler came to power in Germany in 1933. The news for most newspapers at the time was more interesting and enjoyable. There were the everyday stories of Franklin Delano Roosevelt and the economic hopes he brought to the nation. There was the volatile story of prohibition and the antics of bootleggers and congressmen pressing for beer legislation. Then there were the exciting bank robberies of the colorful Bonnie and Clyde, the mob killings in Chicago, Al Capone, and all the rest. And there was always baseball. So it is not surprising to hear accounts from journalists like William L. Shirer, the best-known reporter of World War II and author of *Berlin Diary* and the *Rise and Fall of the Third Reich*. Recalling the coverage of Hitler for *Boston Globe* writer M. R. Montgomery in 1983, Shirer said, "I had the feeling the newspapers didn't want the news."[37] He added, however, that maybe they did want the news but they—like the rest of the country—just handled it with kid gloves out of fear of communism and a growing tolerance instead for fascism if it would keep the Reds in check.

The tenor of the times was not dissimilar to current times in America. World War I was over, and foreign news was not a favorite story among American readers, so newspapers were cutting back on it. The same thing happened following the fall of communism in Europe. As Americans saw that threat dissipate, their interest in foreign news waned for a long time until the attacks of September 11, 2001. But in 1933 there were few correspondents in Europe and, in fact, the CBS radio network had none there when Hitler became chancellor, Shirer recalls, adding that Edward R. Murrow would organize the system of correspondents there later in 1937.[38] Even later, when events were much more ominous for Western powers, NBC and the Mutual Broadcasting Co. withdrew their European correspondents in 1940 because they didn't want to show favoritism in their coverage of the European war.[39]

Therefore, it was the newspapers that carried the burden of reporting Hitler's rise to power, but only a few had bureaus in Berlin in 1933, along with the wire services of course. Still, even the wire services seemed bewildered about Hitler in the early years. The Associated Press, for instance, wrote in 1933 that Hitler had reached the "ambition of a picturesque political career" as if he were some sort of rock star to be applauded. And according to Shirer, the wire services developed a disturbing pattern of reporting the news of Nazis that worsened the gap between truth and knowledge among Americans. For instance, they would put any atrocities into sidebars of main stories about Nazi activities. Editors back in America would usually delete these sidebars, and that was especially the case with smaller papers who were even less concerned about foreign news. Since this pattern remained intact from 1933 to 1938, most Americans knew next to nothing about German atrocities against the Jews for half a decade and remained intrigued by what Shirer called "the little upstart."[40]

Deborah E. Lipstadt, in *Beyond Belief: The American Press and the Coming of the Holocaust*, echoes this belief that U.S. journalists buried news of the Holocaust, even as Germany was burying Jews. She stated that, from the beginning of Hitler's reign in 1933 to his end in 1945 the U.S. press all but missed the story of the Final Solution. A casual reader of U.S. newspapers would have been uninformed about the death camps and the extermination of millions of Jews, she says.[41]

Even the reporters in Berlin seemed to be confused by Hitler's insistence that he wanted peace. Shirer recalls Frederick T. Birchall, chief of the *New York Times*' five-man bureau in Berlin, reporting that the Nazis had no desire to go to war. And the Los Angles Times wrote, "His (Hitler's) anti-semitism is mainly rhetorical."[42]

So it was not until 1938 that most Americans became aware of Jewish persecutions. The lessons in this chapter of history seem clear, and they are ones that have been largely addressed by the dominant news media in America who still scan the international horizons for threats and try to interest the American public in reading or watching. The factor mitigating against more international coverage today, however, is similar to the main one in 1933: media managers want their organizations to produce stories that the American public is interested in and will buy. So editors today are being called on, as they were in 1933, to fight for what they believe the public needs to know, and not just what they want to read or see.

42. "THIS IS LONDON"

Of all the journalists reporting on the eve of the Second World War, the name of Edward R. Murrow was one of the most significant, because it was through Murrow that most Americans first heard about the horrors of the war in Europe. If it was hard to get Americans' attention with the growing trouble in Germany, Austria, and Poland, it was easier for them to empathize with British citizens and the chaos visited on that country by the German bombing attacks that began in 1940. London was the main target of those nightly bomb raids by German planes, and terror was largely their purpose as ordinary citizens lay in the bomb sights of German bombadiers. Murrow and a handful of other journalists risked their lives nightly to report this *blitzkrieg*.

Murrow was among the first phalanx of radio reporters dispatched to Europe to cover the hostilities there. A CBS colleague, Bill Henry, along with Arthur Mann of the Mutual Broadcasting System (MBS) had been the first of the frontline radio reporters in 1939. They were joined by another CBS reporter, William L. Shirer, and William C. Kerker of NBC.[43] Great courage was shown by all these reporters, but it was Murrow who, night after night, told CBS listeners in America of the German air raids on London. As media historians Michael and Edwin Emery note, "The greatest impact on American minds was made by his (Murrow's) 'This is London' broadcasts graphically reporting the Battle of Britain. Murrow's quiet but compelling voice brought images of a bomb-torn and burning London that did much to awaken the still neutral United States to the nature of the war."[44] The poet Archibald MacLeish noted of the "This is London" broadcasts: "You burned the city of London in our houses and we felt the flames that burned it."[45] It was largely because of his tireless reporting of these London broadcasts that Murrow became a pioneer in CBS television news immediately following the war. But it was not fame Murrow was after as he dodged bombs night after night in London. He was there to capture the horror of the German campaign, together with the resolve of the British people in resisting Hitler's awesome intimidation tactics. As writer A. M. Sperber wrote of Murrow's broadcasts:

It was The War of the Worlds come to life, the fantasy of 1938 become the reality of 1940, the rooftop observer reporting on the life and death of cities, no longer an actor in the studio. This was the real thing, broadcasting's first living-room war. A world was ending, and the reporters had become the chorus, playing out their roles on a stage of awesome dimensions.[46]

Murrow had a keen eye for detail and, although working in a nonvisual medium of radio, possessed the ability to paint a distinct verbal picture of what he was witnessing as in this excerpt:

Out of one window there waves something that looks like a bedsheet, a . . . curtain swinging free in the night breeze. It looks as if it were being shaken by a ghost . . . The searchlights straightaway, miles in front of me, are still scratching the sky. There's a three-quarter moon riding high. There was one burst of shell-fire almost straight in the Little Dipper.[47]

Another excerpt shows the passion Murrow conveyed about the terror in front of him and, even more than that, his uncanny ability to articulate the larger picture of the battle scene:

This country is undergoing a revolution, a revolution not by consent but a revolution none the less. This long range pounding from the air . . . should not blind one to the fundamentals of this business. It is a struggle between two ways of life, two systems of governing a people . . . The amount of damage done is only incidental. There is no way for the average man to hit back in this kind of war. In many ways [it] is a race . . . to see which can produce the most fanatics, and which can evolve a relationship between the State and the individual sufficiently attractive to cause him to be willing to be bombed indefinitely . . . [But] there must be equality under the bombs. He must be convinced that after he has suffered, a better world will emerge. His memory will give him "roses in December," but there must be at least the promise that the Spring will bring better roses for all.[48]

For his reporting from London, the Overseas Press Club honored Murrow in 1940 as the best foreign radio news reporter of the year. More importantly Murrow set the standard that other reporters would follow as the war in Europe turned into World War II. And more important than that, Murrow brought the American consciousness into a conflict that ultimately would have to involve them and test their resolve—as it had Britain's—like no other previous war.

43. ERNIE PYLE REPORTS WORLD WAR II

Every war brings out the best in courage of soldiers and of the war correspondents covering them. World War II was no exception, and one of the best journalists it produced was Indiana native Ernest Taylor Pyle, better known by America as just Ernie. Decades before the "embed" system of reporting which the second Iraq War produced, Ernie Pyle was in the foxholes of Europe and the South Pacific with everyday soldiers. Pyle provided close-up profiles of them, their drudgery and their dangers, and sent those dispatches back to America to be devoured by wives, friends, mothers, and fathers. Pyle set the standard for battlefield journalism in World War II and beyond. He won the ultimate journalistic honor when he received the Pulitzer Prize in 1944, and he paid the ultimate price for his heroism in 1945 when he was killed by a sniper on the Japanese island of Ie Shima.

Before the war, Pyle had spent seven years crisscrossing the country gathering stories for his daily feature column which he wrote for the Scripps-Howard newspaper chain. He was eager to cover the war in Europe and was dispatched to England to cover the Battle of Britain in 1940, the year before America entered the war following the December 7, 1941, Japanese attack on Pearl Harbor. Pyle spent most of the war covering Europe and distinguished himself from the front lines in Sicily, Italy, North Africa, and France. When Germany fell, he was sent to the South Pacific where he was killed shortly thereafter. Throughout the war he became the best read American war correspondent, and most of his stories were characterized by the human face of the war, focusing on small bands of soldiers with whom he shared the danger. Pyle's columns appeared in some 400 daily and 300 weekly newspapers. Although reporting on all levels of the military and war effort, his favorite subject was the individual soldier whose courage and resolve he respected and admired. He once said that they were "the guys that wars can't be won without."[49]

Typical of his columns was the following excerpt of a piece called, "Killing is all that Matters," written from Algiers on December 1, 1942, in which Pyle tells Americans how soldiers in battle are changed by the experience:

> The American soldier is quick in adapting himself to a new mode of living. Outfits which have been here only three days have dug vast networks of ditches three feet deep in the bare brown earth. They have rigged up a light here and there with a storage battery. They have gathered boards and made floors and sideboards for their tents to keep out the wind and sand. They have hung out their washing and painted their names over the tent flaps. You even see a soldier sitting on his "front step" of an evening playing a violin.
>
> They've been here only three days and they know they're unlikely to be here three days more, but they patch up some kind of home nevertheless. Even in this short waiting period life is far from static. Motor convoys roar along the highways. Everything is on a basis of "not a minute to spare." There is a new spirit among the troops—a spirit of haste. Planes pass constantly, eastbound. New detachments of troops wait for orders to move on. Old detachments tell you the stories of their first battle and conjecture about the next one. People you've only recently met hand you slips of paper with their home addresses and say, "You know, in case something happens, would you mind writing . . . "
>
> At last we are in it up to our necks, and everything is changed, even your outlook on life.
>
> Swinging first and swinging to kill is all that matters now.[50]

Pyle's legacy lived on after his death. A film on his wartime work after joining Company C, 18th Infantry as the unit fought its way across North Africa was released in July 1945. It was called *The Story of G.I. Joe* and starred Burgess Meredith as Pyle. Additionally, the school where Pyle began his training as a writer—Indiana University—is today housed in Ernie Pyle Hall, and scholarships bearing his name have helped many journalism students receive their training. The majority of Pyle's columns, papers, and letters are housed in the Lilly Library of Indiana University. Pyle's boyhood home in the Indiana town of Dana today receives thousands of visitors and is a State Historic Site.

44. THE FLAG RAISING ON MOUNT SURIBACHI

World War II was covered not only with words in newspapers and over the radio, but also with some terrifically revealing news photography. Photojournalism was an important part of the war's coverage, and the influence of images from the front lines gripped Americans back home and increased their pride and resolve. The American military knew this, and thus the value of heroic images was very high with military commanders. The venues for those photos ranged far and wide from the photo-oriented *Life* and *Look* magazines, to daily papers and small-town weeklies across America. World War II was the first real opportunity photojournalists had to show how important visual imagery is in conveying the heroes and the horrors of war and in transporting readers to the bloody scenes of battle.

Photojournalists caught some singular moments which bespoke victory as a result of self-sacrifice of American troops. Probably the best-known single image from World War II was the Pulitzer Prize-winning photo by AP photographer Joe Rosenthal of the handful of Marines and sailors planting the American flag on Mount Suribachi in the battle for the island of Iwo Jima. Like other memorable photos, such as one of Babe Ruth acknowledging the throngs of fans in his last game at Yankee Stadium, it was not a shot the photographer was originally pleased with. In both of these memorable photos, the actual faces of the subjects are obscured (Ruth was shot from behind as he waved to the crowd), but the images more than did their jobs.

This black-and-white image provided by the National Archives shows a "still" taken from the 16 mm movie series of Marines raising the American flag on the summit of Mount Suribachi, on Iwo Jima. [AP Photo/Files/William H. Genaust]

The photo of the flag-raising at Iwo Jima on February 23, 1945, inspired Americans and made them even more grateful for the jobs their troops were doing overseas. As for the government, they saw in this single photo a chance to raise more funds through the sale of war bonds; enough money that might enable the country to bring a speedier end to the war in the Pacific. The two surviving Marines and one sailor from that photo were quickly taken out of action, returned to the states, and were used by the government as poster boys for a final big push in war bond sales. Their story was told in a 2006 film by Clint Eastwood called *Flags of Our Fathers*. One of the surviving members of the flag-raising squad was Pharmacist Mate Second Class John H. Bradley, USN, serving on Iwo Jima with the 5th Marine Division. Bradley has described the event this way:

> We started up the mountain immediately after the Naval barrage and plane straf-ing was over and we reached the top . . . When we reached the top we formed our battle lines . . . and we all went over the top together . . . We set our line of fire up, the lieutenant in charge placed the machine guns where he wanted them, had our rifle men spotted and immediately we sent patrols to the right and to the left. We went up the mountain almost in the middle . . . When we got there I was with the group that swung to the left and immediately the Lieutenant sent a man around to look for a piece of staff that we could put the American flag on. And the Japs had some old pipes that were laying around there, they used these pipes to run water down below the mountain. And we used this Jap pipe and we attached the Ameri-can flag on there and we put it up. And Joe Rosenthal happened to be there at the right time. He came up a little while after we were on top and much to his sur-prise the picture that is now so famous....the Flag Raising on Mount Suribachi.[51]

It is interesting to note that Rosenthal's famed photo was actually of the second flag that was raised on Mount Suribachi; not the first. Before Bradley's squad raised their flag, a smaller flag had been put up earlier by PlSgt. Ernest Thomas. That flag was so small, however, it could not be seen by troops down the mountain, so the battalion commander ordered a larger flag to raised so all the troops could see it. That was the flag raised by Bradley's group and that was the photo taken by Rosenthal. The photog-rapher used a bulky Speed Graphic camera to capture the image after briefly consider-ing trying to capture images of both the smaller and larger flags in the same frame. He decided to focus instead on the larger flag as it was being raised, and the rest is his-tory. The photo was perceived by the American public as the singular victory symbol of the war. It appeared on the covers of several national magazines, and the government even made it into a postage stamp. As for Rosenthal, he would spend the rest of his life battling rumors—all unproven—that the famed photo was staged.

45. THE LAUNCHING OF *EBONY*

No other publication, with the possible exception of its sister magazine *Jet*, has been more popular with the African American population in America than *Ebony* magazine.

Launched by John H. Johnson in 1945, this monthly magazine has published regularly since its founding, making it one of the oldest and largest continuously published magazines in America. It has survived the magazines it was patterned after, most notably *Look* and *Life*, although the latter was retooled after an absence from the market into a smaller monthly publication. *Ebony*, however, remained strong.

Ebony was certainly not the first black-owned publication aimed at African American readers. That honor would probably go to Frederick Douglass' *North Star*, discussed elsewhere in this book. And, in the 20th Century, there was the notable founding of the *Chicago Defender*, launched by Robert S. Abbott in 1905, which once heralded itself as "the world's greatest weekly." It certainly was the most influential African American weekly newspaper by the start of World War I. Decades later, in 1956, the *Chicago Defender* became the *Chicago Daily Defender*, the largest black-owned daily newspaper in the world.[52] About *Ebony*, Johnson said his objective was to "show not only Negroes, but also white people that Negroes got married, had beauty contest, gave parties, ran successful businesses, and did all the other normal things of life."[53] *Ebony* was also characterized by advertising that jointly featured general merchandise as well as products aimed at blacks. Johnson told the *New York Times* in 1990 that some 12 percent of the readership of *Ebony* and *Jet* were white.[54] The magazines now also have their online editions found at http://www.EbonyJet.com.

The editors state the following about the magazines' current mission: "Our goals are to provide a unique and engaging forum to explore the impact of the world on African Americans and the impact of African Americans on the World."[55]

Johnson was born on January 19, 1918, in Arkansas City, Arkansas, and was he grandson of slaves. His father was killed in a sawmill accident, and his mother took menial wage-earner jobs, eking out a living and moving her family to Chicago. In Chicago, Johnson encountered middle-class blacks for the first time and attended an all-black high school with classmates such as Nat King Cole and Redd Foxx. He studied hard at night, and read many self-improvement books. An insurance company executive heard Johnson speak at an Urban League event, was impressed, and made a scholarship possible for him to attend the University of Chicago. His mother believed in her son's potential and took out a $500 loan in 1942, using her furniture as security, to let Johnson start an empire that began with *Negro Digest*, patterned after *Reader's Digest*, which evolved into *Ebony* and *Jet* and made him one of the richest African American businessmen in history.[56] Ebony grew to be the genre's most popular publication with a circulation of 1.7 million and a monthly readership of 11 million. Johnson Publishing Co. also features a book publishing division and employs more than 2,600 people with sales of more than $388 million.[57] Johnson died in 2005 as one of the most influential African Americans of the 20th Century.

46. *CANDID CAMERA* STARTS REALITY TV

Perhaps no other television phenomenon has so captured American viewers in the late 20th century and early 21st century as so-called "reality television." From shows like

America's Funniest Home Videos, Totally Hidden Video, The Mole, Survivor, Big Brother, The Great Race, Biggest Loser, Extreme Home Makeover, etc., Americans have found themselves captivated by watching "everyday people" deal with interesting and often quirky challenges placed in their paths by the shows' producers. It may come as a surprise to many viewers, however, that the concept for the "reality" show —in fact the first of its breed—hit the television screens not in the 1990s, but in the 1940s. The show was called *Candid Camera*, and what it unleashed has produced great changes in television's prime-time programming.

Produced by Allen Funt, the show premiered on ABC on August 10, 1948, as a television incarnation of a 1947 radio show by Funt called *Candid Microphone.* Its format was simple and featured film taken by a hidden camera of everyday people captured in hoaxes dreamed up by Funt. Examples of these hoaxes included secretaries chained to their desks, money left lying on busy sidewalks, mailboxes that talked to passers-by, a "men's room" sign hung on a clothes closet, and cars moving down the street without engines. The idea was to get on-the-spot reactions from the people passing by and—in the case of the money—finding not-so-subtle ways to reach down and pick it up. Funt told *Psychology Today* in 1985 that he "wanted to go beyond what people merely said, to record what they did—their gestures, facial expressions, confusions and delights."[58]

The show changed its named to *Candid Camera* in 1949 when it moved to NBC, but the network moved it from time slot to time slot, and it didn't get a permanent weekly slot until moving to CBS in 1960. For the next seven years, *Candid Camera* remained among the top 10 shows each week before its network run came to an end. It would reemerge in syndicated form seven years later, from 1974 to 1978) and then for a couple of years in 1990–1992 as *The New Candid Camera*, with Funt still advising the production.[59] In the early years, Funt and his staff worked to overcome numerous obstacles to produce and film the show. This was an age when television equipment was large and bulky, and hiding it from public view was no easy achievement. Yet hiding it was necessary to produce the unscripted or unstaged effects of everyday people reacting to the staged stunts and stimuli. On average, some 50 recorded sequences were filmed for every four to five that were actually aired on the program. Also, this "reality" approach was new to television management, and they weren't sure how much of it would be acceptable, both from ethical and legal perspectives. But Funt was known for censoring any material which unduly breached anyone's privacy or which he considered in bad taste.[60]

An obvious later incarnation of *Candid Camera* was *America's Funniest Home Videos,* which premiered in the late 1980s. But it is not a stretch to see how other shows like *Survivor* and *Big Brother*—although more scripted and with a repertoire cast of everyday (usually attractive) people—came from the same mold as Funt's original creation.

47. HEARST PROMOTES YOUNG EVANGELIST

Although media barons are not in the business of promoting spiritual leaders, a striking exception occurred in 1949 when William Randolph Hearst issued an edict to his editors to publicize a young evangelist as much as possible. That evangelist was Billy Graham, and he was holding a series of tent revival meetings that year in Los Angeles. It would be a city the preacher would return to many times, usually packing college football stadiums with tens of thousands of admirers and spiritual seekers. But in 1949, Graham was only six years out of Wheaton College and a virtual unknown to the nation. That was about to change, and part of that change was due to William Randolph Hearst, publisher of a string of magazines and newspapers such as the *New York Journal* and the *San Francisco Examiner*, and the man who is largely credited with creating the era of "yellow journalism" in the 1890s.

Hearst was a lifelong ideological conservative, so Graham's message of conservative Christianity appealed to him, as did the patriotism he saw evidenced in this young, attractive preacher with a golden voice. In his short time in the ministry, the young Graham had already developed a following but it was the revival meetings in Los Angeles in 1949 that expanded it to a national scale. Hearst heard about the attention Graham was receiving and the reports of how mesmerizing he was to audiences. So he sent a telegram to his newspapers editors that read simply, "Puff Graham," while the L.A. crusade was occurring.[61] Editors did not take lightly any orders from Hearst, and so that is what they did. Immediate national exposure ensued, and the tent

Thirty-year-old evangelist Billy Graham gestures as he speaks to a crowd of 10,000 in Los Angeles, California, November 1, 1949. Thousands attending his tent meetings in Los Angeles publicly announced their decision to accept Christ. [AP Photo]

meetings in Los Angeles stretched to eight weeks when they had originally been set to run only three at best.

Apparently Graham and Hearst never met, and Hearst was not known to be a religious man. Indeed his lifestyle and persona suggested he was not. So many believe it was not Graham's preaching that struck a chord in Hearst so much as seeing Graham as someone who could inspire young people positively, add to America's sense of patriotism, and be a voice for anticommunism, which was important to Hearst.

How important was that exposure of the 1949 Graham tent revivals? Within five years, Billy Graham was featured on the cover of *Time* magazine, and Graham had become a national figure. The evangelist would go on to become a friend and spiritual advisor to every president since Harry S. Truman, reach millions around the globe with his message of salvation, and become one of the most admired men in America. And, for his part, Graham was also influential as a leader in the media, starting magazines such as *Christianity Today* and *Decisions*, and for starting a religious broadcasting and television division featuring shows seen and heard around the world. Graham is also one of the few television evangelists who has managed to steer clear of the kinds of scandals that have gripped other televangelists such as Jim Bakker, Jimmy Swaggart, Oral Roberts, and Richard Roberts.

48. LAUNCHING THE USIA

The flow of information around the world has always had a huge impact on how the citizens of the world view the West and, in particular, the United States of America. The fact that most of that information flow is controlled by western media has been a source of frustration to those developing nations who feel their voices have been silenced. Adding to the information coming from the western news media has been the information flowing from western nations themselves. And no western nation has spent more money or effort in getting its news and views out to the far reaches of the world than the United States.

In 1945, as World War II came to an end, the U.S. government decided that the Office of War Information should continue on in peacetime, albeit under a different name. So the Office of International Information and Cultural Affairs was launched and was placed under the State Department. Three years later, the office was divided into an Office of International Information and also an Office of Cultural Exchange. The act creating that split was the 1948 Smith-Mundt Act. A relatively small budget of $12 million was allocated to the two offices, about one-third what the OWI had been working with. Critics of the lesser funding would complain that this shows the lack of interest by the U.S. government in building and maintaining relationships with other countries around the world during peace time, but others would say at least the United States funded such an international communication effort. In any event, the intent behind these offices was probably to produce more one-way communication and use the offices as a way to get the American story out to other parts of the world.

World War II had no more than ended when America began worrying about the communist threat that Russia might pose. The country had consolidated its power in the East by tightening its control on satellite states in the region. The Korean War in 1950 raised the communist threat to a new level in the United States. All of a sudden, more appropriations were being allocated to getting America's story out. In 1952, the revamped International Information Administration had an $87 million budget, and one-fourth of that was to go to the new Voice of America (VOA). The next year, the name, "United States Information Agency" was adopted and its budget was in excess of $100 million. The main voice of that agency abroad was the VOA, and it was being delivered in 40 different languages over 92 transmitters. It had a worldwide audience estimated at 43 million listeners.[62] Overseas, the U.S. Information Agency was called the "U.S. Information Service" and it was hard at work in spreading American news and views in a variety of ways. In 70 different countries, the USIS set up and maintained information libraries, most in locations separate from U.S. embassies and easily accessible to the public in those countries. The USIS also started funding lecture tours by U.S. college professors, artists, musicians, scientists, and business people who would interact with nationals in the various countries and build cultural bridges between the United States and these nations. But the USIS was mainly in the public relations business, and it would distribute thousands of news releases and bulletins, interfacing with the news and entertainment media in the various countries. The openness of the USIS libraries and events, many of them run by local entities dubbed "America Houses," would continue for decades until the terrorists attacks of 9/11 would require greater security in 2001. The libraries and events would go behind metal detectors, and some of the libraries would be transferred physically to armed embassy grounds.

The role of the USIA, and especially VOA, has been a subject of debate for many years, especially during its first two decades of the 1950s and 1960s. Journalists believed the agency should deliver objective facts about America, but politicians have seen the USIA as more of a public relations effort which emphasizes the positives of the United States, while minimizing the negatives and putting a positive spin on those negatives. The debate was polarized even more during the mid-1960s as the United States became more deeply involved in Vietnam. A strong attempt to legitimatize the objective nature of the USIA came in 1961 when the agency asked CBS news pioneer Edward R. Murrow, who had successfully taken on Sen. Joseph McCarthy and deligitimized his communist "witch hunt," to direct the agency. Disappointed with the direction that television news was taking, Murrow agreed and took charge of the USIA for two years until he retired in 1963.

President Jimmy Carter reorganized the USIA in 1977, combining it with the educational and cultural affairs divisions in the State Department. A new International Communication Agency evolved wherein the VOA and USIS would continue operations as before. But five years later, the USIA symbol was again being used, and its budget was increased to nearly $700 million by 1990. The VOA received more than $170 million of that, and the agency played a large role in disseminating information during the 1989 Fall of Communism in Europe and in the student protest movements in China. By 1995, the VOA had a 24/7 service, broadcasting around the world in

45 languages with some 130 million people listening in. The USIS maintained information libraries in 125 countries.

49. THE FIRST NETWORK TELEVISION NEWSCAST

On May 3, 1948, CBS Television launched a new era when it began the first-ever television network newscast, The CBS-TV News, tapping former radio newsman Douglas Edwards as the first host. The title of "anchor" would not be used for another four years and was first used in describing Walter Cronkite's role in "anchoring" CBS coverage of the 1952 presidential conventions. Although the network had covered a lot of news stories during the startup years of commercial television following World War II, it was not until 1948 that CBS decided to air a nightly news show. By 1947, it was running a Saturday evening newscast, then two newscasts each week before moving to its nightly program in the spring of 1948. In so doing—and in hiring correspondents of the caliber of Edwards and his contemporary Edward R. Murrow and producer Fred Friendly—it would cement itself as a bastion of news enterprise for many years to come.

Edwards' 15-minute nightly newscast would compete with NBC's 1949 launching of the *Camel News Caravan*, anchored by the more animated John Cameron Swayze and named for its sponsor, Camel cigarettes. But Edwards' stoic style would wind up winning the network ratings race. That would change in the late 1950s after NBC replaced Swayze with anchors Chet Huntley and David Brinkley, an anchor duo who became highly popular. Their success led CBS to replace Edwards with Walter Cronkite in 1962, and Cronkite became a legend in television news.

Edwards, who died in 1990 at age 73, had joined CBS Radio in 1942 and anchored its regular news show, *World News Today*. Prior to that, he worked as a radio newsman in Atlanta and Detroit. CBS renamed the newscast *Douglas Edwards with the News* in the mid-1950s, and the show reached an audience regularly estimated at some 30 million viewers, showing how popular the new medium of television could be in delivering the news to America. Edwards would go on to anchor the CBS nightly newscast until 1962 and cement the network's reputation as the premier television news organization of the day until stepping down for Cronkite and returning to CBS radio as one of its leading journalistic lights. During Edwards' tenure, both CBS and NBC found their nightly newscasts to be so popular that they expanded them from 15 to 30 minutes and, in later years, experimented with hour-long versions before going back to the half-hour format.

CBS and NBC dominated national television news coverage as the only two networks doing news. ABC was a latecomer and was first organized out of the old NBC Blue Network in 1948. It would not present serious competition until the late 1970s, showing the immense popularity of Cronkite, Huntley, and Brinkley and the entertainment identification most viewers had of ABC. Of course this was the age of broadcast television (cable networks would not become a threat for viewers until the early 1990s), so CBS and NBC network newscasts owned the television news audience for at least four decades.

50. MURROW CONFRONTS MCCARTHY

The era of the early 1950s, when America was trying to find a balance between opposing perceived threats from Communists while—at the same time—worrying about trampling individual liberties, was not unlike the Post 9/11 chapter of American history. In this latter-day period the same tension exists, although the Communist threat has been supplanted by the international terrorist threat of Al Qaeda. The 1950s was a time when Communist sympathizers existed in America alongside citizens who had allegiance to America's democratic ideals. It was hard sometimes to tell the two apart, and it was hard to know which Communist sympathizers were benign and which might be threats.

The media can learn a lot from the way pioneering broadcast journalists like Edward R. Murrow and Fred W. Friendly covered the 1950s tension in the era known as McCarthyism. Not only did the news tandem stand up against a real threat to American liberty, but they also stood up to CBS management who worried about taking on a popular U.S. senator who was leading a charge against Communism in the United States. After all, ratings were at stake. So, for a time, Murrow and Friendly were operating alone, flying without a net.

Sen. Joseph McCarthy, R-Wis., pounds the podium as he addresses a group of 3,000 admirers at Constitution Hall in Washington, November 11, 1954. McCarthy backers from many cities came to Washington to stage the rally, which was held to protest the censure move against the senator. [AP Photo/Bob Schutz]

The tension of the time reached a level of near-insanity when the junior senator from Wisconsin, Joseph McCarthy saw an opportunity to make a name for himself by declaring, usually without proof, that many Communists had infiltrated various American institutions including the military, the government, the news media, and the entertainment industry. Those suspected of Communist ties were subpoenaed to testify before a congressional subcommittee, where they were questioned aggressively by McCarthy and other congressmen, required to name names of other suspected sympathizers, and were sometimes charged on the spot with treason. Through much of this era, McCarthy enjoyed great notoriety and popularity from many Americans for leading a charge against Communism.[63]

However, McCarthy crossed the line into bullying and ruining reputations without evidence, and that became too much for some to bear. One of those who had enough was Edward R. Murrow, the pioneering CBS newsman who had made a name for himself covering the German bombing of London and who had two popular shows (*See It Now* and *Person to Person*) on CBS television. Murrow himself was an anticommunist, but he distrusted McCarthy and especially the senator's methods and levels of proof. When McCarthy set his sights on Air Force Lt. Milo Radulovich, calling him a communist sympathizer and forcing him to be drummed out of the service, Murrow snapped. Asking for evidence against the 28-year-old Radulovich, Murrow received none. He decided, against the wishes of CBS President Bill Paley, to do a *See It Now* program in 1953 on the Air Force officer and sent reporter Joe Wershba to the Michigan home of Radulovich. From the telecast, it seemed obvious to Wershba, Murrow, and much of the nation that the young officer was not, in fact, a communist sympathizer. His father had read newspapers which were called subversive in the early 1950s and, apparently just for that, he was discharged from the Air Force as a security risk.[64]

For his part, Murrow concluded on-air, "We believe that the son shall not bear the iniquity of the father, even though that iniquity be proved and, in this case, it was not."[65] As a result of the telecast, the Air Force reinstated Radulovich into the Reserves, and the door was opened for Murrow to do a direct assault on McCarthy in a *See It Now* program on March 4, 1954, again against the wishes of CBS management. Murrow was convinced by now that McCarthy posed a real and imminent threat to Americans' individual civil liberties, and he wanted to expose him. The program revealed the brutal and often-unfounded tactics of Sen. McCarthy, making the senator appear as a bullying buffoon to many Americans. Under the Fairness Doctrine of the day, CBS was obliged to offer McCarthy equal time, in this case 30 minutes, to respond to Murrow's broadcast. His on-air rebuttal was a disaster as he showed his discomfort with being on television and lashed out at Murrow as "the leader of the jackal pack." Response to the broadcasts ran 15–1 in favor of Murrow.[66] Several months later, on December 2, 1954, the U.S. Senate voted to censure McCarthy for conduct unbecoming a U.S. senator, and he was effectively finished as a political and influential source in America.

The entire episode was painstakingly recreated in the 2005 critically acclaimed film, *Good Night and Good Luck*, directed by George Clooney and starring David Strathairn as Murrow and Clooney as Friendly.

51. TV'S FIRST PRESIDENTIAL ELECTION

Until 1952, radio was the only broadcast medium Americans had to keep them informed about presidential elections. It was the most up-to-date form of communication, and listeners would sit huddled around their console receivers to hear the latest returns from the presidential race. The days before television were also the halcyon days of newspapers which would often publish special editions after the regular newspaper had gone to bed to provide readers with even later, breaking news about who the next commander in chief would be. All that began changing with the 1952 presidential election, however, when Gen. Dwight David Eisenhower challenged the Democratic Governor Adlai Stevenson of Illinois. For this would be television's first presidential election, and the new medium's first chance to show how well it could perform under the pressure cooker of a presidential election campaign.

Although 1952 was the first year television covered both the Democratic and Republican national conventions, the first fledgling experiments in televising the nominating conventions actually started in the 1948 presidential race. But coverage then was spotty, and few Americans had the ability to watch the limited coverage because only 400,000 American homes had TV sets in 1948, as compared with 19 million television homes just four years later.[67]

CBS News Correspondent Edward R. Murrow is seen broadcasting national election returns on CBS Television Network in New York City on election night, November 7, 1956. [AP Photo/CBS, Inc.]

The Museum of Broadcast Communication states the importance of the 1952 coverage as follows:

> By 1952, both the Democratic and Republican conventions were broadcast nation-wide on television. The impact of the medium, only recently networked into a truly national phenomenon, was immediate. After watching the first televised Republican convention in 1952, Democratic Party officials made last minute changes to their own convention in attempts to maintain the attention of viewers at home. By 1956, both parties further amended their convention programs to better fit the demands of television coverage. Party officials condensed the length of the convention, created uniform campaign themes for each party, adorned convention halls with banners and patriotic decorations, placed television crews in positions with flattering views of the proceedings, dropped daytime sessions, limited welcoming speeches and parliamentary organization procedures, scheduled sessions to reach a maximum audience in prime time, and eliminated seconding speeches for vice presidential candidates. Additionally, the presence of television cameras encouraged parties to conceal intra-party battling and choose geographic host cities amenable to their party.[68]

Television coverage of the presidential campaigns has brought a sea change to American politics, and those changes began taking place after Democratic and Republican party leaders saw how the medium changed the process in 1952. For one thing, until the early 1950s, the Democratic and Republican presidential nominees were actually selected, as well as confirmed, at the parties' national nominating conventions. After television entered the picture, putting the parties and their infighting on the national viewing screen, leaders realized the candidates should be selected before the conventions so the conventions themselves could be seen as great displays of party unity. Hence the importance of the campaign primary season began, whereby the party bickering and deal-making were largely over by the time the conventions rolled around. With some notable exceptions, that has proven to be the case since the 1950s.

Additionally, televised party conventions have brought the candidates a larger degree of freedom from the restraints and dictates of the parties themselves. It wasn't long before candidates realized they didn't necessarily need party support to reach the American voters if they could muster a financial war chest large enough for them to take advantage of television commercial time and go to the people directly with their message. The state political primaries, together with television commercials and—of course—TV news coverage itself, has made it possible for more candidates to enter the process than party officials might have liked. The presidential campaigns of the Rev. Jesse Jackson, Ralph Nader, Pat Robertson, Ron Paul, Ross Perot, and even Jimmy Carter were examples of these outsiders who ran strong campaigns and—in the case of Carter—actually won the White House.

Television coverage has made it possible for candidates to remain in the race for nomination longer than the parties might like. A case in point was the 2008 campaigns for the Democratic presidential nomination between Sens. Barack Obama and

Hillary Clinton, which dragged on until the summer of the convention itself. Party officials were hoping for a longer lead-time to display party unity, especially since Sen. John McCain had been the presumptive GOP nominee for months, but Obama and Clinton each had enough money and popular support to keep their campaigns running until it became obvious Obama would garner the nomination.

The largest single expense of any presidential campaign is advertising, and television's coverage of the 1952 presidential election also brought with it the importance of the television commercial. Indeed, it was in that election that Richard Nixon, then vice-presidential running mate of Eisenhower, saved his position by going on television and making his famous "Checkers" speech, attacking stories he had unduly used campaign money for personal expenses. The irony, was that Nixon's television persona would turn on him when he ran against John F. Kennedy for president in 1960.

When television began covering the presidential election in 1952, TV advertising emerged as a vitally important tool of political hopefuls. It was Rosser Reeves, a Madison Avenue advertising executive, who that year first floated the idea of political advertising strategy for TV. Reeves showed Eisenhower media aides that 20-second commercials played during such popular TV programs as *I Love Lucy* would reach more voters than any other form of advertising. Thus the political commercial was born, and it would have a permanent effect on the way presidential campaigns were carried out from that day forward. While the commercials use state-of-the-art techniques that reflect the trends and fashions of the times in which they were made, the fundamental strategies and messages have tended to remain the same over the years, so that familiar types of commercials have emerged.[69]

52. NBC LAUNCHES *TODAY*

It seems that from the beginning of television, the *Today* show has always been there, starting NBC's broadcast day. It was there for television viewers who grew up in the 1950s, and it is still with them today. And what was originally a two-hour show grew in 2000 to take over a three-hour time slot, and in 2007 was expanded to four hours in some markets. A Saturday version runs one hour, and the Sunday *Today* show runs two hours. In every respect, the *Today* show set the standard for the morning news/talk shows for all other competing networks, then and in the future.

Today premiered on NBC on January 14, 1952 and, although it would face a strong challenge in the ratings starting in the late 1980s from morning shows on ABC and CBS, the venerable day-starter for NBC has not missed a beat and regained its status as regular morning ratings leader in the mid-1990s. Former NBC News President Reuven Frank once called the show a "brash experiment" for the pioneering network.[70] But the experiment succeeded beyond NBC's wildest dreams. The idea was that American television viewers would like to start their day with a show that would not only update them on what was happening in the world, but also be light, airy, and friendly enough to help them feel good as they began their day. Much of the success of *Today* goes to the decision to hire an affable, articulated, yet understated host named Dave Garroway, who would anchor the show until 1961 after his second wife committed suicide. Among other things, Garroway was responsible for hiring a young writer for the show whose name was Barbara Walters.

"He set a tone for the whole broadcast that day," Steve Friedman, former executive producer of *Today* said. "We built it around him. Some people were concerned whether he could carry it off, but he did."[71]

The show was the creation of then-NBC Vice President Pat Weaver, who would later serve as the network's chairman of the board and, incidentally, was the father of actress Sigourney Weaver. The show mixed several elements, including in-depth interviews with newsmakers and celebrities, national and international news stories, tosses to local NBC stations for news updates from their markets, features on a wide range of lifestyles and fads, and more than a few quirky attention-getters. The most famous of the latter was a chimpanzee named J. Fred Muggs who served as a kind of show mascot and sidekick for host Dave Garroway.

With the exception of having a chimp share the hosting duties, the format and goals of *Today* have remained remarkably similar over the decades to the original plan. And the success of *Today* has been obvious not only in the ratings but also in the fact that both ABC's *Good Morning America* and CBS's *The Early Show* were patterned after it. *Today* has even spawned international versions of the show ranging from Germany's *Heute* on ZDF Television, to Britain's *Good Morning Britain* on ITV. In large measure,

Past and then-current cast members of the NBC-TV "TODAY" show get together on the set Friday, January 14, 1977, to celebrate the show's 25th anniversary. Standing from left: Gene Shalit, Tom Brokaw, Floyd Kalber, Jane Pauley and Lew Wood. Seated members from left are: Dave Garroway, Jack Lescouli, and Frank Blair. Shalit still appears on the show. [AP Photo]

Today was the prototype for the news and talk show genre which has come to overpopulate American broadcast and cable television networks. NBC envisioned the show as the front half of two bookend shows. The other was *The Tonight Show* which also premiered in 1952, was much more oriented toward entertainment, and which closed out the network's broadcast day.

The hosts for *Today* is a list that reads like the Who's Who of American television news and includes John Chancellor, Hugh Downs, Tom Brokaw, Barbara Walters, Jane Pauley, Bryant Gumbel, Chris Wallace, Matt Lauer, Katie Couric, and Meredith Vieira. Even baseball great Joe Garagiola cohosted the show for a year (1990–91).

A key feature of *Today* has always been its interaction, real or apparent, with the everyday people who throng the street outside the show studio in New York City. Originally, Garroway was positioned for part of the show in front a wall of street-level windows that looked into the outside crowd, who was looking in. In later years, the show's producers actually took the anchors out into the street for portions of the show where they often interacted one-on-one with the crowd of onlookers. This interactive feature of the show seemed to be a harbinger of the importance this element would have in the media marketplace.

By 2007, *Today* had expanded to four hours Monday through Friday, after the third hour had been added in 2000, making it the only three-hour national morning show broadcast. As NBC publicists state, "*Today*'s hallmark has been its ability to revise an entire edition to bring viewers breaking news as it happens. In that fashion, *Today* delivered immediate coverage of such events as Hurricane Katrina, the Tsunami, the September 11 terrorist attacks . . . and the Oklahoma City bombing and trials."[72] Matt Lauer and Meredith Vieira co-host the show along with Ann Curry and Al Roker.

53. PUBLISHING *CHRISTIANITY TODAY*

The news media in America is known much more for its secular bent than its spiritual focus. Indeed, many journalists would say the spiritual falls outside the realm of everyday journalism. But there are exceptions to this. Religion sections of newspapers have become popular with readers, especially in certain geographic markets, and many of these sections have evolved into sections dealing with broader faith and values issues. And in the world of magazines, an entire segment of that industry focuses on religion and spirituality. One of the most dominant of those publications is *Christianity Today* magazine.

World-renowned and respected evangelist Billy Graham developed the idea to "plant the evangelical flag in the middle of the road, taking the conservative theological position but a definite liberal approach to social problems."[73] The result in 1956 was a magazine many Christians in America consider to be the flagship voice of their faith, *Christianity Today*. The launching of this magazine helped to make evangelical Christianity more mainstream in the eyes of many Christians and non-Christians alike. Its first editor was Carl F. H. Henry, and it has always featured an array of voices from conservative to more liberal wings of Christianity including Fuller Theological

Seminary's Richard Mouw to Stephen Carter, law professor of Yale University. It often runs point-counterpoint articles on controversial issues such as creationism vs. evolution. It has often championed the causes of labor, but it also upholds some of the most cherished evangelical's spiritual beliefs as well. A popular reader feature of the magazine is the movie review section where reviewers go the extra mile in analyzing films in relation to their ethical and even spiritual subtexts and on how ethically they make their points.

The magazine exudes a nondenominational focus and does not shy away from issues which depict disagreement within the family of its founder Billy Graham. For example, in the August 2008 online issue, the lead story was about Franklin Graham criticizing a new film about his famous father although Franklin's sister Gigi Graham disagreed and criticized her brother for stating his opinion saying, "I don't know why Franklin felt like he had to make a public statement. I wish he'd just left it alone."[74]

The magazine has had an online presence since 1994, and AOL listed it then as one of its top 10 content providers. Christianityonlinetoday.com was begun in 1996, and today the online magazine is at http://www.christianitytoday.com.

54. THE *TWENTY-ONE* SCANDAL

The scandal in the late 1950s involving the very popular game show, *Twenty-One*, was an event that caused many television executives to examine the nature of television's responsibility to its audiences. It was not the first time that the authenticity of television quiz shows was brought under the spotlight, a phenomenon that was first probed with earlier shows like The *$64,000 Question*. But the investigation and findings concerning the immensely popular show, *Twenty-One*, were certainly the most highly publicized and troubling. Some television historians believe the exposé might not have occurred had the quiz show not found such a charismatic and willing contestant in young Charles Van Doren, an up-and-coming author and instructor of literature at Columbia University who came from a long line of authors and poets. Others, however, believe the house of cards was already starting to crumble for *Twenty-One* as more disgruntled contestants began coming forth with stories of corruption.

The Museum of Broadcast Communication has this to say about the Van Doren phenomenon:

> Van Doren was an authentic pop phenomenon whose video charisma earned him $129,000 in prize money, the cover of *Time* magazine, and a permanent spot on NBC's Today, where he discussed non-Euclidean geometry and recited seventeenth century poetry. He put an all-American face to the university intellectual in an age just getting over its suspicion of subversive 'eggheads.' From the moment Van Doren walked onto the set of *Twenty One* on 28 November 1956 for his first face-off against a high-IQ eccentric named Herbert Stempel, he proved himself a telegenic natural . . . Van Doren's was a remarkable and seductive performance.[75]

Van Doren and Stempel squared off in front of some 50 million Americans on December 5, 1956, ostensibly to display their intellect on a show known for its very tough questions. Unknown to the audience, however, was that Van Doren had been coached ahead of time and that Stempel had agreed to a deal with the show's producers to reluctantly take a dive over a question for which he readily knew the answer.

Charles Van Doren appears as a witness before congress investigating rigged question-answer programs in Washington, D.C. on November 2, 1959. Van Doren testifies he was given answers and coached in mannerisms on the Twenty-One *game show. He won $129,000 on the television quiz show. [AP Photo]*

The question was what movie won the Best Picture Oscar for 1955, and the answer was *Marty*. Stempel found it especially humiliating to lose on that question, because it was one of his favorite films and he even identified with the loner played by Ernest Borgnine in the movie. Nevertheless, he ultimately decided to go along and on the night of December 5, on live television, answered the question with, *On the Waterfront*. Van Doren answered his winning question correctly and was the new champ and remained so for a long time. Ratings for the already popular show increased as Americans fell in love with this romantic looking intellectual.

By the time he was through, Van Doren was more widely known than any other quiz show contestant ever on the air. He was featured on the cover of *Time* magazine and he received some 500 fan letters weekly from adoring viewers. He had accumulated total winnings of $138,000 by the evening of February 11, 1957, when he met the contestant who would unseat him after three ties. She was an attorney named Vivienne Nearing, and his reign as champion had ended. Not wanting to lose the ratings Van Doren generated, NBC immediately offered him a three-year contract with the network worth $50,000 a year and making him a part of Dave Garroway's popular *Today* show.[76]

The following year, however, unhappy former contestants starting going public with allegations that *Twenty-One* producers had rigged the show's results for years. One of those contestants was Herbert Stempel who admitted taking a dive to let Van Doren win. Stempel's confession might have been perceived only as sour grapes had it not been for another former contestant, James Snodgrass, who had gone so far as to mail himself registered letters which forecast the results of the upcoming *Twenty-One* shows in advance. This was the smoking gun that government investigators were looking for, and soon a New York Grand Jury convened to probe the allegations against the network quiz shows. The presiding judge ordered the results sealed, however, and that provoked the House Subcommittee on Legislative Oversight, based in Washington, D.C., to launch its own field investigation. Van Doren and other former contestants denied any complicity in a deception and said they won fair and square. But on November 2, 1959, after a government subpoena found its way to him, Van Doren appeared before the House subcommittee that launched the probe and confessed totally to his involvement in the rigged show.[77] The publicity from the scandal and Van Doren's confession ruined his career, and the entertainment newspaper *Variety* said the scandal "injured broadcasting more than anything ever before in the public eye."[78] Quiz shows would recover their popularity with TV audiences, but not for several years.

A significant result from the quiz show scandals, however, was the realization by everyone involved in television how dangerous it was to have single-sponsored shows where one advertiser could influence the content and direction of programming so much as had *Twenty-One* sponsor Geritol. Following these scandals, network television executives moved to have several different advertisers sponsor each show, thereby diluting the influence on show content from any one sponsor or advertising agency. Congress also made it a federal crime to rig a quiz show, citing television's responsibility as a public trust with programs that viewers thought were real and honest.[79]

55. INTRODUCING THE *MERCURY SEVEN* ASTRONAUTS

On October 7, 1958, the new National Aeronautics and Space Administration (NASA) announced the formation of the *Mercury* Project. On April 1, 1959, America's first seven astronauts—including future U.S. Sen. John Glenn—were announced to usher

The original seven Mercury *astronauts pose in their silver spacesuits in 1961. From left, first row: Walter Schirra Jr., Donald Slayton, John Glenn, and Scott Carpenter. Back Row: Alan Shepard, Jr., Virgil Grissom, and Gordon Cooper. [AP Photo]*

in manned space travel. The other six space pioneers were Gordon Cooper, Virgil I. (Gus) Grissom, Scott Carpenter, Walter M. (Wally) Schirra, Jr., Donald K. (Deke) Slayton, and Alan Shepard. Shepard was chosen to be the first American in space and, on May 5, 1961, he flew a suborbital mission lasting only 15 minutes and 28 seconds but signaling the dawn of a new era of space exploration. His flight came only 23 days after the Soviet Union's Yuri A. Gagarin became the first man in space, and the race for manned space flights began between the United States and the Soviet Union.

Members of the press were mesmerized and, in turn, glorified these astronauts, NASA, and man's journey into space. All the nation's eyes were on America's venture into the last frontier of space and on the men who were made heroes in the media coverage. The story of that glorification occupied center-stage in the 1979 book *The Right Stuff* by Tom Wolfe. The book, of course, was turned into a classic movie of the same name. Here is how Wolfe describes the treatment afforded these seven men, heretofore unknown before they donned astronaut suits:

> As to just what this ineffable quality was . . . well, it obviously involved bravery. But it was not bravery in the simple sense of being willing to risk your life . . . any fool could do that . . . No, the idea . . . seemed to be that a man should have the ability to go up in a hurtling piece of machinery and put his hide on the line and then have the moxie, the reflexes, the experience, the coolness, to pull it back in the last yawning moment—and then to go up again the next day, and the next day, and every next day . . . . There was a seemingly infinite series of tests . . . a dizzy progression of steps and ledges . . . a pyramid extraordinarily high and steep; and the idea was to prove at every foot of the way up that pyramid that you were one of the elected and anointed ones who had the right stuff and could move higher and higher and even—ultimately, God willing, one day—that you might be able to join that special few at the very top, that elite who had the capacity to bring tears to men's eyes, the very Brotherhood of the Right Stuff itself.[80]

The situation was not unlike a fictional scenario found in the John Wayne classic western *The Man Who Shot Liberty Valance*. There is a scene late in this offbeat film where Ranse Stoddard—the local hero played by James Stewart—who has risen to the U.S. Senate largely on his legendary shootout victory over the evil Liberty Valance—confesses to a reporter what really happened that night in the dusty streets of Shinbone. Stoddard revealed that he didn't shoot the gunslinger at all. Instead, it was a friend, Tom, played by Wayne, who fired from the shadows at the last second to save Stoddard's life. The reporter begins scribbling notes furiously, whereupon his editor, who is an ardent Stoddard admirer, takes the notebook from his reporter. He tears out the poisonous page and rips it up saying, "When the legend becomes fact, print the legend."[81]

As Wolfe notes in his book, the media covering NASA were a group of doting admirers of NASA's boy-wonder space kids. In essence, they carried out the same role as did the editor in *Liberty Valence*. Indeed, the nation's press appeared star-struck by the whole sweep of the spaceshot program. The 1960s offered a chance to fantasize about sitting atop a rocket and being shot into outer space. If America could beat the dreaded Russians in the process, how great would that be? After all, this was the generation raised on sci-fi space books and films like *War of the Worlds* and *The Day the Earth Stood Still.* Moreover, it was the generation to whom the popular John F. Kennedy proclaimed that America would reach the moon within the decade of the 1960s.

Journalists were caught up in the mesmerizing aura of it all, just as everyone else was. Objectivity and distance from the story would take some time to be as fully realized as it was being practiced for other kinds of stories. In fact, it would take a major NASA disaster two decades later for journalists to treat NASA and the space program more objectively and learn an important lesson in the process.

56. TRUMAN CAPOTE PENS *IN COLD BLOOD*

In American literary history before 1966, the term "novel" had meant a work of fiction. New York writer Truman Capote changed that, however, when he broke new literary ground in publishing a nonfiction book written as a novel. The book was *In Cold Blood* and it was the true-life story of the 1959 murder of a Kansas farm family and of the two killers who were convicted and executed of the crimes. Both Capote and the new literary genre of nonfiction novels he created were controversial, but there is no denying the story's popularity with the reading public, and *In Cold Blood* became an instant success and long-lasting best-seller. Reflecting on his book, Capote (who died in 1984) said, "This book was an important event for me. While writing it I realized I just might have found a solution to what had always been my greatest creative quandary. I wanted to produce a journalistic novel, something on a large scale that would have the credibility of fact, the immediacy of film, the depth and freedom of prose, and the precision of poetry."[82]

Capote was no stranger to literature when he read about the murder of the Clutter family in Holcomb, Kansas, in a November 16, 1959, short article in the *New York Times.* The 300-word story announced that wealthy wheat farmer Herbert W. Clutter, 48, together with his wife, Bonnie, his 15-year-old son Kenyon, and his 16-year-old daughter Nancy, had all been found dead after being shot at close range by shotgun blasts. No signs of struggle were apparent, and nothing was stolen.[83] The killings appeared to be the work of psychopaths. Capote read the article in his New York apartment with great interest, feeling there was a much deeper story there. He wondered how this placid farming community was reacting to such a horrendous crime, and he wondered what would drive men to commit such an unspeakable act. As do most good writers, Capote used his own interest and fascination as barometers of the public's interest, and he proved to be right.

Some earlier lines of *In Cold Blood* provide a glimpse of what was to come, both in the account of the murders as well as in Capote's own magnetic writing style: "Until one morning in mid-November of 1959, few Americans—in fact, few Kansans—had ever heard of Holcomb. Like the waters of the river, like the motorists on the highway, and like the yellow trains streaking down the Santa Fe tracks, drama, in the shape of exceptional happenings, had never stopped there."[84]

Capote was a writer of eclectic interests. A decade before hearing of the Clutter family killings, the Louisiana-born Capote had published a book called, *Other Voices, Other Rooms* (1948), a novel which paralleled his own childhood experiences growing up in a broken family in the South. *Other Voices* dealt with young teenager Joel Knox who was sent from his New Orleans home after his mother died to live with the father who had abandoned him and his mother and was now living in Alabama. It would be a childhood narrative that would parallel the early life of one of the two Kansas killers and help Capote come to understand him better. The book hit the *New York Times* best-seller list, and Capote became a sought-after writer, going on to publish magazine pieces, and adapting a novella he wrote called *The Grass Harp* into a 1952 play. He dabbled in screenwriting, and then became even more famous when he wrote the moving romantic comedy *Breakfast at Tiffany's*, which became a major motion picture starring Audrey Hepburn.

Capote envisioned his story of the Clutter family's death as an article for the *New Yorker* magazine, but, after starting his interviews in Kansas with the help of lifelong friend Harper Lee, he believed it would be worthy of becoming a book instead. Lee had just finished writing *To Kill a Mockingbird*, but agreed to help Capote with the Kansas interviews. As it turns out, the story of *In Cold Blood* would be serialized first in the *New Yorker* in 1965 before being published the following year as a book. Capote and Lee arrived just two days after the funerals for the Clutter family members, and two suspects had already been arrested for the murders, Perry Smith and Richard "Dick" Hickock. Capote and Lee spent time interviewing the surviving family members, friends, relatives, police, and other members of the Holcomb community. Capote used his charm to convince law officers to allow him to spend time with the two murder suspects, and he began a long relationship with Perry, whose earlier life reminded Capote of his own. It took him some six years to complete the story, during which time both Smith and Hickock were found guilty and were eventually hanged.

Throughout the relationship Capote had with Perry, one question nagged at him: Did he see Perry as a means to his own end of achieving fame with this book or did he really care deeply about him? The inner turmoil appeared to take its toll on Capote, and that angst was interpreted in the 2005 critically acclaimed film, *Capote*, with Philip Seymour Hoffman in the title role. Capote never finished another book and did not achieve a greater level of fame despite becoming more of a celebrity following publication of *In Cold Blood*. He did allow *Esquire* to publish four chapters of his unfinished novel, *Answered Prayers*, in 1975 and 1976.

Today, however, *In Cold Blood* stands as the first commercially successful and critically acclaimed journalistic novel, although some have challenged Capote's claim that every word of dialogue is true. Nevertheless, it opened a door through which other literary journalists such as Tom Wolfe would pass, adding their success to that of Capote's.

57. THE KENNEDY/NIXON DEBATES

Presidential political campaigns moved into a new era on September 26, 1960, as some 70 million Americans gathered around their television sets to witness the first-ever televised debate between the Democratic and Republican Party contenders for the White House.[85] Television had just emerged from its first decade of enthralling most of America, and it was inevitable that the political parties would one day pit their presidential candidates in a debate over issues live on this new national medium. The contenders were Republican nominee Richard M. Nixon and Democratic nominee John F. Kennedy. They were two men from vastly different worlds and political ideologies, and they would prove to be just as different in their on-camera personas.

The anticipated debate between the sitting vice president and the U.S. senator from Massachusetts was to be the first of four nationally televised debates, each focusing on different kinds of issues. This first centered on domestic issues, while the focal points of the second and third looked at Asian foreign policy, and the fourth looked at policies

Republican Vice President Richard M. Nixon listens as Sen. John F. Kennedy, the Democratic presidential nominee, makes a point during a live broadcast from a New York television studio of their fourth presidential debate on October 21, 1960. The candidates' performances in this debate are often credited with helping lift Kennedy to victory in the general election.
[AP Photo]

with Cuba. Since these debates were on live television, Americans got their first real chance to see the candidates in competition with each other. All eyes were not only on what the men said, but just as important, how they said it and how they appeared on the TV screens. What viewers saw was a healthy and rested Kennedy go up against an awkward and tense Nixon. Historians note that Nixon was still recuperating from two weeks in the hospital following a knee injury in August and that, by the time of the first debate, he was still 20 pounds underweight. His color was pale, he refused the offer of makeup, his shirt was too tight, and it all came across on television. The result was the appearance of a man who was very uncomfortable and uptight. Kennedy's confident, tan, and well rested appearance, on the other hand, translated much better to television viewers.[86] Although the candidates each held their ground in debating the actual issues, most observers felt Kennedy won the debates by a large majority on style points alone. Rika Tyner Allen, writing for the Museum of Broadcast Communications, has noted, "Those television viewers focused on what they saw; not what they heard. Studies of the audience indicated that, among television viewers, Kennedy was perceived the winner of the first debate by a very large margin . . . At election time, more than half of all voters reported that the Great Debates had influenced their opinion."[87]

The 1960 televised debates thus laid the groundwork for all of the television debates that have followed and which have become an important staple in the campaigns of U.S. presidential hopefuls. The formats of the debates have gone through a number of changes, but the impact of them has remained constant. They are deemed one of the most influential aspects of any presidential campaign.

58. THE CUBAN MISSILE CRISIS

For a period of two weeks in October 1962, the world faced the eve of destruction when the Soviet Union placed nuclear missiles on the island of Cuba, only 90 miles south of the Florida coast. The American military went on full alert, ready to invade Cuba and take out the threatening missile sites. And in Cuba, Russian commanders were prepared to launch their missiles should the United States decide to invade. Neither America nor the Soviet Union appeared ready to back down, and leaders of both sides envisioned a very real scenario which would become World War III.

The news media, like the American public, were largely in the dark about what was happening. This was a designed blackout on the part of President John F. Kennedy's administration. The White House reasoned that if Americans knew the extent of the crisis facing them, they would panic. And, the administration believed, if the Soviets knew that the United States knew of its missiles in Cuba, they might be prompted to order the missiles launched at the United States before American forces could take out those sites by way of invasion. In the history of the world, things were never more tense than at this moment. But the White House under Kennedy had exercised message discipline throughout its communication staff and did a good job managing the contacts between officials and journalists. Kennedy and his aides felt it was important that the press exercise self-control over the news they did pick up about the crisis and privately suggested censorship might come should actual hostilities break out between America and the Soviet Union.[88] This crisis would lead both the press and the White House press office to examine the nature of their communication exchanges over the next several years.

Although Cuba is a small island, it was not an insignificant one. Following a revolution led by forces of Fidel Castro in 1959, Cuba became the only communist nation in the Americas. While the Soviet Union perceived it as a point of entry into the Western Hemisphere, the United States saw Cuba and the newly placed Soviet missiles there as a direct threat to American security. Still, Cuba had felt intimidated by NATO missiles placed near its own borders, so Soviet leaders believed their missiles on Cuban soil would balance the equation.

Of course neither the United States nor the Soviet Union really wanted to go to war. They understood their positions as the two dominant nuclear powers on the planet; understood the worldwide gravity of nuclear destruction should they choose to unleash their missiles. Nevertheless, there was this very real stalemate in Cuba and the threat each perceived to its power, should it be seen as backing down to the other. Fortunately, nuclear destruction was prevented at the last minute when Kennedy and Soviet Premier Nikita Krushchev made decisions that would thwart another world war. Both sides eventually declared victory in the arrangement, although it was the United States that actually won in forcing the Soviet Union to remove the missiles from Cuba while giving up little in return.

The whole crisis was played out against a backdrop of worldwide fear over the nuclear weapons that had first been unleashed by America in 1945 on Hiroshima. Improvements had been made in the devices' destructive capacity and in their delivery systems. The Russians now had developed intercontinental ballistic missiles, (ICBMs) and it was felt that 80,000 people killed in the city of Hiroshima would be little compared to the death and destruction the new weapons could deliver. The fact that two unfriendly superpowers each had those weapons in their hands made things even more worrisome.

Cuba entered the picture when a 1953 socialist revolution against fascist dictator General Fulgencia Batista proved successful in 1959. Batista had been backed by the United States as a stopper to communism. Castro was aided in his push against Batista by the Argentine communist revolutionary Che Guevera. The revolution was supported by most of the Cuban peasants who felt oppressed by Batista's policies. After Castro's forces proved successful in downing Batista, the United States helped train Cuban exiles for a planned invasion to overthrow Castro. The training was led by the CIA and, on April 17, 1961, some 1,300 Cuban exiles were put ashore at the Bay of Pigs. The plan was that they would be greeted by supporters and aided in their fight, but no such greeting took place, and three days later the invasion was crushed by Castro's army.

The next year, on August 29, 1962, an American U-2 spy plane took photos of an object that appeared to be a missile site in Cuba. Two months later, other spy photos confirmed that the objects were missile sites. It was obvious the Soviet Union had supplied the weaponry, and the stage was set for a confrontation with the United States. Kennedy called his top military and civilian advisors together. The generals all advised the president to attack Cuba, but the president's brother and U.S. Attorney General Robert Kennedy advised peaceful negotiations instead. The invasion plan, dubbed Operation Mongoose, had already been developed, but was put on hold while the troops were put on alert. In its place, Kennedy chose a Naval blockade of Cuba. However, he called it a "quarantine," inasmuch as a "blockade" was technically a declaration of war. So, on the evening of October 22, 1962, Kennedy decided to go on national television to reveal to the American people what was going on. The blockade had begun, and its purpose was to keep Soviet ships from delivering any more weaponry to Cuba. The media heralded the story of Kennedy's 18-minute radio and television speech the next day. The *New York Times* led its Page 1 with it under the headline, "U.S. Imposes Arms Blockade on Cuba on Finding Offensive Missile Sites." The story read, in part, "A critical moment in the Cold War was at hand tonight. The president had decided on a direct confrontation with—and challenge to—the power of the Soviet Union."[89] The next day, the *Times* would lead with the Soviet response to the U.S. challenge, in which Krushchev warned that the United States' quarantine of Cuba invited—and risked—thermonuclear warfare.[90]

Krushchev was perplexed. He realized the chess game was in play and that the United States had thrown down the gauntlet, demanding the Soviet Union back down. He told Kennedy that the missiles were in Cuba strictly for defensive purposes. He didn't really believe the United States would go to war over Cuba, so he ordered his ships to continue to Cuba, but he also ordered his captains to refrain from firing on U.S. Naval ships. Eventually the Soviet ships turned around, and a Naval shooting war was averted. U.S. Secretary of State Dean Rusk later said, "We were eyeball to eyeball, and the other guy just blinked." On October 26, Krushchev offered to remove the nuclear missiles from Cuba if Kennedy promised not to invade the island. The crisis was over.[91]

Communications had played a troubling role in the development and resolution of the crisis. Kennedy and Krushchev had chosen to write letters to each other rather than delivering coded messages over telephones. But it was a time when a single letter—or its misinterpretation—could mean war or peace. It would take up to six hours for Krushchev to receive a letter from Kennedy, and vice versa. The delay concerned both leaders and their staffs, but so did the ways in which each carefully worded the letters.[92] This was before the age of satellite communications or the Internet, so any real-time communication other than the telephone was unavailable. In later years, national leaders like George Bush and Saddam Hussein would sometimes use a 24-hour television news channel like CNN as a kind of de facto diplomatic channel, carefully planning and rehearsing comments ostensibly made to the world but sometimes essentially targeted to the opposing world leader. This practice began before and during the first Gulf War and has continued since. If nothing else, the Cuban Missile Crisis showed the importance of fast and accurate communication between world leaders and how peace could be threatened simply by slow and misinterpreted communication exchanges.

59. CRONKITE TAKES THE CBS ANCHOR DESK

No listing of significant media moments would be complete without discussing the contributions made by a print reporter-turned television journalist-turned network news institution. That journalist was Walter Cronkite, who over two decades became the best-known and most trusted man in America. Cronkite continued and enhanced the pioneering legacy at CBS that Edward R. Murrow had begun when that network news operation came together.

Cronkite was born in St. Louis on November 4, 1916. After graduating from high school, Cronkite attended the University of Texas but dropped out after two years to become a writer and newsman. He joined United Press in 1939 to cover World War II and was involved in a number of risky reporting assignments. He was one of the "Writing 69th," a group of journalists who went ashore in France on D-Day, flew a bombing mission over Germany, and parachuted with the 101st Airborne.[93]

He joined CBS in 1950 and, like his contemporary Murrow, paid his dues to the entertainment business by hosting *You Are There*, the CBS series that dramatically re-created important historical moments. Murrow was concurrently hosting *Person to*

With a full day's work behind him, CBS news correspondent Walter Cronkite sits while makeup is applied and lights are adjusted so he will appear fresh for his nightly TV broadcast on CBS Evening News with Walter Cronkite. *Cronkite, who was also managing editor of his broadcast, spent a full day preparing and editing the news. Here, on August 29, 1963, he and makeup men and technicians work out plans for the program, which premiered on Monday, September 2, 1963. [AP Photo]*

Person, the CBS celebrity interview series. But both men's passion was news, and that was where they excelled and made their most significant contributions. Cronkite got his chance to show what he could do in television news when he anchored the network's coverage of the 1952 Democratic and Republican Conventions. In 1961, when CBS was still running only a 15-minute nightly newscast, Cronkite took over for pioneering anchor Douglas Edwards on the *CBS Evening News*. The network soon enlarged that program to 30 minutes, and Cronkite found himself in a pitched ratings battle with NBC's nightly news program featuring the popular anchor team of Chet Huntley and David Brinkley. It took five years for Cronkite and the *CBS Evening News* to overtake Huntley and Brinkley for good, but from 1967 to his retirement as anchor in 1981, Cronkite's newscast led the network ratings race.

Cronkite's signature moments on the *CBS Evening News* were many and varied. He soon adopted his famous newscast-closing line of, "And that's the way it is," in much the same way that Murrow had closed his program, *See It Now*, with, "Good night, and good luck." On his first 30-minute newscast in 1963, Cronkite interviewed President John F. Kennedy. The newsman would then anchor CBS coverage of Kennedy's death just six weeks later, momentarily abandoning his trademark objective pose to shed brief tears on the air while announcing the president's assassination. Always interested in war coverage, Cronkite seemed to bring his patriotic journalistic fervor that had served him well in World War II to the Vietnam War, until making a fact-finding trip to the war zone following the infamous 1968 Tet Offensive. Disillusioned by what he saw, he returned to television to opine that, "It seems now more certain than ever that the bloody experience of Vietnam is a stalemate." He said the war was unwinnable for the United States and called upon President Johnson to open negotiations for its end. Presidential aide and future CBS journalist Bill Moyers later said Cronkite's pronouncement was a key factor in LBJ's decision not to seek a second term. The idea was that, if the president lost Cronkite, then he had lost middle America.[94]

Cronkite also proved to be an influential voice internationally. In 1977, he became a de facto diplomatic channel between Egyptian President Anwar El-Sadat, and Israeli Prime Minister Menachem Begin, when he interviewed Sadat and asked if he would go to Jerusalem to meet with Begin. Sadat said he would, and a day later he received an invitation from Begin for such a meeting. Eventually, the two leaders met with President Jimmy Carter at Camp David where the famed Camp David Accord between the two countries came about.

Cronkite's 1981 retirement proved to be anything but that, as he continued to do special reports on television for years to come, hosting many documentaries on PBS, and the cable channels Discovery and the Learning Channel for many years to come.[95] He died in July, 2009.

60. THE FIRST TELEVISION NEWS CONSULTANTS

Formal television news consulting began in 1962, and it seemed like an innocuous beginning for a service that would become the center point of controversy in the

1970s and beyond. For it was in those decades—current one included—that the elitist/ populist debate would certainly extend into television news and the question under scrutiny would be: Does television news report on those issues that are important to the American news consumer, or does it simply pander to the lowest common denominator in its haste to provide more entertainment dressed up as news? The first of these firms was McHugh & Hoffman. It was founded in 1962 by former ad executives Philip McHugh and Peter Hoffman. At its peak in 1985, McHugh & Hoffman consulted in some 100 newsrooms. In 1999, McHugh & Hoffman was reorganized as Convergent Communication.

Certainly a kind of corporatized television journalism has emerged in many local stations, broadcast and cable networks in America. But it is not a recent occurrence, and those who have spent careers in television journalism point to the rise of news consultants as the starting point for blander news content. One such long-time television news reporter and anchor put it this way:

"I was in the news business 22 years, 18 of those in Denver," recalls KMGH's Jim Redmond. "While in Denver I saw deterioration of journalism ethics. All kinds of cases of the steady erosion of truth, justice and the American way and the rise of consultants, along with the crumbling of the wall between the sales side and the news side. It was a slow kind of dissolve that just kept turning legitimate journalism organizations into kind of wordsmithing bordellos."[96]

The use of consultants, focus groups, and marketing studies have become the norm in television news today, and the entry of news consultants in the 1962 opened the door for what would surely have been an inevitable occurrence anyway, given the highly competitive nature of TV news. McHugh & Hoffman was followed a few years later by Frank N. Magid Associates. The latter has some 160 clients today. The main function of these and perhaps ten other consultancies is market research, and television news organizations—both local stations and networks—use them to create strategies that enhance audience size, thereforeratings points, advertising revenues, and profits.

The earliest consultancies like McHugh & Hoffman began working with other industries such as automotive, retailing, and beer, and branched out into television news. In so doing, they simply applied the same focus groups and survey procedures they had been using to help sell beer and cars. This infuriates many journalistic purists who believe they deal in a service that should be handled much more seriously than these.

Much of what news consultants do is applied in a two-stage process. The first consists of compiling information on audiences' preferences for news show content and presentation traits. Then field representatives of the consultancies work with news directors and anchors to apply the collected data to the client's news shows. Among the services that consultancies provide are retreats for news anchors where their presentation skills are groomed and honed to meet the audience preferences that the consultancies have identified in their research. Another service is to offer information to news directors about what kinds of news reports and news series have been popular in other markets. For example, a five-part series on house cats was produced and aired in Boston after the station's consultant told the news director the series was a big hit in Phoenix. Producers at the Boston station viewed the Phoenix tapes, followed the general outline, and produced its own version of this "news" event.[97]

Many news consultants come from the ranks of television journalists themselves. Many former reporters and anchors now work toward advising news directors on how to best the competition while still, hopefully, remaining true to the calling of journalism. Many of these consultants deny they are responsible for what has become known as "tabloid television," and say they often advise clients not to go the way of sensational journalism. However, many of these same consultants say they may be at least partly responsible for the uniformity of content and presentational styles from one TV news show to the next. One such consultant, McHugh & Hoffman's Frank Graham, told the *American Journalism Review*: "In the '70s and '80s there was a generalization by a lot of consultants about what people wanted as TV news." Graham, who is a former television and newspaper executive, continued, "So the stations replicated the standard techniques. But in the '90s it's necessary to understand that each market is uniquely different. The audience in Houston has a set of expectations for TV news that is totally different from Dayton."[98]

Whoever is responsible for taking television news into the world of more entertainment may be beside the point. Because in an age of white-hot competition among television stations and networks alike, the trend is likely to continue until research starts showing the audience has had enough.

61. THE BIRMINGHAM PROTESTS

In 1963, the civil rights movement kicked into high gear when the Rev. Dr. Martin Luther King chose Birmingham, Alabama, to stage protests against unequal treatment for black Americans. His protests were designed to attract the television cameras, because it became apparent in the 1960s that television had become the most powerful informational medium in America. It had the power to move people to action, and action was what King wanted when it came to the civil rights movement. He was not disappointed in the results. King and his advisors understood network television needed concise depictions of drama and message, and they used the white Southern racist violence to provide the drama for which King provided the message.

The City of Birmingham was widely regarded as the most segregated city in America. Some even called it a "southern Johannesburg," alluding to the controversial South African city. Birmingham segregated all public facilities, and local businesses kept separate facilities on their premises for whites and blacks. Everything from restrooms to department store fitting rooms, to lunch counters, movie theaters, and drinking fountains were segregated in Birmingham.

Local politicians and police focused on the maintenance of white supremacy in the city and, at times, even seemed to allow the Ku Klux Klan to provide "enforcement" to keep blacks in check. Over a period of just six years (1957–1963), the city experienced some 18 bombings and 50 cross-burnings. Some were starting to call Birmingham, "Bombingham."

King and other civil rights leaders grew ever more frustrated with attempts by northern white Democrats to solve the problems in cities like Birmingham, so King developed a plan he initially named "Project C." It stood for Project Confrontation. Starting on April 4, 1963, small groups of black activists began staging sit-ins at segregated lunch counters in diners, drug stores, and restaurants. Arrests were immediate and sustained, and a steady group of some 50 marchers protested daily at city hall. They were also arrested. Soon the city's jails became full of civil rights protestors, and when that didn't do the trick, city officials allowed police to use brute force and their K-9 squad of dogs to break up protests in the streets. It was not long before these protests, arrests, and brutal police actions caught the attention of the national media including the news networks of CBS and NBC. Faced with that kind of attention, city leaders decided to make all racial demonstrations unlawful, hoping to shut them down for good. Within three days, King himself had defied the law and led a march to city hall where he himself was arrested.

The protests reached a head when King was thrown into jail and, from solitary confinement, wrote the neoclassic, "Letter from a Birmingham Jail," on April 16, 1963. Those observations provided greater inspiration for blacks, civil rights advocates, and spurred on more protests, greater media coverage, and thus more involvement by the Kennedy administration in the civil rights movement and the plight of blacks in the South. As a result of the television imagery of black Birminghamans being fire-hosed and set upon by police dogs, the television networks provided wall-to-wall

A 17-year-old African American civil rights activist is attacked by police dogs during a demonstration in Birmingham, Alabama, May 3, 1963. [AP Photo]

coverage of this violence against innocent protestors and led to the nation's civil rights legislation.

Among the reporters making a name for themselves for their tireless coverage of the civil rights movement was a young Texas journalist who had joined CBS as a correspondent in 1961 from a CBS affiliate in Houston. His name was Dan Rather, and he was soon promoted to the national news desk from where he zeroed in on the civil rights protests in the South. Because of that kind of coverage and the attention that came with it, Rather was selected to take Walter Cronkite's place as anchor of the *CBS Evening News* in 1981, a position he held for two decades. Rather was inducted into the Academy of Achievement in 2001 and noted, "You can't be a good journalist and not be involved in some kind of controversy." Ironically, it would be a controversy that would cost Rather his anchor seat in 2005 when he aired a poorly documented report alleging President George W. Bush did not fulfill his military service requirements.

The tactics used by King and southern civil rights leaders in attracting media attention in the early 1960s would be borrowed by protestors of the Vietnam War later in the decade and in the early 1970s. Television news had emerged as the mass purveyor of horror images, and changes in public opinion usually followed public viewing of those images.

62. THE KENNEDY ASSASSINATION

The assassination of President John F. Kennedy occurred at 12:30 p.m. CST on Friday, November 22, 1963, in the streets of Dallas as the 35th president of the United States waved to crowds from the back seat of his convertible in the presidential motorcade. The nation sat stunned when the news was delivered first at 12:40 p.m. by Walter Cronkite of CBS, who choked back tears himself. Although live coverage of news events was still years away, the impact of the media—both news and entertainment— was extremely strong nevertheless. Americans turned en masse from their workdays and school days and focused their attention on television and radio in a way that had been unequaled in the then-young history of television. It was a day of shock, sadness, and bewilderment as Americans found themselves leaderless for a short time and— even more heartfelt—realized they had just lost one of the most popular presidents of all time. The Kennedy White House had taken on the alias of Camelot for millions of Americans, and the king was now dead. Into this void stepped television, and its role in helping Americans deal with their grief and vulnerability was hugely important.

Television accomplished this in a number of ways. First, of course, was the wall-to-wall coverage and film of the event itself, solidifying the reality of the assassination and the death of the president in the American mindset. Without benefit of actually seeing how the tragedy occurred, many might have doubted the accuracy of witnesses' reports when interviewed later. The subsequent coverage of the swearing-in of Lyndon Baines Johnson as the 36th president showed Americans that a new leader was in place to ensure the safety of the moment. And, in seeing television footage of the grieving widow Jacqueline and her children, Americans experienced the tragedy on a more personal level. The three networks of NBC, ABC, and CBS also went an extra mile in giving Americans a chance to reflect on the moment, its meaning and its tragic nature by suspending all regular programming for nearly four days, through the period of national mourning. Into that programming window went continuous coverage of the assassination and its aftereffects by the network news staffs. And finally, the coverage of the Kennedy funeral helped to bring at least a temporary closure to the event in the minds and hearts of many Americans.

One of the positive social effects of the media is that it can unite Americans during a time of crisis and grief. The nation has seen it happen many times, both before and after the Kennedy assassination. But the day of JFK's murder and those days immediately following in November 1963, showed for the first time how well television could fulfill that national unifying role. Thomas Doherty framed the significance of the media coverage this way for the Museum of Broadcast Communication:

> The network coverage of the assassination and funeral of John F. Kennedy warrants its reputation as the most moving and historic passage in broadcasting

President John F. Kennedy slumps down in the back seat of his motorcade convertible after being fatally shot in Dallas on November 22, 1963. First Lady Jacqueline Kennedy leans over the president as Secret Service agent Clinton Hill climbs onto the back of the speeding car. [AP Photo/Ike Altgens]

history. As a purely technical challenge, the continuous live coverage over four days of a single, unbidden event remains the signature achievement of broadcast journalism in the era of three network hegemony. But perhaps the true measure of the television coverage of the events surrounding the death of President Kennedy is that it marked how intimately the medium and the nation are interwoven in times of crisis.[99]

In an age of live television coverage and satellite news vans (SNVs), today's journalists might not understand the complexities faced by television in trying get pictures of the Dallas tragedy out to viewers as soon as possible. This was a story that not only broke from the streets of Dallas but continued on at the city's Parkland Hospital where the president was rushed by ambulance, his life in the balance. As examples of the kinds of technical issues television faced that day, the following might suffice: TV cameras needed a warm-up time of two hours to become "hot" enough for operation. Video signals were transmitted nationwide by way of "hard wire" coaxial cable or microwave relay. Field TV cameras had to be physically linked by huge wires, cables, and electrical systems. 16 mm film still was the dominant medium, and that film had to be processed, and then physically delivered, and then edited before being aired.

In every respect, the television coverage of the Kennedy assassination advanced television news as a powerful force in the American media landscape and provided an important blueprint for future speedy coverage of momentous events.

63. A BARBED PRESS ARISES

Wars and social upheaval have always given rise to many dissident voices in the United States, and some of those voices take the form of newspapers and magazines. Often these publications are, in fact, the voice of the movements and causes they support. Others are run by editors who believe journalism shouldn't be shackled to a mainstream, status quo system and push their reporters to do edgier pieces from the viewpoint of those groups and persons outside the mainstream. The 1960s and the counterculture revolution that the decade brought to America was probably the high-water mark for dissident voices in the United States. The decade that brought us the extremely controversial and unpopular Vietnam War also brought us extreme social changes with the civil rights movement and the women's liberation movement. Each cause and movement found its own loyal voices in dissident publications.

Lauren Kessler has said the following about the role of the dissident press in America:

> Most dissident publications attempted to communicate both internally to a group of believers and externally to those not converted to the cause a sense of unity and purpose ... Here (dissidents) could argue and discuss ideas, ask questions,

receive advice, and read about and participate in organizational matters. When it appeared they were in the midst of a losing battle, when they were harassed, ridiculed or ostracized by their own communities, they could look to the pages of their journals for inspiration and comfort. Their publications showed them they were not alone. In their role as external communicators, dissident journals attempted to perform two major functions: educate the "unconverted" public by presenting a forum for ideas generally ignored by the conventional press, and persuade the unconverted that their cause was righteous and worth supporting.[100]

Among the main dissident voices during the 1960s were *The National Guardian*, *I. F. Stone's Weekly* (both of which were launched long before the Vietnam War even started), *Ramparts*, *The Berkeley Barb*, and the Washington D.C. *Hard Times*. Collectively, these publications built upon traditions established by such dissident journalists early in the 20th century as John Reed, made famous in the movie *Reds*, and even dating back to pre-Revolutionary War journalists like Samuel Adams and Isaiah Thomas. Discussion of a just a couple of these newspapers shows how they did what they did.

The Berkeley Barb was founded in 1965 at the height of the antiwar movement in America by Max Scherr. The paper was a sounding board for those who lined up to criticize the "establishment," which meant not only most of the mainstream institutions in America, but certainly the government and the military. The *Barb* claimed a weekly circulation of 90,000 at the height of its popularity, and its image was aided by the fact it took its name from the University of California at Berkeley, which was the epicenter of the antiwar movement during the 1960s and early 1970s. Beyond its antiwar stance, however, the newspaper was also a loud voice for other social and sexual issues going through their own revolutions during that era. This was the decade of free love, burning draft cards and bras to show contempt for the Vietnam War and male chauvinist stereotypes of women. To add to its cachet, the *Barb* was distributed on California street corners by the "flower children" of the day. Like most other dissident newspapers pegged to causes, the Barb died out when the causes gave way to others and when the flower children grew up. The newspaper failed to survive the changed social climate in the 1970s and folded in 1980 after being sold to a sociology professor the previous decade. At its end, it was publishing only about 2,000 copies weekly.

Ramparts was a leftist publication that falls more into the magazine than newspaper category. It focused on politics and new literature and was published from 1962 through 1975. *Ramparts* was launched by Edward M. Keating who envisioned it as a Catholic literary quarterly magazine, but its political aspect kicked into high gear when Robert Scheer was hired as managing editor. Scheer welcomed to the publication such radical writers as MIT linguist Noam Chomsky, black activist Angela Davis, "Chicago Seven" defendant and later California State Senator Tom Hayden, and the *New York Times'* Seymour Hirsch.

Ramparts was a more sophisticated and expensive-looking publication than *The Berkeley Barb* and other dissident publications of the time. Some feel it probably reached more upscale dissident readers than the shoestring underground newspapers did. In the peak years of the antiwar movement, from 1966 to 1969, newsstand sales of *Ramparts* quadrupled to more than 40,000, and subscribers did the same, leaping to more than 244,000. Like *The Berkley Barb*, *Ramparts* was an early and consistent opponent of the Vietnam War and crusaded for other social issues of equality.

The magazine shut down in 1975, for reasons similar to those that would bring *The Berkley Barb* to an end five years later. However, several of its staffers continued to write elsewhere and some founded some significant publications, including *Rolling Stone* and *Mother Jones* magazines.

The dissident press of the 1960s, as typified by these two counterculture publications, raised the banner of a different journalistic orientation in America, that of "advocacy" journalism. Practitioners of this approach have a declared bias on issues, which is usually publicly acknowledged by the publications that carry their work. In fact, a true alternative (or advocacy) publication often declares its position or bias on the publication's masthead and/or nameplate. Advocacy journalists justify their approach by asserting that mainstream media also have biases; they just keep them hidden or implicit. Since the editorial viewpoints of these mainstream publications usually reflect what the majority holds near and dear, there isn't much thought given to that bias. The majority, so the theory goes, are the only ones feeling that a minority viewpoint is biased which, so the advocates argue, is not true. In any event, proponents of advocacy journalism feel there are definite voices that need to be raised for certain issues, and they have no problem in raising them.

64. BIRTHING THE FOIA

To a journalist, access to information is essential. A democracy is built upon the principle that voters know what is happening in society and government, so it seems natural that a freedom of information law would be part and parcel of such a system. However, it was not until July 4, 1966—190 years after the Declaration of Independence—that Congress enacted the country's first Freedom of Information Act (FOIA). This was an act that was long needed in America, because without it there was no federal legal requirement for governmental bodies to conduct their business openly, although many did anyway. With the entry of the FOIA, however, there came a presumption of openness for federal governmental meetings and records and there came an explicit procedure for responding to journalistic requests for government information.

Like any landmark legislation, the birthing of the FOIA took years to complete. The process began when, in 1953, a freshman congressman from California was frustrated by his inability to obtain information from Sen. Joseph McCarthy about the Wisconsin senator's allegations of disloyalty by some government employees. The congressman was Rep. John Moss, and he was infuriated partly because he was a member of the House of Representatives Post Office and Civil Service Committee. If that committee couldn't get any documentation out of McCarthy, who was targeting people as communists in civil service, then who could, Moss reasoned. His frustration would lead ultimately to the creation of the FOIA more than a decade later. In 1955, with the help of two powerful Democratic colleagues in the House, Moss was named chairman of a new subcommittee to explore charges of executive branch practices that denied information to the public and the Congress. Many abuses were found, but road-blocks prevented quick action on a solution. Moss said part of the reason for the 11-year delay is that he had to steer the legislation past three presidents, and there was much presidential resistance to the idea. Every new president, Moss said, wants to tighten up the flow of information in America—especially from the White House—rather than loosen it.[101] President Richard Nixon, taking office two years after the FOIA was passed, went so far as to create the infamous "plumbers unit" to plug information leaks in his administration. But Moss and his colleagues persevered, and the FOIA became the law of the land in the summer of 1966.

The law that emerged created greater opportunities for access to governmental information by not only reporters but also the public in general. Like any legislation, however, the FOIA is far from perfect. Indeed, there are some nine exemptions to the law, and those exemptions allow certain information to be denied to the public. In some cases, such as national security, these exemptions have been abused and politicized. The most celebrated case of such abuse came when President Nixon tried to conceal the damaging Watergate tapes from public scrutiny, claiming executive privilege and danger to the national security. Both claims were found to be groundless, and the president was forced to turn over the incriminating tapes. One of the most common frustrations of reporters is to request a government document and get it, only to find much of it has been blacked out by heavy strokes through passages felt by government officials to fall under one of the nine stated exemptions to the law, including national security. Congressman Moss addressed the problems with the FOIA, noting that there is a need for a "rational system" to clearly identify when national security should not be used as a device to impede the free flow of information. He said Congress must be ever vigilant in overseeing the FOIA, and congressmen should insist on the right to know and the right of disclosure.[102] The FOIA was strengthened in 1974 when Congress overrode President Ford's veto and passed amendments to the law that reduced obstacles to access to government records. For instance, the wording of the national security exemption was tightened to allow withholding of documents that are "specifically authorized under criteria established by an Executive Order to be kept secret in the interest of national defense or foreign policy and are in fact properly classified pursuant to such Executive Order."[103] Overall, the FOIA amendments weakened the security exemption by requiring that agencies mark and segregate classified information so an entire document no longer could be withheld if only part of it required secrecy. As noted earlier, however, this provision has proven only partially successful.

Other presidential efforts to weaken the FOIA have not changed the fact that, despite its problems, the law has been a good one to have around. Journalists around the country have been able to produce insightful investigative pieces by using information obtained through the FOIA that would have otherwise been impossible to access.

65. THE PAPER LION JOINS THE STORY

One of the oldest and longest-lasting traditions of American journalism is the concept of objective reporting. Like many abstract concepts, objectivity connotes different meanings to different people. But traditional journalists usually agree that, whatever else it means, objective reporting calls upon a reporter to distance herself/himself from the story being covered. There have been many notable journalistic exceptions to this arms-length concept, including Elizabeth Cochrane ("Nellie Bly") in the 19th century discussed elsewhere in this book. In the 20th century, perhaps the most singular exception that many journalists believed ushered in a new concept of participative reporting was a sportswriter named George Plimpton.

Plimpton was a staff writer with *Sports Illustrated* magazine in the 1960s when he conceived of the idea of writing about the life and trials of a professional football player by going undercover as a third-string quarterback recruit for the Detroit Lions NFL team. Plimpton wanted to get an insider's view of what professional football exacted from its players and see how difficult it was for a player to make the cuts in NFL camp and emerge with a spot on the team roster. His method reflected his belief in the need to join the story rather than distance oneself from it. As a "participatory journalist," Mr. Plimpton believed that it was not enough for writers of nonfiction to simply observe; they needed to immerse themselves in whatever they were covering to understand fully what was involved. For example, he believed that football huddles and conversations on the bench constituted a "secret world, and if you're a voyeur, you want to be down there, getting it firsthand."[104]

The result of Plimpton's efforts was the 1963 best-selling book, *Paper Lion*, later made into a movie starring Alan Alda as Plimpton. Plimpton went so far in sampling the gridiron action firsthand that he actually took a few snaps in an intrasquad scrimmage, unfortunately losing some 30 yards in the process.

Plimpton's brand of involved reporting, much like that of contemporary Hunter S. Thompson, spurred on other journalists who wondered if a reporter couldn't get more of the *reality* of an event by moving closer to it than distancing himself or herself from it. In fact, the concept of "participative reporting" is often credited to Plimpton. His foray into the world of professional football was only the most high-profile of several similar adventures. He also trained as a goalie with the Boston Bruins NHL team, writing the book *Open Net* about that experience. He returned to football in 1972 and saw action with the Baltimore Colts in an exhibition game against Detroit, and wrote another book called *Mad Ducks and Bears*.

Not only did Plimpton influence the growing participative journalistic movement of the 1960s, but he contributed greatly to the evolution of America's literary brand of journalism. Plimpton was not America's average sportswriter, but instead was a graduate of Harvard and Cambridge universities and editor-in-chief of the influential literary journal, *The Paris Review*. He was also a close friend of Robert F. Kennedy and was with Kennedy when he was assassinated in Los Angeles in 1968. That background, coupled with the fact he chose to write so much about sports in America, brought many readers to the sports page that otherwise might not have visited its pages and contributed to the realization that intellectuals can also be sports fanatics.

66. ROLLING OUT *ROLLING STONE*

When history mixed Vietnam and the civil rights movements together with the disillusioned youth of America and that generation's passion for music, it gave us the 1960s, a decade unlike any other in U.S. history. Tapping into that generation was a young would-be magazine publisher named Jann Wenner with a new publication he called *Rolling Stone*. Ostensibly this was a music magazine, but it proved to be much more as a media and cultural phenomenon that helped to unite a generation of young people and remain relevant to them and their children for decades to come.

"I had a dream," Wenner said in a 2007 *Business Week* interview. "And a vision. And a lot of passion. I was a rock and roll fan and there was no publication for me, of any kind, that would treat it with the respect and dignity and joy that it really represented and deserved. It was either shut out from the mainstream media, or they ridiculed it . . . So what they were missing was one of the major stories of our times which was the emergence of the baby boomer as a driving cultural, economic and political force of this country that would forever change the nature of our culture and our social experience."[105]

Interviewed by the *New York Times* in December of 2005 before *Rolling Stone*'s 1,000th issue hit the newsstands, Wenner explained the magazine's influences by describing the then upcoming anniversary cover:

> It's going to be a version of the past 40 years of people who influenced us and are part of our Gestalt, our zeitgeist. It's Richard Pryor and Jimmy Carter and it's Billy Joel and it's Bono and the Beatles and he Stones and Ike and Tina Turner and Madonna and Prince. It's the big family . . . We have evolved and transitioned well with a lot of cultural changes, and that's great because that is what we do. We cover culture, and we are attuned to that so it keeps us young. It keeps us on the forward edge.[106]

Wenner teamed with music critic Ralph J. Gleason to launch *Rolling Stone* as a magazine weaving the strands of music, politics, and popular culture into one publication squarely aimed at America's generation of unsettled late teens and 20-somethings—the hippie counterculture—in 1967. The magazine was founded in the epicenter of the country's protest movement, which was San Francisco. Having little money for his venture, the 21-year-old Wenner borrowed $7,500 from family and friends, and *Rolling Stone* began. Its original editions looked more like an underground newspaper than the slick magazine it would become, but it differed from the underground papers like *The Berkeley Barb* in a number of ways. For example, Wenner followed more traditional, mainstream journalistic standards than did other counterculture papers. It also avoided the more radical political viewpoints, and attempted to be more objective than its advocacy journalist counterparts. And then there was the fact that the magazine was about music, although Wenner noted in its first issue that music was not the total objective of

Rolling Stone *publisher Jann Wenner poses for a portrait with a reproduction of the cover of the magazine's 1,000th issue, Tuesday, May 2, 2006 in his New York office. [AP Photo/Mary Altaffer]*

Rolling Stone. He wrote that the magazine "is not just about the music, but about the things and attitudes that music embraces." This became the identifying mantra of *Rolling Stone* over the years, and it made the magazine the best-known publication covering music and culture in America.

Helping it to reach that stature were the innovative and enigmatic writers that Wenner called upon to fill its pages. Among them were Cameron Crowe, who went on to movie production fame and even wrote the story of the film *Almost Famous*, a thinly disguised biography of his own start with the magazine. Other writers like "gonzo" journalist Hunter S. Thompson, Joe Klein, and P. J. O'Rourke livened its coverage of political and cultural phenomena and put it into language understood by its readers.

Unlike most of its counterculture competitors of the 1960s, *Rolling Stone* survived the passing of America's protest movement, charging into the 1970s, 1980s, and 1990s and remaining relevant to its baby-boomer core of readers and even their children. The publication began reinventing itself in the 1990s, targeting younger readers and focusing on more titillating and sexy young Hollywood celebrities as well as music. Faced with discontented core readers, however, Wenner took the magazine back to its original editorial mix of music and politics, and the magazine had a circulation of 1.4 million readers in 2008. Some young readers complain that the magazine has a built-in bias still for the music of the 1960s and 1970s, and certainly its list of 500 songs of all time show a healthy number of songs from those decades. But it is hard to argue with success, or with the lasting imprint *Rolling Stone* has made on the media industry and on the country as a whole.

The *New York Times* has noted of *Rolling Stone*, "The magazine became a bastion of serious musical criticism, a voice of liberal angst and iconoclasm and a haven for writers enamored of long-form, exploratory journalism . . . Although four decades have passed since Mr. Wenner introduced the magazine that was the publishing equivalent of finding gold in his backyard, he said his enthusiasms remained rooted in the political and social values of the 1960s and were undiminished by the passage of time or his accumulation of a tidy fortune."[107]

67. COVERING THE TET OFFENSIVE

Volumes have been written about the news media's coverage of the Vietnam War and the impact the coverage of America's first "living room war" had on how the war was received back home in the states. Many historians believe the media's daily, graphic coverage of American soldiers bleeding and dying caused the United States to bring the war to a quicker end than would have been the case without such coverage. And yet the conflict dragged on for more than a decade. In a war of many false bottoms, probably the single-most decisive moment—at least in terms of changing public opinion about how the war was going—came with the 1968 Tet Offensive. This was a quick and well-coordinated progression of assaults by communist North Vietnam on some 100 cities and villages throughout South Vietnam. Some 85,000 enemy troops were launched against U.S. and South Vietnamese forces starting on January 31, 1968. This is the first day of the Lunar New Year and was Vietnam's most important holiday. It not only began on a day normally set aside for celebration, but it was totally unexpected in the minds of many Americans who had been told by the White House that the war was going well and that the enemy had been depleted. Instead, the massive offensive set South Vietnam and U.S. forces back on their heels, resulted in a huge number of casualties, and would require weeks of fighting for U.S. and South Vietnamese forces to retake the captured cities including the former imperial capital of Hue.[108]

Media coverage seemed nearly as massive as the offensive itself, and Americans back home were jerked awake to the reality that the North Vietnamese and their rebel forces, the Viet Cong, were much more alive, tougher, and more determined than ever before. The fact was that the war was not going well, and that it would not end anytime soon. U.S. Commander General William Westmoreland announced to reporters that the war would now take 200,000 more American soldiers and require that the military activate the Reserves. That news, plus the parade of graphic images of the dead and dying airing nightly on American television screens, ratcheted up the protest movement in America to much higher levels and cemented the resolve of war protestors who took their demonstrations to the streets in massive numbers. The American military was not a volunteer force then as it would become with the wars in Iraq, and the Selective Service System was using the draft to recruit all able-bodied men 18 and over. So the threat to the young generation was very real and personal, and it gave another dimension to the spirit of war protest.

A South Vietnamese soldier takes a position on a Saigon street in early 1968, during the Tet Offensive. [AP Photo/Nick Ut]

The infamous "credibility gap" grew wider in the United States, with many wondering: how wide was the distance between what President Lyndon Johnson was saying about the war's progress and the reality of it? Troop levels under Johnson had already risen dramatically, with some 185,000 U.S. soldiers in Vietnam by the end of 1965. By 1968, following the Tet Offensive, that number would peak to more than 585,000. The Vietnam War had essentially become "Americanized" during LBJ's years.

The news media roamed at will on the battlefields of the Tet Offensive, just as they would throughout the Vietnam War. Their reports often seemed to contradict the official story told by Washington under LBJ and President Richard Nixon, who was elected in November of 1968 after Johnson announced he would not seek a second term as president. Watching U.S. soldiers get injured and killed every night was a shocking experience and brought home the rawness of war in ways most Americans had never experienced. The parade of body bags, the crying relatives interviewed back home, the films of American soldiers taken prisoner by North Vietnam and tortured into making public confessions of American wrongdoing all fueled the protests and put more pressure on the White House to end the war. Yet the war would not end until 1975 as Nixon would hold fast to his mantra of "Peace with Honor."

A division had developed among U.S. reporters covering the Vietnam War, and it focused on how the war should be framed. Some reporters—who were seen as rebellious in the early years—began questioning what the military was saying. If what they witnessed contradicted the official military story, they would go with what they saw and note the discrepancy. Also on their agenda was the issue of why America was in this war in the first place. These were reporters like David Halberstam, Neil Sheehan, and Malcolm Browne, and their reporting angered the military and traditional reporters who felt this war should be reported more like World War II, with the press showing more respect in its treatment of the U.S. policy and giving the benefit of doubt to military commanders. The Tet Offensive changed all this, however, and it brought more reporters over to the side of Halberstam, Sheehan, and Browne.

The American journalist with the highest public profile of the day was also the most respected journalist, and he was Walter Cronkite, anchor of the *CBS Evening News*. Cronkite was one who became convinced in 1968 that the war was a losing effort. Returning home from a fact-finding trip to Vietnam, Cronkite stepped outside his normal objective role as a reporter to announce to the nation on his February 27 newscast that, " . . . the bloody experience of Vietnam is to end in a stalemate" and the war was "unwinnable."[109] After that program, White House sources reported that LBJ reacted, "That's it. If I've lost Cronkite, I've lost middle America."[110]

68. THE BIRTH OF *60 MINUTES*

CBS producer Don Hewitt surveyed the television news scene in 1967 and discovered much of what he saw, however important it might be, was also a bit boring. He also realized that short 90-second news packages didn't allow reporters to plumb important stories as they would like to and as those stories deserved. He wondered why there couldn't be a weekly prime time news show that could combine greater depth on topics and still present them in an entertaining, narrative way to the television viewer. The answer to Hewitt's questions was *60 Minutes*, the weekly newsmagazine show which premiered in September of 1968. He was aided in developing the show by Robert Chandler, a CBS executive who had joined the network in 1963 and who became supervisor of its public affairs programming and who helped Hewitt promote the concept to top network executives.

The show's ratings were shaky at first as Hewitt and his first two correspondents, the hard-edged Mike Wallace and the folksier Harry Reasoner, found their way and perfected the show's format. CBS programming management shifted the show from its original Tuesday time slot to Sunday night in 1972, then to Friday night the next year, and then back to Sunday night for good in 1974. But Hewitt was convinced his concept would work if built around a regular repertoire company of correspondents who could make their stories compelling and be versatile enough to cover different kinds of stories, refusing to fall into precast molds themselves.[111]

The show was not just designed to go in-depth on hard news stories but also to feature interviews with politicians and celebrities, feature stories, letters to the editor, and even satire and commentary. A conservative/liberal "Point-Counterpoint" segment was part of the early years' programs, before the commentary "kicker" or ending piece was given to satirical commentator Andy Rooney who usually wound up doing

The 60 Minutes *team poses for photographers at the Metropolitan Museum of Art in New York, November 10, 1993. From left to right are: Andy Rooney, Morley Safer, Steve Kroft, Mike Wallace, executive producer Don Hewitt, Lesley Stahl, and Ed Bradley. The award-winning CBS news show was celebrating its 25th anniversary. [AP Photo/Mark Lennihan]*

it from his cluttered office in the CBS headquarters. Other correspondents who would become well known were added to the staff over the years, but there were never more than four on any one week's show.[112]

The list of correspondents who have worked for *60 Minutes* over the decades reads like a "Who's Who" of television newscasters. Morley Safer was added in 1970 (and was still with the show in 2008), and Dan Rather, who was on the team from 1975 to 1981 until he left to take over for Walter Cronkite as anchor of *CBS Evening News*. The first African American correspondent was Ed Bradley who was added in 1981 and stayed with the show until shortly before his death in 2006, and Diane Sawyer was the first female correspondent for the show, reporting from 1984 to 1989 when she left CBS to coanchor the new ABC newsmagazine show *20/20* with Sam Donaldson. Meredith Vieira was with the team from 1989 to 1991, Steve Kroft was added in 1990, and Leslie Stahl the following year. Both were still with the show in 2008. Scott Pelley, Lara Logan, Anderson Cooper (from CNN), and Katie Couric also were added in recent years. Hewitt remained at the helm until late in lafe and died in August, 2009.

After a shaky start, the *60 Minutes* experience took root in the television viewing habits of America, and the show found its way into the top 10 network shows each week and, for the most part, stayed there. In 1979, it was the highest-rated program in all of television. As late as 2008, one November episode of the program garnered more than 28 million viewers as it featured an interview with President-Elect Barack Obama, and the show has consistently remained in or near the top 20 most-watched shows each week on TV.

The fact that the show immediately followed CBS's *NFL Game of the Week* each Sunday helped its viewership. But Hewitt's underlying concepts for the show, its structure and design, were the elements that kept Americans glued to the tube and has made the show essential weekly viewing for millions of viewers. Hewitt felt audiences must identify with the stories and their people; that they must actually "feel" the stories. He felt strong narratives were needed to help produce this effect and, in a real way, he brought the concept of Truman Capote's nonfiction novel to the television screen. The stories would strive to be painfully accurate, but would also be compelling emotional events. The stories, although they might be about issues, must come through the eyes of interesting individuals interviewed on the show. The mixing-in of offbeat, lighter stories would also help, but the main focus of most *60 Minutes'* segments would be on serious subjects.[113]

60 Minutes would have its bad moments, as well, however. One of these was portrayed in the Russell Crowe-Al Pacino film, *The Insider*, when the show went after the big tobacco companies in 1995 for manipulating the levels of nicotine in their cigarettes to cause them to become more addictive. Having urged tobacco insider Dr. Jeffrey Wigand to come forward and blow the whistle on Brown and Williamson, one of the tobacco giants, CBS management backed off running the full interview under pressure of a lawsuit from the tobacco company. A shortened, less incriminating version was run instead, and Wigand was not identified. It wasn't until the *New York Times* and *Wall Street Journal* were leaked the story and ran it (with the *Times* chastising CBS for caving in to pressure), that *60 Minutes* ran the full interview with Wigand.

69. THE PENTAGON PAPERS

The National Security Archive states that on June 13, 1971, President Richard M. Nixon sat down to scan the day's *New York Times* and found two items which produced startling different reactions in him. To his delight, he saw a front-page wedding picture of his younger daughter Tricia. To his dismay, he saw on the same page a story by *Times* reporter Neil Sheehan which was headlined, "Vietnam Archive: Pentagon Study Traces 3 Decades of Growing U.S. Involvement." This was to be the first installment of a series known as the "Pentagon Papers," a 7,000-page study ordered years earlier by Secretary of Defense Robert S. McNamara.

The war in Vietnam was still dragging on, and the national furor surrounding it had long ago reached a crescendo. Nixon and his secretary of state Henry Kissinger were looking desperately for a way out that would provide Nixon with his oft-quoted goal of "peace with honor." It had been a long and bloody war, with the United States committing more and more troops over the years with little to show for the sacrifices of so many fallen soldiers. National tempers over involvement in the war were at a boiling point. There were many things the American public did not know about why the United States had entered this war and about how it had been conducted at times; things that Nixon felt could damage his presidency were

U.S. Marines carry the body of one of the 18 slain comrades on a South Vietnamese hilltop south of Khe Sahn to an evacuation point on June 17, 1968 during the Vietnam War. The men had died more than a week previously in a clash near a road being built by North Vietnamese forces from nearby Laos into extreme northwestern South Vietnam. An American flag, found on one of the bodies, flies at half staff. [AP Photo/Henri Huet]

they public knowledge. And here was the first of a series that would reveal these troubling secrets. The president felt he had to act and act swiftly to stop the stories that were to follow this one.

The Pentagon Papers had been leaked to Sheehan by Daniel Ellsberg, a former military analyst who worked at the Rand Corporation and had access to the full Pentagon study of Vietnam which was never supposed to be released to the public. Since it dealt largely with the beginnings of American involvement in the conflict, it was considered by many historians to be as much of an indictment of the administrations of President Lyndon B. Johnson and even John F. Kennedy than of Nixon's, but Nixon's paranoia about the war protests had grown so large that he felt attacked by it. Among other things, the Pentagon Papers revealed that plans had been made to invade Vietnam prior to Johnson's public insistence that the United States had no plans to do so. It also revealed that the United States had been involved in a bombing campaign of Vietnam's neighboring country Laos, even though Laos was officially neutral in the conflict. The study also revealed that, even early in the conflict, military officials did not believe the war would likely be won and that continuing the conflict would result in many more casualties than were admitted to the public.

Ellsberg, himself a former Marine officer who served in Vietnam, was fighting his own conscience over the war. He believed the consensus of the Departments of State and Defense: that America had no realistic chance of winning the war. But they also believed that political considerations prevented the Nixon administration from admitting that to the public, so they pressed on, hoping for the impossible in a military victory.[114] Initially Ellsberg tried to secretly convince a few sympathetic senators, including J. William Fulbright, that he should release the Pentagon Papers on the Senate floor. Even thought the papers were classified, the reasoning was that a senator could not be prosecuted for anything he or she might say on record before the Senate. But Ellsberg could find no senator willing to take the gamble.[115] So, still dealing with his internal turmoil over being a whistle-blower, Ellsberg became disillusioned, sought the help of a therapist, and ultimately decided to risk legal action against himself and leak the papers clandestinely to the *New York Times*.

On June 14, 1971, President Nixon ordered his attorney general, John Mitchell, to warn the editor of the *Times* that further publication of the series would result in litigation and that the paper was risking national security in publishing them. Not relying on the "chilling effect" that such warnings often produce, however, Mitchell sought a judicial restraining order against the *Times* on June 15, and he got it. That same temporary injunction was levied against *The Washington Post* when it began publishing the Pentagon Papers. Attorneys for the *Times* immediately went to work to defend publication of the documents and leaned heavily on the First Amendment of the Constitution in so doing.

The journalistic community eagerly followed the judicial proceedings which most believed would have to be settled by the highest court in the land. That proved to be true. Two weeks after the injunction was ordered, the U.S. Supreme Court—in what would become an epic decision—voted 6–3 to reverse the injunction and lift restraints against future publications of the Pentagon Papers. The case was officially named the *New York Times Co. v. United States*. In its decision, the Court greatly strengthened the First Amendment freedom of the press by laying down the interpretation that this amendment provides for "no prior restraint" of publications. Nevertheless, this was the first time in modern history that a presidential administration had been successful in censoring a newspaper for stories yet to be published. It would also be the last. Many observers have called this decision the most important Supreme Court case ever dealing with freedom of the press.[116]

Writing of the decision, the *Times* said on July 1, 1971:

> The Supreme Court freed the *New York Times* and *The Washington Post* today to resume immediate publication of articles based on the secret Pentagon papers on the origins of the Vietnam war. By a vote of 6 to 3 the Court held that any attempt by the Government to block news articles prior to publication bears a heavy burden of presumption against its constitutionality. In a historic test of that principle —the first effort by the Government to enjoin publication on the ground of national security—the Court declared that 'the Government had not met that burden.' "[117]

70. GLORIA STEINEM LAUNCHES *MS.* MAGAZINE

Part and parcel of the protest movements that burst upon America in the late 1960s was the feminist movement which sought to elevate the status of women in the United States and put them on an equal footing with men. With demonstrators on college campuses across the country clamoring for an end to the Vietnam War and with blacks marching in the South for civil rights, it wasn't long before advocates for women's rights began taking to the streets as well and making their collective voices known across America. It seemed inevitable that a national magazine would emerge espousing the cause of the women's movement, originally known as the women's liberation movement, and that magazine would appear in 1971. It was appropriately called *Ms.* for the new title that many women favored in place of a title characterizing women by their marital status.

Ms. was founded by women's right activist Gloria Steinem and founding editor Letty Cottin Pogrebin with a financial subsidy from Clay Felker, editor of *New York* magazine, and a much larger investment from Warner Communications. The magazine was issued originally as an insert into *New York* and then became a stand-alone monthly magazine in the summer of 1972. Six years later, it was published as a nonprofit magazine by the *Ms.* Foundation for Education and Communication. The magazine was a leader in the women's rights movement of the 1970s and early 1980s with Steinem at the helm as editor.[118]

The story of *Ms.* magazine for the next decade and a half is the story of a publication on a mission, but which pursued that mission in a way that didn't always spell commercial success because of friction with advertisers, some of whom felt the magazine's editorial content was too strident. Among controversies the magazine generated was publishing the names of women admitting to having had abortions in a

1972 edition when the procedure was still illegal in most of America. The magazine also took the lead in addressing women's issues such as domestic abuse and day care sexual abuse as well as date rape, sex trafficking, the wage gap, and glass ceiling.

But the story of *Ms.* is also the story of a magazine that didn't do the best job keeping track of the lifestyle changes and interests of its original target audience. These were young women on a mission who had gotten older and had redefined the women's movement into terms that made more sense to them as middle-aged wives and mothers. As a result, many of the magazine's earlier supporters found it losing some relevance to their current lives and issues.

In 1987 the magazine was purchased by Fairfax, an Australian media company and, as part of the purchase agreement, Steinem was named a consultant. The publication changed owners again in a few years, and many readers became disenchanted when *Ms.* seemed to back off its cutting-edge, reformist slant and also changed its design. In 1998, Steinem reemerged as publisher when she and a group of investors developed Liberty Media and purchased the magazine under independent ownership. The magazine was again a nonprofit publication that refused to accept advertising out of concern over advertisers' influence on content.

Author/activist Gloria Steinem, left, joins Planned Parenthood Federation of America President Gloria Feldt, alongside a blow-up of the cover of the reborn Ms. *magazine, in New York, Monday, March 22, 1999. Steinem and Feldt joined 200 activists, journalists, and celebrities at a reception for* Ms. *magazine, which would be relaunched under ownership and management by women after years of corporate control. [AP Photo/Planned Parenthood, Chrystyna Czajkowsky]*

71. WATERGATE

The biggest political scandal of the 20th century also produced some of the best and most significant investigative reporting of that century. It was a classic case of how the news media can carry out its role in society as an independent "fourth estate" and fulfill its "watchdog" role over government and corruption. In its basic form, Watergate involved the financing and carrying out of a break-in with the purpose of wiretapping phones, but it broadened into one of the nation's most unbelievable cover-up attempts by the White House in history. When all was said and done, it also showed that this break-in, shocking as it was, was only the tip of the iceberg for a presidential administration deeply engaged in dirty political tricks.

The story—or series of stories over a period of months—was known simply as "Watergate," and even the name has given birth to the appendage "gate" which has been attached to every scandal from "Billygate" to "Irangate" to "Troopergate" to "Monicagate" and beyond. The era known as Watergate began early in the morning of June 17, 1972, with the break-in at the Democratic National Committee Headquarters at the Watergate office and apartment complex in Washington, D.C. It would

The Washington Post *writers Carl Bernstein, left, and Robert Woodward, who pressed the Watergate investigation, are photographed in Washington, D.C., May 7, 1973, when the announcement came that the* Post *had won the Pulitzer Prize for public service for its stories about the Watergate scandal.*

end August 8, 1974, with the forced resignation of President Richard Nixon. For the news media, this era proved to be the finest hour of the 20th century for investigative journalism. The saga began when five men, one of whom told a judge he was a former CIA employee, were arrested at 2:30 a.m. on June 17 trying to bug the offices of the Democratic National Committee at the Watergate complex. As the subsequent journalistic investigations would show, however, this break-in was just the latest link in a long chain of dirty tricks—some illegal, all unethical—perpetrated by the GOP's Committee to Re-Elect the President (dubbed by many as CREEP).

Several things made this journalistic investigation interesting. First, the reporter assigned to the initial story of the break-in was a 29-year-old rookie who had been with *The Washington Post* for less than a year. His name was Bob Woodward, and he was assigned to cover the arraignment of five men who had just been arrested for the Watergate break-in. Woodward knew enough about arraignment procedures to spot the deviations that occurred in this one, and it was that alertness by a cub reporter that launched the missile known as Watergate. First among the deviations was that an attorney—and only one—was already on hand at the courthouse to represent all five defendants when they arrived, yet none of the five had made any phone calls during or after their arrest. A walkie-talkie found among their equipment suggested at least one other person was involved in the break-in, and it was he or she who contacted the lawyer. The court, assuming that the five men would need representation, had already made arrangements for public defenders, but they were not needed. Then, of course, was the fact that the office broken into was the Democratic National Headquarters, and police found wiretap equipment in the bags of the defendants when they were arrested.[119]

Add to all that the fact that one of the defendants, James McCord, listed his occupation as a security consultant who had worked with the CIA, and Woodward saw that this was no routine burglary. He was soon joined in the investigation by another young *Post* reporter, Carl Bernstein, and the two of them began following one thread after another until, after a period of several months, they traced the break-in and subsequent coverup to the Oval Office itself. At several turns, the reporters wanted to publish more information than their editors felt they had solid documentation for. The restraint showed by the *Post* editors forced the reporters to triple-check most of their key facts, developing multiple sources for these facts and—ultimately—producing a mosaic of stories that sustained repeated attacks by the Nixon administration.[120]

The reporting led to the Senate Watergate Hearings, televised live before a stunned nation, and it led to the arrest and conviction of several of President Nixon's top men including two attorneys general and the White House chief of staff. Ultimately it led to President Nixon's forced resignation as Congress was poised to oust him. Only a pardon by his vice president and successor, President Gerald Ford, saved Nixon from any subsequent criminal prosecution.

The reporting by Woodward and Bernstein was chronicled in detail in the bestselling book the two wrote called *All the President's Men* which of course was made into the critically acclaimed film of the same name starring Robert Redford and Dustin Hoffman. That book and film inspired an entire generation of young people to become journalists as enrollment in the nation's college journalism programs swelled in the two decades following Watergate. The era proved to be the high-water mark for investigative journalism in America and, in many ways, it has not been equaled since. Investigative journalism has fallen on hard times as newspapers have been in an economic cutback mode for several years. Since investigative reporting is expensive, and since readership studies show that complex investigative stories are not as popular as other kinds of less expensive reporting, many newspaper companies have deemphasized this genre of reporting. Yet Watergate remains as an inspiration for those reporters and news media which are still committed to in-depth journalism.

72. THE FOUNDING OF MICROSOFT

In the mid-15th century, a German printer named Johannes Gutenberg invented movable type and perfected an earlier invention of the printing press. Gutenberg joined these two developments to create a new era for information technology in the world. Before Gutenberg, about 30,000 books existed in all of Europe, and each was made by hand. Almost all of them had religious themes. But by the year 1500, just 50 years after Gutenberg's inventions, some nine million books existed in Europe, and they covered a wide variety of subject matter. Such was the importance of movable type and the Gutenberg printing press.

An invention of similar impact would await the late 20th century to be developed, and it would come from two friends named Bill Gates and Paul Allen. The computer industry was growing in the early 1970s, but most observers believed that "microcomputers" or desktop computers would never be anything more than intriguing toys for hobbyists. The parallel might be the belief early radio developers had when they saw home radio transmitters and receivers as toys for "ham" or amateur radio operators who wanted to engage in point-to-point communication. Broadcasting? What was that? What Gates and Allen did was to adapt the computer language called BASIC so that programs written in it could run on a specific microcomputer, the Altair, which was the world's first commercial microcomputer.[121]

Although by 21st century standards the Altair appears hopelessly primitive in comparison with today's complex personal computers, it kicked open the door on a revolution in the way the world sends, receives, stores, and handles information. And it created a new way for society to think, learn, play, communicate, and even make new friends.

So it was that in 1975, before Gates had even turned 21, he and Allen formed the tiny company called Microsoft. It was poised at the dawn of the Information Age. Personal computers were about to explode in popularity, and Microsoft was about to explode alongside it. Eventually, through the process of applying technical expertise to market applications, Microsoft would emerge as the leading maker of computer software in the world. As of 2008, nine out of every ten personal computers depends on operating systems or other software from Microsoft. Gates's mantra of, "A computer on every desk and in every home, each one running Microsoft software," is virtually a reality.[122]

The intersection of a young computer industry and an even younger software development company would prove unbelievably successful for Gates and Allen. The personal computer market was showing strong signs of growth in the mid-1970s, earning nearly $30 million annually.[123] Microsoft, still a tiny company but already a leader in software development, was primed to collect a share of those earnings. Other firms had jumped into the PC market, and Gates's idea was to grab their business by making Microsoft's product so attractive that there just was no practical alternative to buying it. He did this in a number of ways, but one was to offer MS-BASIC at a bargain-basement price. His company's operating overhead was low, and he didn't want to give computer companies a reason to look for other bids. So companies that struck deals with Gates and Allen included General Electric, Commodore, and Tandy, all of which were making personal computers. An early court ruling in 1977 gave Microsoft permission to license their software to anyone, and several companies came forward to acquire Microsoft software licensing. As a result, soon all of the main companies producing low-end microcomputers were running versions of Microsoft BASIC. The company continued to grow and to hire new programming and marketing talent. With its development of MS-DOS operating systems, Microsoft would eventually come to dominate the PC software market and put Gates and Allen on the list of the richest men in the world.[124]

73. WALTERS AND REASONER SHAKE UP THE NEWS

Producers of network television newscasts have traditionally not been known for drawing attention to the drama taking place on their sets and involving their news anchors. Network management has understood that most viewers want anchors who seem like normal people and who are solid, steady and credible. Emotional drama on the news set, while titillating to hear and read about, is not the stuff of which security and credibility are made. So it was with some chagrin that ABC executives saw their evening

Barbara Walters, shown on opening night on the ABC Evening News *with coanchor, Harry Reasoner, on October 4, 1976. [AP Photo]*

newscast turn into a show sometimes reaching tabloid proportions from 1976 to 1978 when they decided to match Barbara Walters, co-host from NBC's *Today* show, with the senior, seasoned, and likeable journalist Harry Reasoner from CBS's *60 Minutes*. Almost from the start, the two anchors seem to clash on the set, and insider reports leaked to the press about problems and jealousies between the two professionals (who had grown up and worked largely in two different cultural eras) didn't help.

What was to be a television news event in putting a female anchor on the evening newscast, turned out to be more of a television soap opera that the late *60 Minutes* executive producer Don Hewitt later called "a disaster."[125] Reasoner had gained popularity with American viewers in the 1960s and 1970s as one of the original correspondents on CBS's groundbreaking news magazine *60 Minutes*. Those critics who decried matching him with Walters at the anchor desk called it another step by ABC to turn the news into entertainment, asserting that Walters was more of a celebrity than a serious journalist. The same criticism would be leveled against Katie Couric three decades later when she resigned from the *Today* show to become anchor of the *CBS Evening News*.

The tension between Reasoner and Walters was real. Av Westin, then-executive producer of the *Evening News*, said he had a single order from top management of getting them off the air while ABC developed their replacements. ABC was languishing in third place in the network news ratings, and something had to be done quickly. Writer Douglass K. Daniel put it this way:

Westin found the newsroom divided into two camps. "The whole thing was such a mess," he remembered. "The two of them had been pissing at each other. We knew that we were going to replace them." One of Harry's associates told Westin that Barbara owed him four and a half minutes of airtime, a sign to Westin of how silly things had become. "They both wanted out of it, too," Westin said. "Barbara was unhappy, Harry was unhappy. Harry's male chauvinism was rampant. Now . . . the anchors no longer appeared in the same shot. It was as if they were in different locations. Nor did they acknowledge each other's presence, even at the end of the program."[126]

Accounts differ between Harry Reasoner and then-ABC News chief Roone Arledge as to why the Reasoner-Walters team broke up, although both agreed the tension perceived by the audience wasn't good for the show. Arledge said in his memoir, "One of them had to go. Deciding which was coldly simple, Barbara was the future of ABC News. Harry wasn't. Because while there were other Harry Reasoners in television, there was only one Barbara Walters." Reasoner simply said he decided to execute his "Barbara Walters escape clause." Walters called the episode "the worst period in my life."[127]

In the end, both anchors left the *Evening News* desk in 1978, with Reasoner returning to CBS News and Walters moving on to other successful projects with ABC News, most notably the new *20/20* newsmagazine show that the network developed, and later, the syndicated morning show, *The View*.

74. LAUNCHING ESPN

Sports reporting has always an important part of journalism in America. At times it seems the appetite for sporting news is bottomless, and the history of American journalism is full of great stories about athletes and the contests that demand seemingly superhuman strength both internally and externally. So it was no surprise that a television network would arise to meet the needs of sports fans across the country, a phenomenon similar in the magazine world to *Sports Illustrated* or the *Sporting News*.

When television was still exclusively a broadcast medium, a sports network was too specialized for the mass audiences needed for traditional television networks. But when cable television took root in the United States, the door was opened for the first sports network. Such a network began to emerge when, in 1978, Bill Rasmussen formed Entertainment Sports Programming Network, Inc. (ESPN) to broadcast sporting events for cable TV operators nationwide via satellite. Rasmussen was an out-of-work sports announcer who had begun looking for ways to broadcast University of Connecticut basketball games via cable TV operators in the region. He found the means in an RCA satellite for which he leased time. ESPN was born. It was a pioneer among basic cable TV networks and has been one of the most successful, if not the most successful of such cable channels.[128]

The following year, 1979, ESPN began broadcasting on a limited-time basis, and by 1989 it was broadcasting 24/7. ESPN became so popular that the ABC television network acquired it in 1984, and the link helped both companies combine sports broadcasting budgets and talent. A big boost for ESPN came in 1987 when it began broadcasting NFL games, and the following year saw the creation of ESPN International. Major League Baseball broadcasting joined the ESPN lineup of sporting events in 1989.

The sports network continued to expand and diversify in the 1990s. ESPN Radio Network was launched in 1991 as a tandem venture with the existing ABC Radio Network. Two years later, ESPN2 went on the air, and in 1997 the company purchased the Classic Sports Network and launched ESPN Classic. ESPNU would join the lineup of channels, and in 1998 ESPN, moved into the magazine world, publishing *ESPN: The*

Chris Berman hosts ESPN's 20th Anniversary Special from in front of the all-sports cable channel's headquarters in Bristol, Connecticut. The show aired September 7, 1999. [AP Photo/Espn]

Magazine. Then, in 2003, ESPN HD was introduced to service the high-definition television audience.

ESPN had become cable's largest network as 1984 began, reaching nearly 29 million households in the United States. It was to benefit greatly from a 1984 court decision that deregulated the televising of college football games, and it picked up many such games on a regular basis, which in turn boosted its advertising revenue. Today the ESPN "College Game Day" has become a must-see staple for serious college football fans around the country, and the avid sports fan can find college football and basketball games all across the spectrum of ESPN channels. Success bred success and resources increased with ESPN's acquisition by ABC and the subsequent acquisitions of ABC by, first, Capital Cities Communication and, later, the Disney Co.[129]

75. FROM FILM TO REAL-TIME REPORTING

A major change in television news reporting occurred when the industry was able to move from shooting and editing stories on film, to shooting and editing on video tape. The term usually given to this process is "electronic newsgathering" or ENG. It is used to mean a number of things: from a single news reporter taking out a camcorder to get a story, to an entire crew taking a satellite truck to report live from the scene of breaking news. The switch from film to ENG made the whole process of production fun, faster, and smoother as the post-field work processes of processing the film was eliminated, and the editing process morphed from an actual cutting room procedure to a faster and cleaner electronic process in the editing booth. And, when ENG is used to refer to the use of point-to-point land-based microwave signals from live, remote locations back to the studio, then the former process of actually distributing the film from location to studio was eliminated as well, and live, real-time reporting became possible.

Videotape has been around in primitive form since the early 1950s, and CBS first used it to play a delayed broadcast of *Douglas Edwards and the News* from New York to the Pacific Time Zone on November 30, 1956.[130] The following year, *Truth or Consequences* became the first entertainment program to be shown in all time zones on videotape.[131] But the early Quadruplex machines were bulky and didn't allow for freeze-frames or picture searches. Also the tape heads wore out quickly. Nevertheless, the "Quad" machine became the standard for two decades until the mid-1970s, and their big contribution was the use of four recording heads on a revolving drum that allowed for more sights and sounds to be recorded and at a higher rate of speed.[132] Starting in 1976, the Type C format was developed and opened the door for regular use of videotaping in news broadcasting. Sony had introduced a prototype for the first widespread video cassette in 1969 and continued to improve it as part of its Betacam family in the early 1980s. The developments went digital with Sony's D-1 video format, followed by the D-2 and D-3 formats. To record the tapes, Sony's Betacam camcorder became the standard in the television news industry.

As electronic newsgathering replaced the practice of filming news stories for the nightly network and local television news shows, TV news entered the modern era where speed ruled even more than it had before. The development of communication satellites and the ability of television news crews to go remote with SNVs in the 1980s allowed for regular live reports from the scene of breaking news. As the network of communication satellites grew and became more sophisticated, along with the uplink and downlink equipment, the process of real-time reporting was introduced on the world stage. It is often said that Vietnam was America's first "living room war," where the American public saw nightly graphic images of U.S. soldiers being wounded and killed. That is true, but this war was not able to be covered in real time, and there were usually delays of a day or more between the story being shot on the battlefield and its being shown on American television screens. The first war involving U.S. troops to be covered real-time was the first Gulf War which began in 1991 with the U.S. bombing of Baghdad. Reporters on the ground were reporting developments as they were unfolding, trying to sort out rumor from fact, and also trying to prepare for the outbreak of chemical warfare at any time. The phrase, "gas mask reporting" was part of the jargon of the first Gulf War as network and cable TV reporters sometimes did their stand-ups from behind the clear-plated, bulky gas masks they wore. Probably more than any other image, this showed the danger reporters faced when engaged in live reporting as the conflict surged around them.

If government leaders in Washington, D.C. complain about how real-time reporting destroys the comfort zone of time before they must react to crises, television and on-line journalists feel the same pressure. The time available for fact-checking has shrunk to zero when a journalist is engaged in real-time reporting. Resource-rich news organizations can and do have producers and assistants checking facts while their reporters and anchors are on air, and feed the information to them through ear pieces. The classic comedy about television news, *Broadcast News*, showed how that process works in a scene where executive producer Holly Hunter is feeding information into the ear-piece of anchor William Hurt even as he is narrating live a program about an ongoing air scramble of U.S. fighter jets in Libya.[133]

76. THE BIRTH OF *NIGHTLINE*

One of the most important ongoing international stories of the 20th century gave rise to one of the most important and unique news programs on American television. The story was the taking hostage of 52 American diplomats for 444 days from November 4, 1979 to January 20, 1981. The news program was ABC's *Nightline*. It is important to understand the hostage crisis before discussing the role *Nightline* played informing the American public of it.

On November 4, 1979, Iranian militants broke into the U.S. Embassy in Tehran and took some 70 American embassy officials and staff hostage. The ordeal would last well over a year before all hostages were released following the end of Jimmy Carter's presidency and the entry of Ronald Reagan into the White House. The crisis was spurred on by the return of the exiled Ayatollah Khomeini in February 1979. With him came rampant anti-Americanism which reached a head when the militants took over the embassy.[134]

ABC launched its program on November 8, 1979, only four days after the Americans were taken hostage in Tehran.[135] Roone Arledge was president of ABC News then and saw both journalistic and marketing justifications for starting the program. ABC was losing the late-night audience to NBC's *Tonight Show* with Johnny Carson. Why not compete with a high-quality nightly news magazine that kept American television audiences updated on the issue on everyone's lips: the American hostages in Iran? At this point, the show was called, *The Iran Crisis: America Held Hostage* with the day of capture updated nightly to reflect how long the incident had lasted. Veteran ABC journalist Frank Reynolds was tapped originally to anchor the special reports, but soon the anchoring duties fell to ABC News State Department correspondent Ted Koppel. The name of the show was changed to *Nightline* and the first network late-night news magazine show was born. As of 2009, *Nightline* was still on the air, and Koppel had served as its anchor for 25 years, until 2005.

Koppel's *Nightline* was a different kind of news program in a number of ways. It seemed a merger of the news magazine format that CBS' *60 Minutes* had made famous and the extended interview format of *Meet the Press*. Typically the show featured an introduction by Koppel, a taped piece from a *Nightline* correspondent like Dave Marash or Jeff Greenfield, then a live interview or interviews with individual experts on the night's topic. Most shows were devoted to a single topic. Several times, however, the format of the show would change to a 90-minute town hall forum, done on remote locations and focusing on an important issue in the news. Two such subjects were the Israeli-Palestinian relations, and the War in Iraq. *Nightline* would move from four nights a week to five nights, and from a half-hour to an hour-long program, then back to a half-hour over the years. Along the way it garnered the respect of everyone in the news business, and it received many honors for its coverage and for Koppel's steady, balanced, and persistent interviewing style. The program managed to avoid focusing on the more titillating stories that other news magazine shows like *Dateline* and *20/20* would focus on.

Nightline was known for covering a diversity of subjects ranging from politics, economics, education, science, social trends, entertainment, and—of course—breaking news. The show also innovated with live coverage from such remote locations as the base of Mount Everest and even from Antarctica.

Despite its significance as America's only late-night news and public affairs show on broadcast networks, the show had not done all that well in head-to-head ratings competition with the *Tonight Show with Jay Leno* and *Late Night with David Letterman* until ABC revamped *Nightline* in 2005. For a time, ABC executives considered dumping the show in favor of its own late-night talk show and even tried to lure Leno over to ABC as CBS had lured Letterman away from NBC. But Leno decided to stay at NBC in 2008, and that boded well for the continuation of the historic news program that had greatly improved in the ratings race.[136]

Koppel decided to leave the show in 2005 following earlier attempts by ABC management to either change the program or drop it entirely in favor of an entertainment-oriented late-night show. Following Koppel's departure, the show remained on the air, although its format changed considerably. A troika of anchors was brought aboard in the persons of Cynthia McFadden, Martin Bashir, and Terry Moran, and would alternate duties in hosting the show. Also, the single-topic format was changed to three or four different subjects being broached in each half-hour program. The show's ratings had actually improved so much that it surpassed the Letterman show in two 2008 sweeps periods.[137]

77. "JIMMY'S WORLD" OF IMAGINATION

A basic tenet of American journalism is, no matter what the reporter's orientation or writing style, the story produced must be a work of nonfiction and as reflective of reality as is humanly possible. Indeed, journalism separates itself from other forms of literature at the dividing line of fiction and nonfiction. From a professional standpoint, there is no greater sin that a journalist can commit than to make up a story—or even parts of a story—that just flat did not happen.

That is what makes the case of *The Washington Post*'s Janet Cooke so startling. It would unveil one of the darker secrets of journalism, that storytelling fraud exists, and it would be echoed by two other highly publicized cases in years to come. The cases of Cooke, Stephen Glass, and Jayson Blair would provide a shocking, "collection of moments" in journalism history. In each case, a gifted reporter and writer made the decision to cross that dividing line of fact and fiction and produce works of fiction cloaked as nonfiction stories. They were not the first, nor the last, American journalists to do this. But the fact each worked for a premier news organization and that one of them even won the Pulitzer Prize for her fake story makes their cases significant in journalism history.

On September 28, 1980, one of the best newspapers in America, *The Washington Post*, ran a story entitled, "Jimmy's World: 8-year-Old Heroin Addict Lives for a Fix."[138] The story, by Janet Cooke, resulted in one of the most embarrassing incidents for a U.S. newspaper and certainly the most embarrassing for the *Post*. For the story, purporting to be about a real-life boy who had been addicted to heroin by his mother's boyfriend, turned out to be a hoax. In this case, it was the reporter herself pulling it. She was not manipulated or used by someone else trying to pass off fiction as reality. She dreamed it up herself, wrote it, and submitted it to her metro editor, who was Bob Woodward of Watergate fame.

As it turned out, there was no real-life Jimmy, but there were real-life effects to the story. Much like the fallout from the later Carol Stuart murder case in Boston, police in Washington, D.C. turned the neighborhoods upside down looking for someone who did not exist. In this case it was young Jimmy, and police wanted to get him out of the trouble he was in. For her part, Cooke refused to reveal his true identity, citing reporter-source confidentiality. Then, of course, there was the problem that the story eventually won journalism's highest honor: the Pulitzer Prize. Upon discovery of the hoax, *Post* editors returned the prize and apologized to its readers.

Responding to the incident later, Woodward said he had no reason to distrust Cooke's reporting, although other reporters mentioned the possibility that the story might at least be embellished. But Woodward said he chalked those comments up to newsroom rivalry and professional jealousy. City editor Milton Coleman also had dismissed the suspicions of other reporters for similar reasons. Even when a reporter noted Cooke's obvious unfamiliarity with Jimmy's neighborhood and the fact she couldn't point out his home, the story still went ahead. Even U.S. News & World Report reprinted Cooke's story in its October 13 issue and headed it, "The Story That Shocked the Nation's Capital."[139]

In the end, the story was probably believed because it fed upon white readers' uninformed perceptions of how horrible and immoral life must be in the city's black nieghborhoods. As such, it was an example of racial stereotyping, made even more believable because it was a black reporter who was doing the stereotyping.

The Janet Cooke hoax was a main topic of discussion in newsrooms and at journalistic conferences for more than a year. In the wake of the incident, many editors tightened their policies regarding keeping sources confidential, demanding that their reporters at least share the identity of those individuals with their editor if conditions seemed significant enough to warrant that.

If Janet Cooke was the journalistic hoax of the 1980s, then Stephen Glass provided the hoax of the decade during the 1990s. Like Cooke, Glass was a young, bright reporter and writer who seemed to have everything going for him as a 25-year-old staff member for *The New Republic*, the prestigious magazine of political news and commentary which boasts it is "required reading" on Air Force One. Glass gained such fame in his short time with the magazine that he also contributed articles for other national magazines including *George*. He was also an occasional journalistic panelist on C-Span, commenting on the workings of Washington, D.C.

The CBS newsmagazine *60 Minutes* devoted an entire program segment in 2003 to the hoax perpetrated by Glass. Correspondent Steve Kroft put it succinctly when he told viewers:

> Every profession has its share of scandals, hoaxes, and con men. And journalism is no exception . . . Stephen Glass, a 25-year-old rising star at *The New Republic*, wrote dozens of high-profile articles for a number of national publications in which he made things up. As *60 Minutes* first reported in May, he made up people, places, and events. He made up organizations and quotations. Sometimes, he made up entire articles. And to back it all up, he created fake notes, fake voicemails, fake faxes, even a fake Web site—whatever it took to deceive his editors, not to mention hundreds of thousands of readers.[140]

In describing how he made his journalistic hoaxes work, Glass said he began by writing nonfiction stories but then would think it would be great to have a good quote to spice it up here and there. So Glass began inventing quotes. Maybe he would put a fake quote after a real quote, or an untruth following a true statement. Before long, however, it became easier and more enjoyable just to invent quotes, facts, and—before long—some entire stories. Glass had earlier worked as a fact-checker at the magazine, so he knew how to subvert that process by creating fake interview notes.[141]

His undoing would prove to be a story ostensibly about an organization he called the National Association of Hackers, focusing on a 15-year-old computer hacker who extorted money from a company called Jukt Electronics for agreeing to stop hacking into their system. Word of the story was picked up by *Forbes* online magazine, which tried to do its own piece on it, only to find there were no real people or organizations—including the National Association of Hackers or Jukt Micronics—that Glass had written about. When the *Forbes* editor contacted Glass's editor at *The New Republic*, and the young reporter's house of cards began to tumble. When the full extent of his duping was revealed, Glass was fired from the magazine.

But the journalistic hoaxes of American history were not over yet. In 2003, a gifted reporter for the prestigious *New York Times* tried his hand at fabricating truth, and it proved very successful for him—for awhile. Jayson Blair, 27, repeatedly plagiarized parts of his stories and invented others out of whole cloth before—like Glass and Cooke—he was discovered and resigned. As the *Times* itself reported, Blair "committed frequent acts of journalistic fraud while covering significant news events in recent months."[142] The paper continued, "The widespread fabrication and plagiarism represent a profound betrayal of trust and a low point in the 152-year history of the newspaper."[143]

Among Blair's journalistic sins were the fabrication of comments which he used as direct quotes, vivid descriptions of scenes that did not exist, the use of material from other writers and publications without crediting them, and the creation of details to make editors and readers believe he was on the scene of stories when he was actually somewhere else, writing about them from a distance. In all, the *Times* reported its investigators had found problems with some 36 of 73 stories which Blair wrote since being assigned to the national desk.[144]

These moments of journalistic fraud, all dutifully exposed and publicized by the news organizations victimized by their reporters, have served to cause problems for the overall credibility of journalists, the believability—and therefore impact—of their stories, and the freedoms that editors allow their reporters to have in covering the news.

78. TED TURNER LAUNCHES CNN

When Atlanta entrepreneur Ted Turner decided to take advantage of the new cable industry and create a nationwide "superstation" out of his Atlanta station WTBS, he launched an enterprise that would become the first 24-hour television cable news network which we know as CNN. It would not take long for this upstart enterprise to gain the respect of journalists working for the broadcast networks, and that occurred in early 1991 when the CNN news team of Bernard Shaw, John Holliman, and Peter Arnett—under the direction of producer Robert Weiner—became the only news team to be able to report live from Baghdad as American planes dropped bombs on the city

CNN founder Ted Turner, right, gives the double thumbs up as he is applauded by Christiane Amanpour, CNN's chief international correspondent, left, after Turner and Amanpour participated in a panel discussion at the CNN 25 World Report Conference in Atlanta, Wednesday, June 1, 2005. [AP Photo/Ric Feld]

at the start of the first Gulf War. That episode is detailed elsewhere in this book as another media "moment."

But the idea for CNN and its launching were certainly significant in and of themselves. At the time, there were no other television stations or networks doing 24-hour news programming. With the success of CNN, however, has come other such enterprises such as MSNBC and Fox News Channel. A sizeable share of American television viewers, in fact, have found themselves somewhat addicted to the up-to-the-minute nature of live, 24-hour news stations like CNN. And today there is not only CNN Domestic, which Americans see, but also CNN International, seen around the world.

Turner's career in television started in 1970 when he assumed control of a struggling, independent UHF station in Atlanta. Turner's WJRJ (which he renamed WTCG) was running fourth in the local ratings out of four stations. Like many non-network-affiliated stations, Channel 17 was running mostly syndicated programming, no original programming except for a minimal amount of news in order to keep its FCC license to operate. Within three years of Turner's takeover, however, WTCG was making money and was gaining an audience by running old movies and reruns of popular series. Turner saw the potential in the growing cable television industry and arranged to have the WTCG signal microwaved to many southeastern cities and states, where

---

THE DAWN OF CABLE TV

Traditionally, the American television industry has existed under a so-called "two-tiered structure," denoting the two levels of network broadcasting and local television station operations. Local stations have the opportunity to affiliate with a television network to increase their audience by receiving network programming. With the advent of cable television, however, another tier was added to television's traditional structure. Now cable "networks" are created without affiliated local stations, and the cable network programs are received directly by viewers nationwide via local cable television companies.

Cable television can be traced all the way back to 1949 as a means of getting broadcast signals to rural Americans who lived in areas unable to receive the broadcast signals. The first of these cable ventures may have been in Lansford, Pa., when the owner of a radio and television sales and repair shop decided to build what was probably the first community television antenna. Financing such a tower was a problem, however, so the merchant, Robert J. Tarlton, organized local viewers into the Panther Valley Television Co., who chipped in to build the transmitter which would beam Philadelphia broadcast signals over a mountain to viewers in Lansford, 65 miles away. Other communities followed suit, building even larger towers to pull in signals from beyond the nearest broadcast market, thereby increasing the number of channels and diversity of programming available to their viewers.

It was not until 1974–75, however, that cable television grew into an important national phenomena and started to change the structure of American television altogether. Two events occurred to make this possible: One was the move toward deregulation of broadcasting by the FCC. The other was the development of communication satellites. The FCC had been restricting retransmission of broadcast signals by local cable operators, but began easing those restrictions in the mid-1970s. And since 1975 cable program networks like HBO have been using RCA communication statellite Satcom 1 to transmit signals to far-flung cable companies around America. Not only did such satellites make it easier to transmit programs from a single location, it also enabled local cable providers to have a broader range of networks and programs available to them. Much of this programming wound up on the cable operators' pay channels.

It wasn't long before other cable networks joined HBO—ESPN and CNN were two of the most significant—and cable television began sapping masses of TV viewers from the broadcast networks and local broadcast stations. As a result the market shares held by the broadcast networks of NBC, CBS, ABC, and Fox are today much weaker than what they were in the pre-cable era. But the day of local, independently owned community antenna cable companies has given way to an age of the MSO, or Multiple System Operator, which are companies that have bought out the local cable operators and merged them into large cable companies. Among the largest of these MSOs are Comcast, Time Warner, Charter Cable, and Cox Communications.

---

local cable companies would pick it up and show it to their audiences. Soon that signal was beamed via satellite to cable systems in other parts of the country, and WTCG morphed from a local Atlanta station to the first "superstation" in America.[145] In fact, today's cable network model is based in large part on the WTCG model. In 1979, the Turner Communications Group changed its named to Turner Broadcasting System and changed the name of WTCG to WTBS.[146]

Using the infrastructure he had in place in Atlanta in June of 1980, Turner launched the country's first 24-hour cable news network, or CNN. Since its launch, CNN has grown to be included as a staple on many cable and satellite television networks and even has a specialized closed-circuit network in the CNN Airport Network. It also has two radio networks. The company has some 36 bureaus around the world and more than 900 affiliated local stations. Although it has a large viewership internationally, CNN remains second in popularity to BBC World News, based in England.

The network has had a huge effect on the way television covers news and the way Americans process it. Much of its success is based on its ability and willingness to go live to events as they are unfolding and to stay with them until they are resolved or they lose importance. For example, on Thanksgiving Day of 2008, CNN beamed live, hour-after-hour coverage of the terrorist attack on Mumbai, the commercial and tourist capital of India where hundreds were killed or injured. The concept of "real-time" reporting is often seen as originating with CNN's live, sustained reporting from developing events. Pentagon officials and media theorists have developed a concept called the "CNN effect" to describe the impact of such real-time coverage on policy decisions made by government officials. Most believe such coverage forces government leaders into making quicker decisions than they otherwise would, because as the public sees the graphic images of unfolding crises, it demands responses from government.[147] Today, CNN is owned by Time Warner, Inc., which also owns the other cable networks created by Turner Broadcasting System. It continues to have a significant effect on the television news industry, especially in the area of political coverage. CNN's coverage of the 2008 presidential election made it one of the most watched networks throughout the latter weeks of that campaign.

79. MTV BRANCHES OUT

A year after Ted Turner launched his CNN as the nation's first 24-hour cable television news network, the country's first 24-hour cable television music channel was launched by another company, Warner Amex Satellite Entertainment. On August 1, 1981, MTV (Music Television) came into existence with the words, "Ladies and gentlemen, rock and roll," spoken on camera by John Lack, one of its creators. This brief introduction was then followed by MTV's first music video called "Video Killed the Radio Star," by a band called the Buggles.[148] From that beginning, this new music network began to take the nation's young people by storm and would grow into not only a cultural phenomenon in music television, but it would also carve out a new way of delivering news and information to young television viewers.

According to the Museum of Broadcast Communication, the key to MTV's initial success was its delivering of low-cost programming in the form of music videos. It wasn't the first time music videos were available—they had been provided free as promotional vehicles by record companies—but MTV made these videos—as well as many new, originally produced music videos—available to viewers on a 24-hour, nonstop basis. In effect, MTV became a television version of a Top 40 radio station, complete with "video jockeys," the counterpart of radio's disc jockeys. In 1985, MTV launched a second video channel, VH1 (Video Hits 1) which often plays softer rock and adult music. MTV Europe was launched in 1987, and it was followed by service in Asia and Latin America.[149]

MTV has not only broken ground in music but also in fostering a new approach to news, one aimed at the younger audiences drawn into watching the music channel.[150] Many traditionalists in the news media may have scoffed at MTV-style news, but the fact is MTV has generated interest in younger voters who have lost interest in the more traditional forms of political coverage on TV and in print. The example of the 2004 presidential election coverage is a case in point. Much as *Rolling Stone* magazine used music as the common thread to reach young people and then intertwined political and cultural news into its editorial mix, MTV has done the same on the television side. MTV used two different tactics to interest young viewers in the Bush-Kerry presidential election of 2004. The network utilized different kinds of "correspondents" who would interview candidates and deliver news and commentary about the election. Within its stable of celebrity journalists were Drew Barrymore, Christina Aguilera, and hip-hop music artist P. Diddy (Sean John Combs), who interviewed both Sen. Hillary Rodham Clinton and the Rev. Jesse Jackson from the floor of the Democratic National Convention.

MTV made its move into nontraditional political coverage to try and bring younger voters into the election process. Statistics were showing most 18–24-year-olds were avoiding news coverage from the traditional broadcast and print media venues. In 2002, for example, the Pew Center found these people spent nearly 40 percent less time with the news than had their predecessors before 1994. Young people were finding traditional news coverage boring and irrelevant to the issues they cared about. And for those between the ages of 25 and 29, the drop-off was smaller (23 percent) for the same years, but it was still significant. As for political news, a 2004 Pew study found that people between the ages of 18 and 29 were showing only minimal interest in political news, at least from traditional sources. Only 23 percent of people in that age group reported they "regularly learn something" from network news.[151]

MTV answered this challenge by framing its coverage of the entire 2004 presidential campaign in a "Choose or Lose" series comprised of different news reports from both national party conventions and additional half-hour and hour-long programs that covered the race and issues from several different orientations. In addition to P. Diddy, its correspondents were Gideon Yago, a 26-year-old who anchored the coverage in a way not too unlike traditional anchors, with the exception of his age; Aguilera, who seemed to draw her authority from the fact she was covering issues related to sex and who, by her own admission, knew something about that topic, and Barrymore, the popular actress who said she was a representative of "polticially disaffected youth."[152] Taken altogether, MTV's coverage was a big leap from traditional coverage, but it seemed to work with young Americans who found themselves more interested in the election than they otherwise might have been.

As the 2008 presidential campaign rolled around, "Choose or Lose" was back, and interest among these same young demographics had peaked, especially given the youthful Barack Obama as a candidate, and MTV again did its part in furthering interest among young voters in that presidential election. For this coverage, the network used 51 "citizen journalists" to comprise "Street Team '08" who submitted videos, blogs, photos, and more from around the nation. The reporters came from each of the 50 states plus Washington, D.C., and submitted weekly multimedia reports tailored for mobile, handheld electronic devices. "Recent MTV research shows young people believe their generation will be a major force in determining who is elected in the upcoming . . . elections," said Ian Rose, MTV's vice president of public affairs, "and Street Team '08 will be a key way for our audience to connect with peers, as well as get informed and engaged on the local and political issues that matter to them most."[153]

80. LAUNCHING *USA TODAY*

The case could be made that no other single newspaper had such a modeling effect on other newspapers in America during the 20th century than a newspaper launched in 1982 by the Gannett media empire under the supervision of flamboyant but savvy Allen Neuharth. That newspaper was *USA Today*. Within a decade, newspapers across the country were changing their design to conform to the successful features of this upstart newspaper. Among those *USA Today* design innovations were the widespread use of color, the user-friendly yet comprehensive weather page, the introduction of "infographics" (innovative charts and graphs which delivered the story of a societal trend or dissected a phenomenon quickly and graphically), and easy-to-read Page 1 teasers or index boxes linked to inside pages.

But *USA Today* was more than a package of innovative design elements. For one thing, like the Fox Network on television, it was initially seen by many industry observers as a superfluous media launch. In a time when some large daily newspapers around the country were closing up shop or being folded into their morning counterpart publications, why would anyone want to start up a *new* daily newspaper? Even more puzzling was why a company as savvy as Gannett (which already owned a large stable of dailies) thought they could defy the fundamental nature of the industry and offer up a *national* daily newspaper. With the exception of the *Wall Street Journal* and possibly the *New York Times*, American newspapers are all oriented toward local markets and they derive the lion's share of their revenue from local advertising. Television owned the national audience and national advertisers. Yet here was a newspaper that dared to claim the entire nation as its hometown and somehow planned to find enough advertisers interested in reaching such a far-flung audience of readers.

To a large degree, *USA Today* was a newspaper built upon market research. Most of the newspaper's features are those which research said Americans wanted in a newspaper: more color, a user-friendly way of navigating the newspaper, shorter stories, more upbeat stories, news about celebrities and cultural trends in America, a comprehensive sports section, a weather page that made sense, a newspaper that would be easy to read for the person on the move, and informational blurbs about things happening in every one of the 50 states. The resulting newspaper that Gannett editors produced contained all of this and more. It also featured an op-ed page that had so many diverse viewpoints that some critics claimed robbed the newspaper of an identifiable editorial soul.

It is highly doubtful that any company other than Gannett could have produced what would become the leading circulating daily newspaper in America with a daily circulation in excess of 2.5 million readers.[154] This media empire could afford to take the kinds of losses which *USA Today* would originally generate before becoming a success in the 1990s. Also, the company's network of newspapers across the country provided a ready-made system of satellite printing plants which could electronically receive the pages sent to it from *USA Today* headquarters, print it, and truck it out to the far corners of the country in time to be read the next morning. Finally, the company already had a huge editorial staff in place at its many newspapers across the country, and it put into operation a system of "loaned" journalists who would leave their home newspapers for a period of months, move to Arlington, Virginia, where *USA Today* was based, and join its staff of permanent employees for awhile before returning home.

USA Today has drawn a lot of criticism from traditional journalists who have called it "McPaper," for what is perceived as a quick and superficial treatment of the news. Editors at *USA Today* counter, however, that they are not trying to be a traditional newspaper, but are the best at what they are designed to be: a national newspaper for busy readers, many of whom are traveling when they pick up a copy of *USA Today*. In sum, the newspaper has become extremely successful as a risky startup in a decade when other newspapers were failing.

81. THE FOX NETWORK PREMIERS

By the mid-1980s, cable television had found a welcoming audience in America, and the three broadcast networks of NBC, CBS, and ABC found their market shares diminishing. Industry observers began talking more and more about audience fragmentation as viewers deserted the traditional broadcast networks for the newer cable channels. Many observers believed cable would sound the death knell for the broadcast networks, or at least for network news programs. Why would viewers continue to watch broad-based, general-interest channels when new channels more specialized to individual tastes were popping up everywhere on the TV dial? Wasn't this the same picture that confronted the general-interest magazine industry of the 1960s when television siphoned off its advertisers and specialized magazines had to arise to save the industry?

So the idea of someone creating a fourth broadcast network, and airing yet another network news program, didn't seem to make sense to many industry insiders. Yet it was precisely at this point that Rupert Murdoch, owner of the media empire News Corporation, decided to bring the Fox Network into the broadcast mix. The network launched on October 9, 1986. Although well-funded, the new network appeared shaky at first but would wind up two decades later leading the broadcast network ratings race, as Fox finished in first place in 2007 for the first time since its launch.[155] Helping to propel Fox to that lofty position was its breakout show that had caught America by storm a few years before, *American Idol*.

Fox was anything but a shoestring startup. In 1985, News Corporation paid $250 million for half of TCF Holdings, the parent company of the 20th Century Fox movie studio. Two months later, the company bought a half-dozen independent television stations in six of the largest television markets in America. The plan called for the company to set up an independent television system, and produce and distribute programming to its stations and other independent stations wishing to affiliate with Fox. The network expanded its station holdings and affiliates in the 1990s with improved, aggressive programming, but probably the biggest single boost for Fox came in 1993 when the network outbid CBS for rights to broadcast the National Football League's NFC games. The contract also lured the popular broadcast team of John Madden, Terry Bradshaw, and Pat Summerall away from CBS. The NFL Sunday broadcasts were so huge among viewers that Fox became a legitimate network contender almost overnight, and it wasn't long before former CBS-affiliated stations decided to become Fox affiliates instead.

Added to the success of the NFL deals were popular Fox shows in the 1990s like *Beverly Hills, 90210*, *Melrose Place*, and *Party of Five*. Programs like *The X-Files* and *The Simpsons* would help cement the network's appeal to viewers. The guiding genius behind Fox was not only Murdoch but also entertainment executive Barry Diller, who seemed to have a sixth sense in seeing a hole that existed in the network television programming landscape. In many ways, almost from the beginning with shows like *Married . . . with Children*, Fox pushed back the boundaries of what was considered "safe" programming on broadcast network television. Sex, violence, and more graphic language and content were now appearing on a broadcast networks as opposed to a cable television channel.

Author Daniel Kimmel notes that Fox was ridiculed at first as being the "hanger network," because its transmitting signal was so weak that some viewers actually used wire coat hangers as antennae to help receive it in their homes. But employing a canny and aggressive marketing strategy and cutting-edge programming, Fox took advantage of television market segmentation and dared to challenge current standards of programming taste. The Fox success formula seemed pretty basic, yet also profound: network management must "be nimble, be opportunistic, and be aggressive." Kimmel, the Boston correspondent for *Variety*, believed the success came as a result of timing and incisive analysis of television market research. In responding to what they found, Fox pioneered in the areas of counter-programming and "narrowcasting," which is essentially another term for specialization. Again, the analogy to the success of special-interest magazines holds true. As a result of pitting an over-the-top sitcom like *Married . . . with Children* against CBS's venerable news magazine, *60 Minutes*, on Sunday evenings, the show created buzz, especially with the younger, Gen-X crowd.[156]

The impact of Fox has been felt across the television landscape as it has since it launched the popular Fox News Channel and fit it into the conservative ideological niche of America. Probably the greatest contribution of the Fox Network, however, is that it showed that the death notices of broadcast television in America were indeed premature, even in an age of mounting competition from cable.

82. THE *CHALLENGER* DISASTER

The journalistic love affair with NASA, its astronauts, and the space program in general began in the early 1960s. It lasted for years—until problems started mounting which resulted not only in failed missions but also lost lives. On January 27, 1967, one of the original *Mercury Seven* astronauts, Gus Grissom, and his two shipmates, Edward White and Roger Chaffee, were killed in an *Apollo 1* launch pad fire. Three Soviet astronauts lost their lives when their *Soyuz 11* craft depressurized during re-entry, and another Soviet astronaut lost his life in 1967 when his *Soyuz 1* parachute failed to open on re-entry.[157] But the most significant NASA tragedy, in terms of numbers of lives lost and the dampening effect it had on the space program for years afterwards occurred on January 28, 1986. This was the explosion shortly after launch of the space shuttle *Challenger* that resulted in the deaths of its six-member crew plus the first "teacher in space," Christa McAuliffe, who had been selected from some 11,000 applicants for that program designed to reinvigorate America's interest in NASA's space efforts.

From the beginning, Shuttle Mission STS-51L was plagued by problems. Liftoff was first set for 3:43 p.m. EST on January 22, 1986. It was reset to the next day and then the next, due to delays in another mission and finally was reset for January 25. The reason was bad weather at the designated site for an aborted landing in Dakar, Senegal. But bad luck plagued the launch date, and it was reset again when launch processing was unable to meet new morning liftoff time. Then a forecast for inclement weather at Kennedy Space Center caused the launch to be rescheduled for 9:37 a.m. EST, January 27. However, it was delayed yet another day when ground servicing equipment could not be removed from orbiter hatch. Engineers had to actually saw the fixture off and drill out an attaching bolt to solve the problem. But while this was happening, heavy crosswinds swirled and other mechanical problems ensued causing the liftoff to finally occur at 11:38 a.m. EST on January 28.

Inside the rocket's body, however, all was not well. Cold launch temperatures had contributed to a failure of O-rings on one of the solid rocket motors. As a result of this failure, hot exhaust gases escaped out of the side of the solid rocket motor that, in turn, led to a major structural failure of the launch vehicle.[158] To everyone's horror, 73 seconds into the mission, the *Challenger* exploded, killing all seven people aboard. In addition to Christa McAuliffe, fatalities included Francis Scobee, Michael Smith, Judith Resnik, Ellison Onizuka, Ronald McNair, and Gregory Jarvis.

Subsequent investigations showed everyone involved, including the major news media, failed to probe conditions surrounding the reaction of the spacecraft's

The space shuttle Challenger *explodes 73 seconds after takeoff on January 28, 1986, at Kennedy Space Center in Florida. The seven crew members perished in the explosion. One of the shuttle's booster rockets, whose faulty O-rings were blamed for the disaster, shoots off to the right. [AP Photo/Steve Helber]*

"O rings" that failed to work properly in cold weather, the kind existing at the time of the launch. Had this problem been probed and stories done on it, the disaster might have been averted. A veteran journalist who had covered many NASA launches in the past was William Broad of the *New York Times*. Broad told *Columbia Journalism Review* several months later, "Clearly, knowing what we know now, if (journalists had) really dug into it they might have been able to save seven lives. Standing back, it looks like the whole edifice (NASA) was rotten to the core."[159] Not all journalists were buying the rosy picture NASA had been selling, however. In 1979 and 1980, two articles appeared in *Science* and the *Washington Monthly* magazines challenging the safety record of NASA and asserting the agency was succumbing to budget pressures and was cutting safety measures.[160] In the *Science* article, R. Jeffrey Smith noted a decision by Rockwell International to save time and money by not testing engine parts separately. Smith noted this resulted in nearly a half-dozen engine fires during those tests. His conclusion: "a shuttle that many feel will be the most risky spacecraft ever launched."[161]

In the *Washington Monthly* article, writer Gregg Easterbrook noted there were no ejection seats for crew members, but there were plenty of used rocket parts—in some cases ones that had been used 100 times—despite space wear and tear.[162] Even more disturbing, in hearings after the *Challenger* disaster, a top engineer for rocket-builder Morton-Thiokol said he had advised against launch because of the cold weather's effect on engine parts. And he told journalist Bill Moyers that "We all (Morton-Thiokol engineers at the launch site) thought it was going to blow up on the pad . . . Bob Lund turned to me and said he had just whispered a prayer of thanks."[163] Seventy-three seconds later, *Challenger* exploded as it began its climb to space. Several red flags had appeared from 1981 to 1985 in NASA projects. Yet Boot found six major publications including *Time*, *Newsweek*, the *Philadelphia Inquirer*, the *Christian Science Monitor*, the *New York Times*, and *The Washington Post* shows these episodes were reported only in piecemeal fashion.[164]

After the *Challenger* disaster, journalists across the country began treating NASA as they treat other government agencies: as one vulnerable to the possibility of mistakes, accidents, human error, outside pressure and—ultimately—with the desire to succeed.

83. THE WALL COMES DOWN

On November 9, 1989, the West's most visible symbol of repression was first breached and later demolished, chunk by chunk, as elated Germans danced atop the hated Berlin Wall. The structure, which had come to be known as the "iron curtain" had physically separated West Berlin from communism's German Democratic Republic of East Germany for 28 years since the start of its construction in 1961. Upwards to 200 people lost their lives as they were killed, trying to reach freedom, by East German border guards. As the wall was breached on the night of November 9, the event was covered live by television and seen around the world. The images provided an utter clarity of the end of an era of European communism.

The fall of the wall may have seemed like an instantaneous event, but it was not. One writer likened it to, "a singer who labors for years in obscurity before becoming an 'overnight success.' "[165] The actual breach of the Wall by Eastern Germans was allowed by border guards who had misread an order. Although history may call it an accident that brought down the separator of communism and democracy, many observers feel the end was in sight as communism was already crumbling in Eastern Europe.

The news media, especially the western media, was influential in bringing East Europeans to a point of hope and defiance against their Communist leaders. Television producer Tara Sonenshine noted that, "Television was, for the people of East Germany, a window through which they could witness the revolutionary changes taking place . . . It allowed them to take part in the broad movement to unseat communism around the world. It filled them with courage . . . it gave them information and knowledge with which they could challenge the old ways of looking at the world."[166]

East German Chancellor Erich Honecker seemed to have been living in denial that his communist system was crumbling, although his country was showing obvious signs of disarray ranging from pollution, to a bad economy, to the Stasi, the secret police force that was shutting down East German enterprise. In the months preceding November, many East German citizens took vacations in Hungary, a country that had a weak border with the West. The hope was that it would be easier to emigrate to freedom there. Instead of seeing this flight as a sign of mass unrest, Honecker derided the refugees as moral outcasts and then forbade travelers to leave for Hungary. So East Germans then turned to Czechoslovakia, cramming themselves into the West German Embassy in Prague until Honecker agreed to let them go to West Germany. Some East Germans who craved democracy decided to stay home and protest, inspired by the rhetoric of Russian leader Mikhail Gorbachev, who realized communism was on its last legs in East Europe. Regular demonstrations ensued in cities like Leipzig, and they gained such popularity that the government was worried about shutting them down. Then Honecker welcomed Gorbachev to East Berlin in October, and the protestors' inspiration was now on their soil. Gorbachev suggested to Honecker that he loosen the grip he had placed on civil liberties, but Honecker refused.

A huge protest demonstration took place in Leipzig where some 70,000 East Germans poured into the streets. Police were ordered to pull back, and the spirit of protest won the night. Honecker was voted out of office by the Politburo on October 17 as Egon Krenz took charge, promising to initiate democratic reforms and ease travel restrictions to the West for East Germans. On November 9, East German Politburo member Gunter Schabowski announced to journalists in Berlin that those travel restrictions would be lifted for his country's people. The order was intended to go into effect the next day, but Schabowski got it wrong and told reporters they would be implemented immediately. East Germans began to approach the checkpoint gates of the wall en masse. Border guards were confused, thinking their standing order to shoot was still in effect. But there were so many people approaching the gate, they decided to stand down. The gate was open, and there was no closing it from that point forward.[167]

One of the reasons why the media coverage of this event was so important was it showed how influential live television can be in international diplomacy. In fact, live television results in real-time diplomacy in which government leaders often feel forced to make responses to events more quickly than they would normally like. Time can be a priceless asset for the political leader confronting a crisis, allowing a cushion before a decision is made. A journalist sees time differently, however: Speed is of the essence, especially to television reporters. As the night of November 9, 1989, revealed, technology has reduced the interval between gathering the news and delivering the news to zero. The cushion of time is gone. In 1961, a 2 1/2-day interval separated the start of construction on the Berlin Wall and its viewing on American television screens. So President Kennedy had a cushion of time to deal with how to react. By 1989, however, that cushion had disappeared as events in Berlin were covered live. Although euphoria was gripping East Germany, President George Bush resisted being caught up in it, and live television captured that as he noted cautiously being "very pleased" he added a statement he would probably later regret, saying that he wasn't going to dance on the wall.

84. THE CAROL STUART MURDER CASE

Journalists like to think of themselves as being more skeptical than the average person, unwilling to take too much at face value. They also like to think of themselves as unwilling to buy into stereotypes but treat each incident as the facts seem to shape it. So it was a surprise to many journalists to find both of these bubbles burst by a tragic murder that occurred in Boston in 1989. In this case, journalists put way too much stock in what seemed a *likely* story and, in the process, inflamed some long-held urban stereotypes that were not true, at least in this murder. As a result, the public, its law enforcement agencies, and even city hall itself were aroused to take inappropriate action following the media coverage.

On the night of October 23, 1989, Charles Stuart and his pregnant wife Carol had just attended a childbirth class at Boston's Brigham and Women's Hospital. The couple seemed excited over the pending birth, and life seemed very good indeed. Charles was manager of a trendy fur store, and Carol was a young lawyer. They had just pulled away from the area in their car, so Charles' story later went, when a black man with a gun and raspy voice came out of nowhere at a stop light and forced his way into their car. He demanded Stuart drive him to Mission Hill, then robbed and shot them both, hitting Charles in the stomach and Carol in the head. Still conscious but bleeding from his wound, Charles sped away and called 911 on his car phone, asking them to send help. Police responded immediately and, as it happens, a film crew for the CBS television series, *Rescue 911*, was shadowing the Boston EMT unit that received the police call to assist the Stuarts. So that moment was captured as it happened and later aired time and again on television.

While Charles Stuart survived the shooting, Carol died later that night following the caesarean-section delivery of her son Christopher, who was two months premature. He would die 17 days later. The media dutifully reported the crime, providing detailed accounts of Charles Stuart's story of how the tragedy unfolded. Stuart even provided a description of the assailant. Police sprang into action, conducting a thorough search of Boston's black neighborhoods and settling on a man answering the description named Willie Bennett. Stuart even picked Bennett out of a photo lineup, and the case appeared headed toward a speedy resolution.

As a media story, the Stuart murder case—to that point—followed a familiar tragic theme: a young white urban couple, both professionals with a good life ahead of them, are attacked by a black man from the ghettos with nothing to lose. Their lives are ruined, the suspect is caught and goes to prison. The Boston media portrayed the young couple as having their dream world shattered. Several politicians attended Carol Stuart's funeral, while others called for the death penalty for the then-fugitive assailant Charles described to police. One Boston city councilman longed publicly to meet the assailant alone in the street so he could kill him with his own hands. Mayor Raymond Flynn ordered all available detectives to work on the case. As a result of the hysteria, hundreds of men in Boston's predominantly black Mission Hill area were detained only because they were black. One, Bennett, was arrested for the crime.

The problem was that, apart from the fact Carol Stuart was dead and her husband was shot in the stomach, the story as told by Charles Stuart was untrue. Not only had Bennett not committed the crime, but there was never any black assailant. In fact, there was never any assailant other than Charles Stuart himself. Had police not asked doctors treating the Stuarts if Charles' wound could not have been self-inflicted? In fact, the question was asked and the answer was probably not, because the stomach wound was so severe. Someone wanting to wound himself would probably have picked a less dangerous area of the body, doctors said. But in this case, "probably" wasn't good enough.

The criminal case against Willie Bennett fell apart when Matthew Stuart, Charles' brother, told police he believed Charles committed the crime himself. Matthew confessed that he himself had driven to meet his brother that night to help Charles commit an ostensible insurance fraud. When he arrived at the scene and saw Carol had been shot and his brother in pain, however, Matthew realized something other than insurance fraud had been planned. He said he took the gun and a bag of valuables that Charles handed him and disposed of them. Police later learned Stuart was having financial problems and was romantically interested in an intern at his fur salon. The tragedy came to a conclusion when Charles Stuart, apparently perceiving that the noose was tightening around him, took his life the night of January 4, 1990, by jumping from the Tobin Bridge into the Charles River below. His body was found in Boston Harbor.

About the phenomenon, reporter Margaret Carlson wrote: "Stuart tapped into assumptions about race and crime so powerful that they overwhelmed skepticism about his tale."[168] And ABC *Nightline* correspondent Jeff Greenfield noted that the whole episode resulted in a scenario where, "To be black is to be guilty."[169] And former Chicago reporter Ellis Cose said the media made the case much more believable by portraying an ordinary couple as extraordinary who were victims of scum. He added this scenario is played out in the media every few weeks.[170] Phil Balboni, then news director for WCVB-TV in Boston asked, however, "Why would anyone doubt the word of a man suffering from such a horrible gunshot wound himself?"[171]

After the pieces of the puzzle came to light and the news was reported about Stuart's suicide, journalists around the country held many conversations about how their own stereotypes might make them vulnerable to falling for pat stories like the one Charles Stuart spun for police and the news media. Like other media events that have occurred, the Stuart murder case provided a point of reference for journalists who wish their stories to be the result of fact and not stereotype. And the discussions didn't end in the newsroom. In Massachusetts, legislators and Gov. Michael Dukakis supported a bill that would have created a commission to probe the way news media and police officials handled the Stuart murder case, in hopes that this kind of manipulation wouldn't occur again.[172]

Bernard Shaw, left; Peter Arnett, center; Robert Wiener, and members of the CNN crew in Baghdad shortly before leaving Iraq. Photo taken January 19, 1991. [AP PHOTO/Dominique Mollard]

85. LIVE FROM BAGHDAD

The history of journalism is full of heroic stories about journalists covering wars. Some of these stories are told elsewhere in this book. Several of these historic moments produced big changes for the ways in which future battles and wars would be covered. One of these most heroic moments, which would usher in the age of live war coverage and cause a minor news network to become a major one, is the story that follows. In this moment, three reporters for Ted Turner's Cable News Network, better known as CNN, set the early standard for covering modern war in the Middle East. Bernard Shaw, Peter Arnett, and John Holliman, under the direction of producer Robert Wiener, covered the American bombing of the Bagdad live on a January night in 1991 from an upper floor of the Al Rashid Hotel as bombs fell all around the hotel. For all this crew knew, the next one would fall on the hotel itself. Because of Wiener's resourcefulness in securing a satellite-based audio feed and the courage shown by the news team, the young network was the only news organization to be able to broadcast that bombing raid live and did so for 17 straight hours until it was over. This was the night that put CNN on the map as a premier international news organization. Formerly referred to derisively by other newsmen as "Chicken Noodle News," this Baghdad coverage put CNN on the path of becoming America's foremost international news network. It also moved war coverage from taped to live, and brought with it all the questions and problems that live coverage of the fog of war entails.

Wiener sensed the importance of having CNN put a crew on the ground in Baghdad early, long before the deadlines which President George H. W. Bush gave to Iraqi president Saddam Hussein for removal of his troops from the invaded Kuwait. The time Wiener spent in Baghdad acclimated him to the cultural norms of Iraqi politicians and he used the knowledge to aid CNN in setting up equipment to cover the eventual bombing live. When the attack came, crews from other major news organizations were sent to the basement of the hotel while CNN's crew remained upstairs, defying Iraqi soldiers, and reported the bombing live with the natural soundtrack provided by the airbursts exploding just outside their open windows.

The device the crew used to report live was called a "four-wire," which gave them direct two-way audio linkage to CNN's headquarters in New York City.

The courage shown by this news crew, as well as their ingenuity, became important benchmarks in the history of war reporting from which future reporters, producers, and news organizations would benefit. Peter Arnett would stay on in Baghdad long after other Western reporters were ordered out of the country as the ensuing short war (dubbed "Desert Storm") played out. Arnett's later coverage became controversial as it was supervised by Iraqi officials as a condition of its airing.

The crew assisting Wiener in this project also included a young Nik Roberts, who would become a senior CNN correspondent in the Middle East in the years to come, helping anchor that network's coverage of the second war with Iraq which would begin in 2003.

86. NBC'S EXPLODING PICKUP TRUCK

By its very nature, news reporting is supposed to deal with relatively spontaneous and/or significant events that are real and were not staged for the media. So-called "re-creations" of events, unless they are clearly labeled as such, are not perceived by mainstream media as being ethical. Nevertheless, in a supercharged environment of competitive television news, history has shown that even the most highly respected television networks and local TV news stations have been tempted to cross the line. In one highly publicized news faux pax, one major network actually participated in setting up the staged event for dramatic purposes. That network was NBC, the news program was *Dateline NBC*, and the staged event was an exploding pickup truck designed to show consumers how unsafe the gas tank on this vehicle was if struck from a particular angle. The only problem was *Dateline* did not tell viewers they were watching a staged explosion.

On November 17, 1992, NBC aired the episode which carried a segment featuring some 14 minutes of a debate on the safety of certain older GM trucks and how a spate of consumer lawsuits asserted they were prone to catch fire when hit from the side by other vehicles. The debate was topped off by a 57-second segment showing dramatic footage of how one such GM truck caught fire when struck sideways and its fuel tank erupted. The footage, ostensibly a real collision, was meant to show that, when those trucks were struck from the side, their gas tanks would burst into flames. Viewers saw an example of a low-speed accident involving a GM truck in which the gas tank exploded. What they were not told was that experts hired by the show had rigged the truck with remotely controlled rockets to make sure the fuel tank exploded. The effect was dramatic as the tank burst into flames, and producers for the show felt they had scored coup in the competitive battle with other newsmagazines, such as CBS's *60 Minutes* in alerting the public to a significant danger for GM truck owners while, at the same time, garnering a lot of viewership through this moment of high drama.

The staging might have gone unnoticed had it not been for the prying eyes of investigators hired by General Motors to study the tape for possible clues as to its authenticity. The investigators noticed that the truck's gas tank actually emitted smoke a split second before the side impact. That finding spurred on a more intensive GM-led investigation which involved searching almost two dozen auto salvage yards for old GM trucks, and the probers located enough evidence to refute almost every aspect of the televised crash sequence. General Motors then filed a defamation lawsuit against NBC. GM publicized its findings and rebuttal to the *Dateline NBC* episode on February 18, 1993, and announced its lawsuit against NBC, which the network settled soon afterwards. NBC News President Michael Gartner admitted the mistake and Jane Pauley, cohost of *Dateline*, read an on-air apology. Four of the show's producers were dismissed by NBC, and the on-air reporter for the segment was transferred to a local television station. Gartner resigned after noting about the on-air apology, "The more I learned, the worse it got. I was troubled by almost every aspect of the crash. I knew we had to apologize. We put 225,000 minutes of news on the air last year, and I didn't want to be defined by those 57 seconds."[173]

Commenting on the episode, Mortimer R. Feinberg and John J. Tarrant wrote in their book, *Why Smart People Do Dumb Things*, "At some point, it became more important to provide a satisfying climax than to maintain integrity. After all, let's face it: the thrust of the 'Dateline' segment was hardly likely to be that there was nothing to the lawsuits against GM, that the trucks were perfectly safe. The people putting on the show had an objective—not the holding of a real test to gauge the riskiness of the truck, but rather a ratings building conflagration. Once the group had locked onto that target, it looked for the best means of hitting it."[174] The troubling incident at NBC was certainly not the first time the news media has participated in staging an event purported to be real, but it was the most highly publicized hoax in the late 20th century. It caused news directors, producers, and editors around the country to re-examine their practices and commitment to reporting real—as opposed to pseudo—news. Other such instances would follow, however, as the competitive pressure of television ratings continued to result in a blur between news and entertainment.

87. THE OKLAHOMA CITY BOMBING

American journalists were handed two sad opportunities to show how they could react to covering tragedies of unbelievable impact in the last decade of the 20th century and the first year of the new millennium. One was the Oklahoma City bombing which claimed 168 lives, and the other was, of course, 9/11 which killed almost 3,000 people. Journalists learned many lessons in covering each of these tragedies which were remarkably similar in their coverage and impact.

The case of the Oklahoma City bombing gave journalists an example of the kinds of risks associated with disaster coverage. Not just physical risks, which were minimal since journalists were kept at arms length from the building's vulnerable carcass, but risks associated with first day coverage accuracy and continual sensitivities to the surviving victims and relatives and friends of the many people killed.

There was some physical risk involved for journalists and photographers converging immediately on the Alfred P. Murrah Federal Building just after 9 a.m. on Wednesday, April 19, 1995. Their police scanners had picked up news of an explosion in the building, but most journalists in and around the city didn't need a scanner to know something huge had just happened because they heard and felt it themselves in all corners of the city. On that tragic morning, many reporters and photographers arrived at the scene along with—and a few even before—the emergency personnel from fire and police departments. As the chaos of the first hour unfolded, photojournalists were snaking their way through the rubble at the base of the nine-story building. April is a month known for strong winds in Oklahoma, and that made the building's hollowed-out carcass sway and threaten to rain debris down on anyone below. There were even reports that other bombs might still be awaiting detonation in the building. It was, by all accounts, an unsafe scene. One rescuer, nurse Rebecca Anderson, lost her life when she re-entered to the rubble to assist survivors. Shortly, however, police had removed nonemergency personnel from the scene and draped the scene in yellow police tape.

Rescuers at the scene described the area around the building as "organized chaos." An Oklahoma City police officer, Sgt. Jerry Flowers, was one of the first on the scene. He wrote the following about the blast site:

> Black smoke was shooting in the air. People, both old and young, were covered with blood. Some were holding towels and clothing articles against their bodies trying to stop the bleeding. Babies and adults were lying on the sidewalk. Some appeared to be dead . . . Everywhere I looked was blood, misery and pain. I saw a car hood burning in the top of a tree. Debris, rocks, bodies, burned cars, glass, fire, and water covered Fifth Street. A large hole about thirty feet in diameter was where a small circle drive used to be in front of the Murrah Building.[175]

One lesson reporters learned from just the first day of this coverage was one that police reporters know well: Be wary of imputing blame for crimes. More than one of the first day stories intimated that the bombing was the work of Middle Eastern terrorists, and broadcast reports mentioned two Arab men who were questioned in an Oklahoma City hotel room. While these speculative reports were being filed, an Oklahoma highway patrolman arrested the man who would ultimately be charged and convicted of the crime, and he was an American named Timothy McVeigh, who planned and executed the crime with the help of codefendant Terry Nichols.

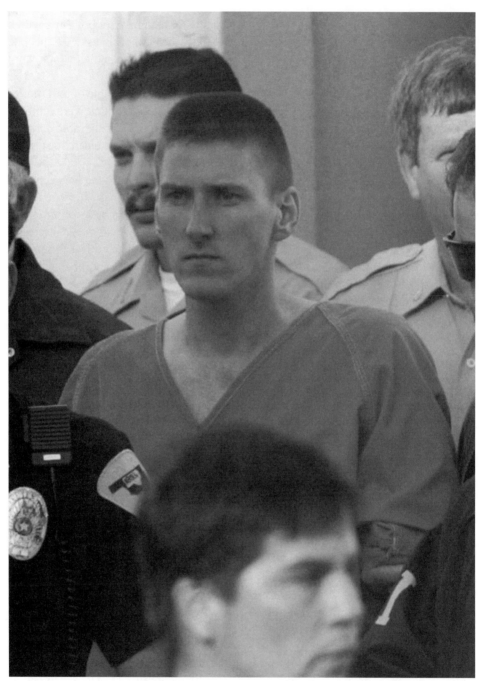

Oklahoma City bombing suspect Timothy McVeigh is escorted by law enforcement officials from the Noble County Courthouse in Perry, Oklahoma, Friday, April 21, 1995. The April 19 bombing of the Alfred P. Murrah Federal Building claimed the lives of 168 people. McVeigh was convicted Monday June 2, 1997, of the crime. [AP Photo/David Longstreath, File]

Ed Kelley, editor of Oklahoma City's *Oklahoman*, said his newspaper immediately dispatched as many people as possible to the crime scene. Extensive coverage of the event called for long hours from the *Oklahoman* staff, who worked more than 150,000 hours of overtime. Some 70 additional pages were produced within one month just to tell this tragic story. The story was deemed too much for the city desk alone, so editors called upon all staffers at the newspaper. Each editor was assigned a different aspect of the coverage like crime, damage, casualties, and community and family support. One person alone was assigned the casualty list and, for 28 days, did nothing but obituaries and life profiles. For its coverage, the paper won a prestigious award from the Society of Professional Journalists.[176]

McVeigh had sped away from the blast scene immediately after the lighting the fuse, not realizing that the concussion from the blast apparently blew off his license plate from his Mercury Marquis. That was the main reason he was stopped about an hour after the explosion: for driving without a license plate. The officer making the stop then sensed something else was afoot when he saw a pistol in the car and arrested McVeigh for carrying a loaded firearm. He was identified later as a suspect in the bombing and taken into federal custody. Two years later, McVeigh was convicted in federal court on eight counts of first-degree murder (there were eight federal officers killed in the blast), and several other charges relating to conspiracy and using a weapon of mass destruction. McVeigh was executed in Terre Haute, Indiana, in 1999. Nichols received a life sentence for his part in the crime.

The Oklahoma City bombing was the worst act of terrorism committed on American soil up to that moment. It would be eclipsed almost six years later, in 2001, with the terrorist attacks on New York City and the Pentagon in Washington, D.C. Oklahoma City is, however, still the worst act of domestic terrorism, since the attacks of 9/11 were committed by foreign members of Al Qaeda. Reflecting on lessons learned in covering the Oklahoma City bombing, one journalist who had been on the scene for several weeks said the following:

> On a professional level, I had been confronting burnout with this business of journalism going into April 19, 1995. I wondered if there was any real reason for journalists to go running around, exposing the pain, problems and perils of others. By the end of my first day of bombing coverage, I had found a new meaning in this profession. Such journalism puts all humanity on the same page in the hymnal of brotherhood, understanding, and support. Such journalism is washed clean of the manipulation and sensationalism of pseudo-news and trash reporting. Such journalism deals openly with the gut questions that friends and families of the dead and suffering are desperately seeking answers to. Questions like what happened and why did it happen? What can we learn from it?[177]

Following the attack on Oklahoma City, Americans felt a vulnerability they had not felt for more than a century when the country was torn apart by civil war. But many were sure something this tragic could never happen again. That is, until the morning of September 11, 2001.

88. THE O. J. SIMPSON TRIAL

No trial in recent memory has shaken up America and been the focus of so much attention and controversy as the murder trial of athlete-turned-actor O. J. Simpson. The former running back of the Buffalo Bills who picked up acting roles in films such as *The Towering Inferno* and the *Naked Gun* series, was arrested and charged in the summer of 1994 with the brutal murder of his former wife, Nicole Brown Simpson, and a restaurant employee named Ronald Goldman. From the initial discovery of the two bodies outside of Brown's condominium in the posh Brentwood neighborhood of Los Angeles, to the long and slow freeway chase of Simpson's white Ford Bronco by a phalanx of LAPD cars, to the lengthy trial that ensued and the dramatics created by Simpson's large defense team headed by the flamboyant Johnnie Cochran, this trial had it all in terms of media allure. In a larger and more important sense, however, the murder trial of a high-profile African American, the last-minute so-called "race card" played by his lead defense attorney, and the surprising acquittal cast a spotlight on black and white Americans and how differently they view the practice of justice in the United States. The episode also had a lot to say about the status of celebrities and hero-worshiping in America, especially when those celebrities are accused of real-life crimes.

The murders had been particularly gruesome, even by contemporary U.S. crime standards. Both Brown and Goldman had been stabbed several times, with Brown's neck wounds nearly severing her head. The severity and repeated nature of the wounds pointed to a crime of passion, and evidence at the scene—as well as past reports of

In this June 21, 1995 file photo, O. J. Simpson holds up his hands before the jury after putting on a pair of gloves described as the infamous bloody gloves during his double-murder trial in Los Angeles. Mike Gilbert, a sports agent who profited off O. J. Simpson alleges the football star confessed to murdering his ex-wife and admits that he helped Simpson outwit prosecutors with the gloves. How I Helped O. J. Get Away with Murder: The Shocking Inside Story of Violence, Loyalty, Regret and Remorse, *was published in 2008. [AP Photo/Vince Bucci, File Pool]*

domestic problems between Brown and Simpson—pointed to him as a prime suspect. An arrest warrant was issued on June 17, 1994, five days after the bodies of Brown and Goldman were discovered. Simpson was to turn himself in as more than a thousand reporters waited for that event at the police station. He did not show up, however, and instead a friend and defense attorney, Robert Kardashian, read a long letter from Simpson to the press. Simpson denied involvement in the murders and then included the statement, "Don't feel sorry for me. I've had a great life."[178] It sounded like a suicide note, and police issued an all-points bulletin for Simpson's arrest. Simpson's Ford Bronco was spotted on the 405 freeway in Los Angeles, with his friend Al Cowlings driving. An LAPD officer approached the van as it stopped, but Cowlings yelled that Simpson had a gun and was ready to kill himself, causing the officer to back off. He began a pursuit of the Bronco, however, and was soon joined by many other squad cars and police helicopters, and they were joined by other helicopters from local television stations. The whole chase, seldom reaching high speeds, was played out on live, national television. NBC even diverted coverage from the deciding game of the NBA Finals to cover the pursuit live.

The chase went on for some 50 miles as thousands of spectators thronged its path when it left the freeway and proceeded on surface streets. Many signs and banners could be seen, and some encouraged Simpson, who was a role model to many Americans at the time, to try to get away. The pursuit ended when Cowlings pulled the Bronco into the driveway of Simpson's Brentwood home, and Simpson got out and surrendered to police. Simpson was arrested, charged with the murders, and was placed on suicide watch in the L.A. County Jail. He pleaded not guilty to the crimes. On July 7, a California Superior Court judge ruled there was sufficient evidence to try Simpson for the crimes, and Simpson again pleaded not guilty.

The trial began on January 25, 1995, and it was covered live by the new cable channel Court TV after presiding judge Samuel Ito heard several arguments and motions regarding placement of cameras in the courtroom and ruled there could be just one camera. But the trial was front-page news and occupied center stage on television for its duration. Adding to the color of the event was the "Who's Who" of a defense team that Simpson assembled including Cochran, F. Lee Bailey, and Alan Dershowitz, among others. L.A. County Prosecutor Christopher Darden argued Simpson committed the murders in a fit of jealous rage, while the defense team said he didn't do it and was set up by police fraud, racial bigotry, and sloppy investigative procedures that contaminated the crime scene. A key media moment—especially for television—came when Cochran urged Darden to have Simpson try on the infamous "bloody glove" and its mate found at the crime scene. One glove had been soaked with blood, reacted to the drying process and was otherwise mangled under scientific probing. With the cameras going, Simpson tried to fit the glove on his hand, but they were too small. Cochran used that as a centerpiece of his closing arguments to the jury saying, "If it doesn't fit, you must acquit." Cochran also asserted Simpson was being victimized by the racial bigotry of at least one investigating officer.

Finally, after more than eight months of testimony, fireworks, and internal drama provided by both the defense and prosecuting teams, the jury deliberated for just three hours before returning a verdict of not guilty while more than a 100 million Americans watched the moment live on television. Some of the jurors said later they thought Simpson probably committed the murders, but that the police and prosecution had mangled the case so badly that real evidence was unattainable.[179] Simpson would later lose a civil wrongful death trial filed by the victims' families, who would find getting the monetary judgment from Simpson was no easy matter. But the criminal trial verdict caused white and black Americans to evaluate their concept of justice in America and exposed the issue of how much an issue race and money are when it comes to the findings of guilt and innocence. From a media standpoint, the Simpson trial made media coverage of criminal trials more important than ever as a form of real-life television drama.

Americans saw what many considered poetic justice 13 years to the day after Simpson's acquittal on the double murder charges. On October 3, 2008, Simpson was found guilty of 12 counts involving armed robbery and kidnapping in a Las Vegas hotel as he tried to retrieve sports memorabilia he believed was taken from him unlawfully. Simpson faced the possibility of life in prison for those offenses. That verdict announcement was also heavily covered by the media, but did not match the attention the 1995 verdict received.

89. EXPOSING BIG TOBACCO ABUSES

In large measure, the high-water level of investigative reporting in America that had been reached in the 1972 and 1973 coverage of Watergate had been steadily ebbing over the years in the face of more market-oriented news. This was happening on television and even in newspapers as competition for viewers and readers increased and the public's interest in long, complex stories decreased. The situation, as decried by such frustrated editors as *The Atlanta Constitution's* Bill Kovach (who would leave newspapering to direct the prestigious Nieman Fellows Program at Harvard), seemed dire to many journalists. Some were asking whether any newspaper could launch another Watergate-type investigation without first consulting the marketing department. So when a CBS producer for the acclaimed program *60 Minutes* began digging around in Louisville, smelling smoke that might evidence a serious fire, it was welcome news in the halls of journalism. Perhaps investigative reporting had more life left in it yet.

The situation was this: In 1993, Dr. Jeffrey Wigand, vice president of research and development for Brown & Williamson Tobacco Co., was fired for what he said management described as "poor communication skills." In reality, he was released for objecting to a chemical process called "impact boosting," which had the result of increasing the addictive attraction of cigarettes. The irony of management's "reason" for Wigand's firing was not lost on history. For it was Wigand who communicated the company's abusive practices to CBS producer Lowell Bergman and *60 Minutes* star correspondent Mike Wallace. But the nicotine practice was not limited to Brown & Williamson. It was a process that all of the CEOs of the seven biggest tobacco companies swore to Congress was not happening, although it was. Bergman worked with

Wigand to bring this story to light, an exposé which caused trouble for the fired executive and one for which CBS delayed airing the full Wigand interview for fear of a massive lawsuit from Brown & Williamson.

Ultimately, after other media including the *New York Times* and *Wall Street Journal* printed the story, CBS allowed *60 Minutes* to air the interview in its entirety. Among other reasons for the media significance of this story was the fact it showed the tension—and often competing goals—that media managers have with their news departments. Management, especially at publicly held media companies, are first concerned about the bottom line and shareholders' reactions to it. Journalists are concerned first with exposing wrongful practices. The desire by *60 Minutes* to air a controversial interview with Wigand, which would allege that one of the largest tobacco companies in America was engaged in abusive health practices, was a risk CBS management was unprepared to take. At least initially. Faced with a complicated lawsuit threat by B&W which could potentially cost owners their network, management shelved the story until it became public knowledge by other media. The battle between the news department and CBS corporate management was similar to the battles fought in the early 1950s by journalist Edward R. Murrow against CBS management as he went about exposing Sen. Joseph McCarthy as a fraud out for political gain at the expense of ruining reputations of innocent people.

Fast-forward to 1993, and the same kind of journalistic/management tension was still found at the same network. Today that tension is just as pitched at most of the nation's news media companies. Nevertheless, the coverage of big tobacco company practices in 1993 had a happy ending for journalism. In a larger vein, the coverage may have saved many lives of individual Americans who saw it and decided smoking was not worth it. As a result of this kind of intensive, national coverage by CBS, the *New York Times* and the *Wall Street Journal*, the nation's largest tobacco companies were successfully sued for more than $350 billion by 46 states and were forced to change their marketing campaigns for cigarettes and to fund public service announcements about the dangers of smoking.

*Tobacco whistle blower Jeffery Wigand speaks to the Louisville Forum annual meeting in Jeffersonville, Indiana, Thursday, February 24, 2000. The Oscar-nominated movie,*The Insider *was based on Wigand's fight against the tobacco industry. [AP Photo/ Patti Longmire]*

MIXING NEWS, EMOTION, AND OPINION

American reporters separate fact from opinion as much as possible. Further, most traditionalists believe journalists should not bring their emotions into their reporting. There are times, other journalists insist, that emotions can actually help a journalist capture the spirit of an event or its people, and still other journalists assert that reporters are not robots and cannot possibly distance themselves emotionally from the people and events they cover.

Recent reporting trends, especially on cable television news programs, have shown that this debate is far from over and that some high-profile journalists today are pushing the edge of traditional journalistic approaches. The popularity of individual cable news journalists/commentators like Anderson Cooper, Lou Dobbs, and Bill O'Reilly suggests strongly that more and more Americans are preferring the way cable television does news. And the way that cable is doing that has relevance to the topic of the media's influence on government action. That style, as evidenced by the above-noted cable journalists, is being called various things from "emotional journalism," to "passionate journalism," to "personality journalism," to "opinion journalism," to just flat-out editorializing. One of the obvious differences between cable news programs is that, while network newscasts appear under the names of *NBC Nightly News*, *CBS Evening News*, and ABC's *World News Tonight*, cable news programs are titled for their news personalities. So we have Fox's *Special Report with Britt Hume*, and *Fox Report with Shepard Smith*. CNN has *Lou Dobbs Tonight*, and *Anderson Cooper 360* (also known as *AC 360*) in addition to the many commentary shows featuring everyone from Geraldo Rivera, to Hannity and Colmes, to Bill O'Reilly.

One CNN journalist-commentator is Lou Dobbs, anchor of the nightly *Lou Dobbs Tonight* newscast. Dobbs believes in reporting news as he sees it and is not afraid to comment on the events, as well as report the facts. He once stated in a *New York Times* interview, in fact, that he feels traditional notions of journalistic objectivity are often a "cop-out" and that more journalists should call a lie a lie if that's what facts indicate it is. Dobbs has been extremely outspoken on the issue of Mexican immigration policies and hit the Bush administration hard for not—in his view—tightening the U.S.-Mexican border enough. The following excerpt from Dobbs is indicative of his mixing of commentary and news:

> Reports this week that the Border Patrol is notifying the Mexican government of the locations of Minutemen volunteers are being denied by U.S. Customs and Border Protection. True or not, the Bush administration continues to follow absurd policies on both issues of border security and illegal immigration . . . Only a fool, Mr. President, Sen. Kennedy, Sen. McCain, would believe you when you speak of new legislation. You don't enforce the laws now. Would you do so if the law were more to your
> liking?

While both Dobbs and Cooper anchor nightly CNN programs touted as news shows, O'Reilly's program on the Fox News Channel, *The O'Reilly Factor*, seems more clearly categorized as commentary in a political talk show format. To many Americans, O'Reilly has become the leading conservative news commentator. He may come from the world of more objective reporting (he once led an investigative reporting team at Boston's WNEV-TV), but it is obvious to even casual viewers that his Fox program is opinion and not news.

—Anderson Cooper, *Dispatches from the Edge: A Memoir of War, Disasters, and Survival.* New York: HarperCollins, 2006.
   —"Dobbs's Outspokenness Draws Fans and Fire," Rachel L. Swarns. *New York Times,* February 15, 2006, pp. B1 & B4.
   —"Dobbs: Bush, Congress tell working folk to go to hell," www.cnn.com.

90. THE BIRTH OF THE WORLD WIDE WEB

No single media development has produced greater change in the fabric of American life and the way information is retrieved and processed than the Internet. Many feel its impact and influence dwarf even that of television. Indeed, television viewing is now done by millions of Americans on the Internet. A quick answer to who developed the Internet would focus on one man, Tim Berners-Lee who invented the World Wide Web. Lee was an Oxford engineer who seemed to commit his life to developing, refining and fine-tuning his invention.[180] Lee was working with Swiss associates in a physics lab in 1989 when he came up the web concept because he was having trouble keeping track of all his research notes on myriad computers in different offices. So he proposed a means of making it easier for scientists to look in on what their colleagues were doing. He felt this would advance science faster and farther than ever before. Lee envisioned this web to function something like the human brain does, often by mere associations. So he began work with a trio of software engineers, and the scientists had a prototype of the web in operation within just a few months. He realized that a discovery no one knew about wouldn't help the scientific world much, so he set about promoting and explaining it at scientific conferences around the world. In its simplest form, the Web would be a system—much like a spider web—that would link all information to all other information. And it would be accessible by a simple means of association which became the concept of "keywords."

The means by which this was made possible to all was a relatively simple computer language known as HTML, which stands for "hyptertext markup language." Also needed was a kind of addressing system that would let computers find each other. The idea was that each and every computer contains a unique address or universal resource locator (URL). Berners-Lee also developed a protocol that actually connects computers, and that is what we know as HTTP, or "hypertext transfer protocol."

Taking Berners-Lee's inventions to the next level in 1992 were several top research organizations in Germany, the United States, and the Netherlands, all of whom committed themselves to the Web. Enthusiasm soon grew beyond the scientific community and a key time for the Web's development was an eight-month stretch in 1993 when the Web's use multiplied geometrically some 414 times.[181] Lee decided against entering private industry and cashing in on the many offers that came his way and stayed instead at his MIT academic job, figuring out ways to expand upon the usefulness and ease which the Internet offers to people the world over.

MICHAEL MOORE'S *MOCKUMENTARIES*

If Jon Stewart and Stephen Colbert are making the news of the day more entertaining for television viewing audiences, one could make the case that filmmaker Michael Moore has done the same thing for film-goers. Moore studied journalism at the University of Michigan–Flint and began his career writing for his school newspaper, *The Michigan Times*. He dropped out of college and worked as editor for the liberal *Mother Jones* magazine before trying his hand at making documentaries and using film to make the points traditionally made by journalists in news stories.

In 1989, Moore unveiled what he calls a "muckraking documentary that took General Motors CEO Roger Smith to task for closing a Buick plant and throwing thousands out of work." The film became very popular, especially for a documentary, and used humor and irony to make its points in attacking GM. These would become trademark characteristics of future Moore films which, while humorous at times, nevertheless dealt with deadly serious issues facing the country. In 2002 he released *Bowling for Columbine* which took America to task for being so lax on domestic gun sales and which drew its name from the horrific high school shooting spree in Colorado. Then he set his sights on what he perceived as wrongheaded and excessive reactions by the Bush Administration in the wake of the 9/11 terrorist attacks. The film, *Fahrenheit 9/11* became the highest-grossing documentary of all time. Moore followed that up with *Sicko*, which focused on what Moore saw as a twisted and sickening health care system in America which hurts more patients than it heals.

Clearly, Moore's films have awakened many Americans to issues they might not otherwise have pondered, while infuriating others who have ideological disagreements with his liberal thinking. About his influence on filmmaking, producer and director Carl Deal has said, "Michael's body of work has changed the landscape for all documentary filmmakers. He's kicked open the doors, he's broken the rules. He's made clear that you can actually make a commercially viable documentary film."

Filmmaker Tia Lessin became a disciple of Moore's after seeing *Roger and Me*. "There was no 'Daily Show' back then, no Jon Stewart," she said. "Michael did things on camera no one was doing, said things no one was saying. I was determined to get a job on that show, and by golly I did."

Time Magazine featured Moore on its July 12, 2004, cover with the headline, "Michael Moore's War." The article inside noted, "Taking aim at George W., a populist agitator makes noise, news, and a new kind of political entertainment." The article went on to underscore the popularity and controversial nature of Moore's films and his influence on his audience and disciples in filmmaking.

—"Mike's Books and Films," www.michaelmoore.com.
—"Biography for Michael Moore," www.IMDb.com.
—"Michael Moore approves their messages," by John Flesher, Associated Press, September 9, 2008, www.boston.com.
—"Michael Moore's War," *Time*, July 12, 2004.

Although Berners-Lee can be credited with the invention of the World Wide Web, he would be the first to admit he was only drawing upon a string of inventions and developments that had begun with the 1947 invention of the semiconductor, which then led to digitization and compression of information and graphics. This semiconductor became the basic building block of the technology that finally made the Internet possible. Following the invention of the semiconductor came Web coding and the Netscape browser which widened access to the Internet. The name "Internet," came from the development in 1969 for a U.S. military-created computer network called ARPAnet, short for Advanced Research Projects Agency Network. The network was built by the Pentagon as a means for military contractors and universities carrying out military research to exchange information. Fourteen years later, in 1983, the National Science Foundation took over the project, and the NSF network became, in turn, a connector for thousands of other computer networks. The "Internet" seemed a good name for the mainline system that interconnected networks. Add in some good databases, the first provided by Mead Data Central with its Lexis and Nexis systems, and a growing list of Internet service providers (ISPs) in the 1980s (CompuServ and America Online were the first providers), and you had the ground laid for Berners-Lee's invention of the World Wide Web.

91. THE LAUNCHING OF GOOGLE

A significant phase in the development of the Internet was the launching of what has become the dominant search engine for sites and content on the World Wide Web. That search engine is Google, and it was founded in September 1998, by Larry Page and Sergey Brin. In its first decade, the company had grown to more than 10,000 employees worldwide. Eric Schmidt, former CEO at Novell, joined Google as its chairman and CEO in 2001.

It is ironic that one of the most significant developments in Internet history was founded at a time when the so called "dot.com bubble" was bursting for so many startup companies that misread the Web as a certain way to profits. But as those companies were sinking their money into individual web sites, creating a competitive environment of millions, Page and Brin decided to go in a different direction and develop an *index* to those millions of sites and make it easy for computer users to find information on those sites relevant to key words they would punch into the Google search window. The genius of Google comes not only in the massive database it has created using "crawlers" who roam throughout the Web looking for new and existing sites (and some seven million blogs), but in *rating* the content of those sites as to the relevance of the key words or phrases the user punches into the search window. That rating system is reputed to be one of the most closely held trade secrets in American business.

Page, who moved from the role of founding CEO to president of products in 2001, is a graduate of the University of Michigan where he received a bachelor's degree in computer engineering. He displayed his creative skills while still in college by constructing a working inkjet printer out of Lego bricks. He met his future business partner Sergey Brin while the two were pursuing graduate degrees in computer science at Stanford University.

Brin is a native Russian who studied math and computer science at the University of Maryland, earning a bachelor's degree in those fields. He received a National Science Foundation Graduate Fellowship and went to Stanford where he met Page. Brin had college research interests in search engines and extracting data from unstructured or nontraditional sources. He serves as president for technology at Google.[182]

Google was actually an outgrowth of research done by Page and Brin at Stanford. The two wound up dissecting the structure of the World Wide Web, which had just been created in 1993 by another engineer, Tim Berners-Lee. Page and Brin were looking for a way to get people to the specific content items they were looking for in this informational ocean that the Web had given people access to. As *Wired* magazine has noted, "It was Larry Page and Sergey Brin's attempts to reverse engineer Berners-Lee's World Wide Web that led to Google. The needle that threads these efforts together is citation —the practice of pointing to other people's work in order to build up your own."[183]

Page had done a research project on backlinks, which he called "BackRub," feeling that the Web was structured on a whole system of citations which Berners-Lee called links. He believed if he could develop a system of counting and qualifying each backlink or citation on the Web, then retrieving desired information from this information warehouse would be much easier, and the Web would become a more useful tool for everyday users as well as professional researchers. So Page began designing a "crawler" that could essentially browse the far corners of the Internet and its some 10 million documents (at the time). That is when Brin joined the work, and the two of them realized the project was beyond the scope of a college research effort.

Page began implementing his project in March, 1996. He aimed the crawler at his own Stanford homepage and turned it loose to roam where it would. The crawler quickly began working out from the homepage to other sites. But crawling through the Web and finding links was only part of the plan. To be really helpful, the two researchers would have to develop a system of rating the importance of the sites to the informational cues input by the user. Certainly the number of "hits" to a page link would be helpful in determining the importance of that link, but a more sophisticated ranking system would depend upon applying some complex mathematical analysis, and that's where Brin's mathematical expertise entered in. The result of the collaboration was the Google search system of site ranking where more popular ones would climb to the top of the search list and less popular ones would drop toward the bottom. The researchers saw that their BackRub system worked automatically as a search engine and that it actually produced better results than the existing ones of Excite and AltaVista. Writer John Battelle concluded about the researchers' project, "Not only was the engine good, but Page and Brin realized it would scale as the Web scaled . . . the bigger the Web, the better the engine. That fact inspired the founders to name their new engine Google, after googol, the term for the numeral 1 followed by 100 zeroes. They released the first version of Google on the Stanford Web site in August, 1996—one year after they met."[184]

NOTES

1. http://thinkexist.com/quotes/lincoln_steffens/, as retrieved on August 21,2008.

2. Lincoln Steffens. *The Shame of the Cities*. American Century Series, New York: Hill and Wang, 1957, 19ff.

3. Dennis L. Wilcox and Glen T. Cameron. *Public Relations Strategies and Tactics*, 8th ed. Boston: Allyn & Bacon, 2007, p. 52.

4. "The Sinking of the Titanic, 1912," as retrieved on August 21, 2008. www.eyewitnesstohistory.com.

5. John Tebbel. *The Media in America*. New York: John Y. Crowell, 1974, pp. 357–358.

6. James Pollard. *Presidents and the Press*. Washington, D.C.: Public Affairs Press, 1964, p. 7.

7. Ibid., p. 12.

8. Katharine Q. Seelye. "Another White House Briefing, Another Mutual Day of Mutual Mistrust," *New York Times*, February 27, 2006, C1.

9. Ibid.

10. Louis L. Snyder and Richard B. Morris. *A Treasury of Great Reporting*. New York: Simon & Schuster, 1962, p. 312.

11. Ibid.

12. Ibid.

13. Michael Emery, Edwin Emery, and Nancy L. Roberts. *The Press and America: An Interpretive History of the Mass Media*, 9th ed. Boston: Allyn & Bacon, 2000, p. 254.

14. Ibid.

15. Walter Lippmann. *Public Opinion*. New York: Macmillan, 1922, p. 13.

16. Walton E. Bean. "The Accuracy of Creel Committee News, 1917–1919: An Examination of Cases," *Journalism Quarterly*, XVIII, September 1941, p. 272.

17. Emery, Emery, and Roberts. *Press and America*, p. 256.

18. Paul Starr. *The Creation of the Media*. New York: Basic Books, 2004, p. 278.

19. George Creel. *How We Advertised America*. New York: Harper & Brothers, 1920, p. 3.

20. http://jeff560.tripod.com/first/html. Retrieved on August 22, 2008

21. http://www.kdkaradio.com/pages/15486.php. Retrieved on August 22, 2008.

22. Gerald Tyne. *Saga of the Vacuum Tube*. New York: Ziff Publishing, 1943.

23. "Company Overview," NBC Universal, as retrieved on August 23, 2008, www.nbc.com on November 10, 2008.

24. "Mary White," *The Emporia Gazette*, May 17, 1921, www.journalism.ku.edu.

25. "The Prince of Publishing: The Early Years of Henry R. Luce," http://www.evancarmichael.com/Famous-Entrepreneurs/1955/The-Prince-of-Publishing-The-Early-Years-of-Henry-R-Luce-html.

26. Time, Inc. "About Us," http://www.timeinc.com/aboutus/. Retrieved on August 23, 2008.

27. National Broadcasting Company, Museum of Broadcast Communications, as retrieved on August 25,2008,http://www.museum.tv/archives/etv/N/htmlN/nationalbroa/nationalbroa/htm.

28. Ibid.

29. "Corporate Info," National Broadcasting Company, as retrieved on August 26, 2008,http://www.nbc.com/nbc/header/Corporate_Infos.html.

30. Barry Mishkind. "CBS Section of the Broadcast Archive," as retrieved on August 26, 2008,http://www.oldradio.com/archives/prog/cbs.htm.

31. Ibid.

32. Robert Clark Young. "The Richest Girl in the World," *The Southern Humanities Review*, Spring 2005, Auburn University Southern Humanities Council.

33. Tebbel. *Media in America*, pp. 332 & 334.

34. Ibid.

35. Ralph G. Martin. *Cissy*. New York City: Simon & Schuster, 1979.

36. Richard J. Hand. *Terror on the Air! Horror Radio in America*. Jefferson, NC: McFarlane & Co., 2006, p. 7.

37. M. R. Montgomery. "Reporting on the Third Reich," *Boston Globe Magazine*, January 20, 1983, pp. 11–13.

38. Ibid.

39. Ibid.

40. Ibid.

41. Deborah E. Lipstadt. *Beyond Belief: The American Press and the Coming of the Holocaust*. New York: Free Press, 1986.

42. Montgomery. *Boston Globe Magazine*, p. 13.

43. Emery, Emery, and Roberts. *Press and America*, p. 340.

44. Ibid.

45. Erik Barnouw. *The Golden Web*. New York: Oxford University Press, 1968, p. 151.

46. A. M. Sperber. *Murrow: His Life and Times*. New York: Bantam Books, 1987, p. 174.

47. Ibid.

48. Ibid., p. 184.

49. "Reporting America at War," PBS, www.pbs.org. Retrieved on September 1, 2008.

50. Ernie Pyle. "Killing Is All That Matters," one of Pyle's stories archived in the Indiana University School of Journalism, Bloomington, Indiana, as retrieved on September 2, 2008,http://journalism.indiana.edu/resources/erniepyle/wartime-columns.

51. "Oral History: Iwo Jima Flag Raising," adapted from a John Bradley interview in Box 3 of World War II Interviews, Operational Archives Branch, Naval Historical Center, http://www.ehistory.osu.edu/osu/sources/oral/oralview.cfm?oralid=5 as retrieved on September 5, 2008.

52. "Newspapers: The *Chicago Defender*," as retreived on September 5, 2008, http://www.pbs.org/blackpress/news_bios/defender.html.

53. Douglas Martin. "John H. Johnson, 87 Founder of Ebony, Dies," *New York Times*, August 9, 2005, as retrieved on September 5, 2008, http://www.nytimes.com/2005/08/09/business/media/09 johnson.html. As retrieved on September 7, 2008.

54. Ibid.

55. "About Us," EbonyJet.com, as retrieved on September 7, 2008, http://www
.ebonyjet.com/general.aspx?logoid=484&contentid=308.

56. Martin. *Cissy*, 1979.

57. "John H. Johnson," *ChickenBones: A Journal for Literary & Artistic African-American Themes*, as retrieved on September 9, 2008, http://www.nathanielturner
.com/johnhjohnson.htm.

58. P. Zimbado. "Laugh Where We Must, Be Candid Where We Can," *Psychology Today*, 1985, as retrieved on September 9, 2008, http://www.museum.tv/archives/
etv/C/htmlC/candidcamera/candidcamera.htm.

59. Amy Loomis. "Candid Camera," The Museum of Broadcast Communication,
as retrieved on September 10, 2008,http://www.museum.tv/archives/etv/C/htmlC/
candidcamera/candidcamera.htm.

60. A. Funt. *Eavesdropping at Large: Adventures in Human Nature with Candid Mike and Candid Camera*. New York: Vanguard Press, 1952.

61. Nancy Gibbs and Michael Duffy. *The Preacher and the Presidents: Billy Graham in the White House*. New York: Center Street, 2007.

62. Emery, Emery, and Roberts. *Press and America*, p. 275.

63. Michael Jay Friedman. "Edward R. Murrow: Journalism at Its Best,"
as retrieved on September 12, 2008,http://usinfo.state.gov/products/pubs/murrow/
friedman.

64. Katie Couric. "Remembering Milo Radulovich," *CBS Evening News*,
November 20, 2007.

65. Ibid.

66. Friedman. "Journalism at Its Best."

67. "The Living Room Candidate," www.livingroomcandidate.org.

68. "Presidential Nominating Conventions and Television," Museum of Broadcast Communication, http://www.museum.tv/archives/etv/P/htmlP/presidential/
presidential.htm.

69. "The Living Room Candidate," www.livingroomcandidate.org.

70. http://www.richsamuels.com/nbcmm/.

71. Ibid.

72. "About 'Today,'" http://www.msnbc.com/id/29055142. Retrieved on September 14, 2008.

73. Christian Smith. *American Evangelicalism: Embattled and Thriving*. Chicago, IL: University of Chicago Press, 1998.

74. "Franklin Graham Criticizes Film about His Dad," August (Web Only) 2008,
Christianity Today, as retrieved on September 20, 2008, www.Christianitytoday.com.

75. "Quiz Show Scandals," The Museum of Broadcast Communications, as
retrieved on September 20, 2008www.museum.tv/archives/etv/q/htmlq/.../
quizshowsca.html.

76. "American Experience: The Quiz Show Scandal," as retrieved on September 22, 2008, www.pbs.org.

77. Stone, Joseph. *Prime-time and Misdemeanors: Investigating the 1950s TV Quiz Scandal: A D.A.'s Account*. New Brunswick, N.J.: Rutgers University Press, 1992.

78. "Quiz Show Scandals," as retrieved Septbember 22, 2008, www.museum.tv/ archives.

79. Anderson, Ken. *Television Fraud: The History and Implications of the Quiz Show Scandals*. Westport, Conn: Greenwood, 1978.

80. Tom Wolfe. *The Right Stuff*. New York: Bantam, 2001.

81. *The Man Who Shot Liberty Valence*. Warner Brothers, 1965.

82. "American Masters: Truman Capote," as retrieved on September 25, 2008, www.pbs.org/wnet/americanmasters/...trumancapote/.../58/.

83. *New York Times*, November 16, 1959.

84. Truman Capote. *In Cold Blood*. New York: Vintage, 1994.

85. "The Kennedy-Nixon Presidential Debates, 1960," The Museum of Broadcast Communications, as retrieved on September 27, 2008, www.museum.tv/archives/ etv/k/htmlk/kennedy-nixon/kennedy-nixon.htm.

86. Ibid.

87. Ibid.

88. Emery, Emery, and Roberts. *Press and America*, p. 396.

89. *New York Times*, Page 1A, October 23, 1962.

90. Ibid., October 24, 1962.

91. Fergus Fleming. *The Cuban Missile Crisis: To the Brink of World War III*. Chicago: Reed Publishing, 2001, pp. 4–20.

92. Ibid.

93. Albert Auster. "Walter Cronkite: U.S. Broadcast Journalist," The Museum of Broadcast Communications, as retrieved on September 29, 2008, http://www .museum.tv/archives/etv/C/htmlC/cronkitewal/cronkitewal.htm.

94. Arthur Unger. " 'Uncle Walter' and the 'Information Crisis," *Television Quarterly*, Winter 1990.

95. Richard F. Snow. "He was There," *American Heritage*, December 1994.

96. Jim Redmond, interview with author, August 20, 2007.

97. *Journal of Broadcasting and Electronic Media*, September 1, 2007.

98. Lou Prato. "Don't Bash Consultants for Tabloid TV News," *American Journalism Review*, November 1993, as retrieved on September 30, 2008, www .ajr.org.

99. "Assassination and Funeral of President John F. Kennedy," Museum of Broadcast Communication, as retrieved on October 1, 2008, http://www.museum.tv/ archives/etv/K/htmlK/kennedyjf/kennedyjf.htm.

100. Lauren Kessler. *The Dissident Press: Alternative Journalism in American History*. Beverly Hills, Calif.: Sage, 1984, p. 158.

101. Laird B. Anderson. "FOIA Founder Looks at Law Today," 1988–89 Society of Professional Journalists FOI Report, p. 13.

102. Ibid.

103. Ibid.

104. "George Plimpton, Urbane and Witty Writer, Dies as 76," *New York Times*, September 26, 2003, retrieved on October 3, 2008, http://newyorktimes.com.

105. Jon Fine. "An In Depth Interview with Jann Wenner," a "Fine on Media" blog by Jon Fine of Business Week, as retrieved on October 3, 2008, http://www.businessweek.com/innovate/FineOnMedia/archives/2007/11/an_in-depth_int.html.

106. Timothy L. O'Brien. "Will You Still Need Me, Will You Still Read Me?" *New York Times*, 3:1, December 25, 2005.

107. Ibid., 3:4.

108. "Wars and Battles: Tet Offensive, 1968," http://www.u-s-history.com/pages/h1862.html.

109. *CBS Evening News* transcript, February 27, 1968.

110. Dennis Simon. "The War in Vietnam, 1965–1968," http://faculty.smu.edu/dsimon/change-viet2.html.

111. Don Hewitt, in an interview on NBC with Bob Costas, 1989.

112. Frank Coffey. *60 Minutes: 35 Years of Television's Finest Hour.* Los Angeles: General Publishing Group, 1993.

113. Don Hewitt. *Minute by Minute.* New York: Random House, 1985.

114. "Pentagon Papers: Federal Government, American Constitutional Crisis," as retrieved on October 5, 2008, www.u-s-History.com.

115. Ibid.

116. Thomas S. Blanton, ed. "The Pentagon Papers: Secrets, Lies and Audiotapes," National Security Archive Electronic Briefing Book Number 48, as retrieved on October 7, 2008, posted online June 5, 2001, at www.gw.edu/~nsarchiv/NSAEBB/NSAEBB48.

117. "Supreme Court, 6–3, Upholds Newspapers on Publication of Pentagon Report," Special to the *New York Times*, Thursday, July 1, 1971, as retrieved on October 10, 2008, www.nytimes.com/books/97/04/13/reviews/papers final.html.

118. Jane Johnson Lewis. "Ms. Magazine," as retrieved on October 11, 2008, http://womenshistory.about.com/cs/periodicals/p/p_ms_magazine.htm.

119. Bob Woodward and Carl Bernstein. *All the President's Men.* New York: Simon & Schuster, 1994.

120. Ibid.

121. Adam Woog. *Bill Gates.* San Diego: Lucent Books, 1999, p. 7.

122. Ibid., p. 9.

123. Ibid., p. 45.

124. Lauren Lee. *Trailblazers of the Modern World: Bill Gates.* Milwaukee, Wisc: World Almanac Library, 2002.

125. Don Hewitt, in an interview on NBC with Bob Costas, 1989.

126. Douglass K. Daniel. *A Life in the News: Harry Reasoner.* Austin: University of Texas Press, 2007, pp. 172–173.

127. Ibid., pp. 174–175.

128. ESPN, Inc.: Company History, as retrieved on October 13, 2008, on www.espn.go.com.

129. Ibid.

130. AMPEX Corporation. "Corporate Background," as retrieved on October 13, 2008, on www.ampex.com/03corp.html.

131. "Daily NBC Show Will be on Tape," *New York Times*, January 18, 1957, p. 31.

132. Sterling Head et al. *Broadcasting in America: A Survey of Electronic Media*, 8th ed. Boston: Houghton Mifflin, 1998, p. 133.

133. *Broadcast News*. 20th Century Fox, 1987.

134. "The Hostage Crisis in Iran," The Jimmy Carter Library and Museum, as retrieved on October 19, 2008, http://www.jimmycarterlibrary.org/documents/hostages/phtml.

135. "Nightline," WCHS ABC 8, as retrieved on October 16, 2008, http://www.wchstv.com/abc/nightline.

136. Paul J. Gough. "Leno Move Good for 'Nightline'," December 9, 2008, as retrieved on October 17, 2008, on THR.com Television, http://www.hollywoodreporter.com.

137. Ibid.

138. Janet Cooke. "Jimmy's World," *The Washington Post*, September 28, 1980, A1.

139. "The Story That Shocked the Nation's Capital," *U.S. News & World Report*, October 13, 1981.

140. "Stephen Glass: I Lied for Esteem," CBS News, *60 Minutes*, August 17, 2003, as retrieved on October 17, 2008, http://www.cbsnews.com/stories/2003/05/07/60minutes/main552819.shtml.

141. Ibid.

142. "Correcting the Record: Times Reporter Who Resigned Leaves Long Trail of Deception," *New York Times*, May 11, 2003, as retrieved on October 18, 2008, www.nytimes.com.

143. Ibid.

144. Ibid.

145. "Corporate History," Turner, a Time/Warner Company, as retrieved on November 27, 2008, on http://turner.com/about/corporate_history.html.

146. "The State of the News Media 2008: Audience." Project for Excellence in Journalism as retrieved on November 27, 2008, http://www.stateofthenewsmedia.org/2008/.

147. "The CNN Effect: How 24-Hour News and Coverage Affects Government Decisions and Public Opinion," A Brookings/Harvard Forum, as retrieved on November 27, 2008, on http://www.brookings.edu/events/2002/0123media—journalism.aspx.

148. "Music Television," The Museum of Broadcast Communications, as retrieved on November 28, 2008, http://www.museum.tv/archives/etv/M/htmlM/musictelevisi/musictelevis.htm.

149. Serge R. Denisoff. *Inside MTV*. New Brunswick, NJ: Rutgers University Press, 1988.

150. Lisa A. Lewis. *Gender Politics and MTV: Voicing the Difference*. Philadelphia: Temple University Press, 1990.

151. Pew Research Center for the People and the Press. *Cable and internet loom large in fragmented politically news universe*, 2004. Retrieved on November 28, 2008, from http://people-press.org/reports.

152. Dr. Geoffrey Baym. "Political News for the Hip-Hop Generation: MTV and the 2004 Presidential Election," pp. 3–4, presented to the NCA Central States Regional Convention in April 2006, Indianapolis, Indiana.

153. "MTV's Choose or Lose Taps Local Reporters to Cover Presidential Election," December 20, 2007, as retrieved on November 29, 2008, http://www.mtv.com/news/articals/1576844/20071219/id_0.jhtml.

154. "Top 100 Newspapers in the United States," Infoplease as retrieved on November 29, 2008, www.infoplease.com.

155. David Bauder. "Fox Wins TV Season on Strong 'Idol' Finish," Associated Press, May 23, 2007, as retrieved on November 30, 2008, www.breitbard.com.

156. Daniel Kimmel. *The Fourth Network: How Fox Broke the Rules and Reinvented Television*. New York: Ivan Dee, 2004.

157. William Harwood. "Astronaut Fatalities, Spaceflight Now," as retrieved on November 30, 2008, http://spaceflightnow.com/shuttle/sts114/fdf/fatalities.html.

158. "Fatal Events Involving NASA Astronauts," as retrieved on November 30, 2008, http://www.airsafe.com/events/space/astrofat.htm.

159. William Boot. "NASA and the Spellbound Press," *Columbia Journalism Review*, July/August 1986, p. 24.

160. Ibid., p. 26.

161. Ibid.

162. Ibid.

163. "The Public Mind: The Truth about Lies," PBS, November 1989.

164. Boot. "NASA and the Spellbound Press," p. 24.

165. Jim Willis and Simone Notter. "Fall of the Wall Celebrated in Berlin," *The Oklahoman*, November 10, 1989. p. 1A.

166. *Nightline*, ABC, November 10, 1989.

167. "The Wall Comes Down: 1989," CNN as retrieved on December 2, 2008, www.cnn.com/SPECIAL/cold.war/episodes/23/.

168. Margaret Carlson. "Presumed Innocent," *Time*, January 22, 1990, p. 10.

169. *Nightline*, ABC, January 22, 1990.

170. Ellis Cose. "Turning Victims into Saints," *Time*, January 22, 1990.

171. *Nightline*, ABC, January 22, 1990.

172. "New Study Sought on Boston Murder Case," Associated Press, February 10, 1990.

173. William A. Henry III. "NBC Goes BOOM!" February 22, 1993, as retrieved on December 3, 2008, http://whatreallyhappened.com.

174. Mortimer R. Feinberg and John J. Tarrant. *Why Smart People Do Dumb Things*. New York: Simon & Schuster, 1995, pp. 157–158.

175. *In Their Name: Oklahoma City: The Official Commemorative Volume*. New York: Random House, 1995, pp. 34–35.

176. Ed Kelley, comments to the seminar, "Understanding and Reporting the Disaster Scene," November 8, 1995, the University of Memphis, Memphis, Tennessee.

177. Jim Willis. "Journalists Heal Wounds During Bombing," *Edmond Evening Sun*, April 19, 1985, p. 5.

178. "O. J. Simpson Trial News: The Suicide Note," CNN, retrieved on www.cnn.com, August 29, 2008.

179. "Jurors Say Evidence Made the Case for Simpson," CNN, October 4, 1995, as retrieved on November 25, 2008, www.cnn.com.

180. John Vivian. *The Media of Mass Communication*, 9th ed. Needham Heights, Mass: Allyn & Bacon, 2009, p. 239.

181. Ibid.

182. Google Corporation Information, retrieved from www.google.com.

183. John Battelle. "The Birth of Google," August 2005, as retrieved on December 4, 2008, www.wired.com.

184. Ibid.

Part IV

The 21st Century: 2000–2009

The first decade of the 21st century produced some startling developments for America and the media, starting with the tragic and devastating losses suffered in 9/11 and ending with the nationwide government-mandated shift from analog to digital broadcasting. If these first few years are indicative of the changes to come, then the rest of the 21st century should be a century of revolutions in the way America receives and processes information and in the very way individual Americans get to know each other and communicate with each other. The 21st century is the era of media convergence where all the different media formats discussed thus far have come together in all-encompassing online formats.

92. 9/11

When that first airplane hit the first of the Twin Towers in New York City on the morning of September 11, 2001, America looked to the media for understanding. But by the time the second plane hit and the towers crumbled, the media had a story on its hands that, for a time, seemed just too big and too hard to get its arms around. Part of the reason for that was the emotional weight involved in covering the worst act of terrorism ever experienced on American soil. In attacks on the Twin Towers, on the Pentagon in Washington, D.C., and on Flight 93, nearly 3,000 people lost their lives while going about their daily tasks. The attackers were members of the international terror network Al Qaeda, and the pain they inflicted on America was felt, then articulated, by the nation's journalists. That journalists are not immune from emotional punches is a fact brought home loud and clear by the attacks of 9/11, so it made this story a textbook case of how journalists need to fight off—or at least fight through—their own emotions to tell a story factually and comprehensively.

The south tower begins to collapse as smoke billows from both towers of the World Trade Center in New York, in this September 11, 2001, file photo. In one of the most horrifying attacks ever against the United States, terrorists crashed two airliners into the World Trade Center in a deadly series of blows that brought down the 110-story Twin Towers. [AP Photo/Jim Collins/ FILE]

It seems fitting to note what a few writers have had to say about the role emotions play in their work. Joan Didion once said, "I write entirely to find out what I'm feeling." In their more introspective moments, many journalists would probably utter the same statement. E. M. Forester, author of *A Passage to India* once asked, "How can I know what I think until I see what I say?" Again, most journalists would agree, especially after the events of 9/11. As Henry David Thoreau chided, "How vain it is to sit down to write when you have not stood up to live." All of these statements suggest strongly that there is a vital connection between a journalist's emotions and personal life experiences and the work that they do in reflecting reality for their readers and viewers.

One *New York Times* journalist, Katherine E. Finkelstein, described how an event like the attacks on the Twin Towers cannot help but be felt by any writer, especially one such as she who experienced it first hand:

> I fought against the tide of employees, past one rescue command center and down to the entrance of the north tower, where the dust and paper storm felt thicker. I was feet from the door through which employees were being evacuated. The sunlight was gone, the air thick with ash. People waiting to leave were backed up the stairwell in what looked like an endless line. It is hard to say what I heard or saw first. A low and ominous rumble, in a split second turning into a roar. A vast black cloud forming at the top of the south tower, then sinking quickly as though the building were made of fabric, not steel. People yelled out, "It's going to go!" . . . I am running for my life up a street I have known all my life, being chased by a building.[1]

Among the normally stoic television journalists who showed emotional strains on the air was the late Peter Jennings of ABC's *World News Tonight*. Anchoring live coverage of the Twin Towers attack as the buildings began crumbling, Jennings said:

> We do not often make recommendations for people's behavior from this chair but as (Lisa) Stark was talking, I checked in with my children . . . who are deeply distressed, as I think most young people are across the United States. So if you're a parent, you've got a kid . . . in some other part of the country, call them up. Exchange observations.[2]

As in other moments of national crisis, most notably the 1963 assassination of President John F. Kennedy, the nation's news media served to put all Americans on the same page of mourning and unity. The coverage of the 9/11 tragedies provided the media another huge opportunity to do that again, and most journalists carried out that responsibility very well. This moment also served to get journalists talking to one another around America about how best to handle their own personal emotions when covering important news stories.

93. EMBEDDING WAR REPORTERS

Probably the most significant effect on journalism produced by the Vietnam War was the change in rules by the military on how journalists could cover wars involving U.S. troops. Having come through America's first "living room war" in which reporters roamed the battlefields at will showing all its carnage, the government cracked down on war correspondents in subsequent American military actions. The Nixon administration realized how difficult it was to conduct a prolonged war without the support of public opinion, and it felt the constant TV images of American soldiers dead and dying produced that lack of public support.

So it was when American troops would later go ashore in the invasion of Grenada, and when U.S. troops were sent into Panama against general Manuel Noriega, journalists were kept at arm's length from the fighting. They were required to get their news from military briefings and to be ushered in pools to the battlefronts *after* the battles were over. When American troops were sent to Kuwait and Iraq in 1991 for the first Gulf War, a variation of the pool system remained in effect with journalistic access kept at arm's length and closely monitored by many public affairs officers. After the war, the clamor among journalists was so loud that the military decided to revise its rules of coverage when the second Gulf War was launched in 2003. It was determined that selected reporters would be allowed to be "embedded" with frontline American troops. Perhaps the military realized that, in a digital age, it would be even harder to keep journalists at arm's length from the fighting. In any event, the Pentagon's director of media relations Victoria Clarke sent out invitations to major media to send reporters to specially designed courses for war correspondents. These mini-courses were set up to orient reporters to combat situations. A part of the course was also to test the actual physical readiness of these correspondents to go into combat. The so-called "embed system" was born, and it would generally prove to be a win-win scenario for both the military and the media.

As a result of the embed system, the Iraq War would receive coverage unlike any other since Vietnam. In fact, it received better coverage thanks to the satellite communication technology that allowed much of it to be covered live, or for video to be released to the public shortly after the battles. The news organizations were required to outfit their reporters with equipment and vehicles but, in return, the correspondents could tell the battlefield news as they perceived it. The media were elated and took full advantage of Clarke's invitation, and hundreds of journalists went to the reporters' boot camps. Major news organizations spared no expense in outfitting their troops, and Time Warner, which owns CNN, committed some $30 million to cover the war, going so far as to buy a fleet of Humvees for its correspondents.[3]

The results proved good, and journalists acquitted themselves well both in covering the action and in following what few ground rules existed. Among those rules were that they not disclose positions of American coalition units. The embed coverage produced a sharper image of this war than the first Gulf War, and it also put a more human face on it, since journalists were embedded with individual soldiers with frontline units. The Pentagon was pleased because the strategy and fighting was going well on its side, and they were willing to put up with the sometimes graphic images showing American blood

DANGER ZONES FOR JOURNALISTS

The Committee to Protect Journalists keeps track every year of the number of journalistic casualties in wars and conflicts. In its December 18, 2008 report, the CPJ noted that—for the sixth straight year—Iraq was the deadliest country in the world for the press. A total of 11 deaths of journalists was reported in Iraq in 2008. That number dropped sharply from the record of 32 journalists killed there in each of 2006 and 2007. The committee noted, "The decline in media deaths is consistent with an overall improvement in security conditions in Iraq."

All of those killed in Iraq in 2008 were local journalists who worked for Iraqi news outlets. In addition, two media support workers died during the year in Iraq. Since the war began in March 2003, some 136 journalists and 51 media workers have died while working there, and it has become the deadliest killing field for journalists in recent history.

The CPJ also reported that conflicts in Pakistan, Afghanistan, Sri Lanka, and India together claimed 13 journalists. Worldwide, wars and conflicts claimed the lives of 41 journalists as they went about reporting the news.

American journalist Daniel Pearl, whose story was made into a film called *A Mighty Heart*, was the best-known American journalist who died in modern conflicts related to the war on terrorists. A *Wall Street Journal* bureau chief following news leads or terrorists in Pakistan, Pearl was kidnapped and murdered by terrorists there in 2002.

In August 2005, American reporter Steven Vincent and his translator Nour Alkhai were covering sectarian violence when they were kidnapped by the same people they were reporting on. The kidnappers shot Vincent dead, making him the first U.S. journalist murdered in Iraq. His translator was shot three times, but she survived the experience. Vincent had written several stories on the war in Iraq for publications such as the *Christian Science Monitor*, the *New York Times*, and the *National Review*.

Two other American journalists suffered near-death experiences while covering the war in Iraq, while a soundman and cameraman with one of them were not so lucky. CBS reporter Kimberly Dozier was severely injured in an Iraqi car bombing that killed her soundman James Brolan and cameraman Paul Douglas in 2005. Dozier suffered severe injuries to her lower body in the attack and spent several months in recovery. In 2006, ABC reporter and anchor Bob Woodruff and his cameraman Doug Vogt were severely injured when their convoy was attacked near Taji, Iraq, about 12 miles north of Baghdad. Both Woodruff and Vogt suffered shrapnel wounds, and Woodruff required extensive reconstructive surgery to his head as he came close to death. Both men eventually recovered, and both Woodruff and Dozier have returned to their respective networks and continue to report on the effects of the wars in Iraq and Afghanistan.

—"For sixth straight year, Iraq deadliest nation for press," Committee to Protect Journalists, www.cpj.org/reports/2008.

—"Casualties of War," *NOW on PBS*, http://www.pbs.org/now/shows/318/index.html.

being spilled on the battlefield. The military knew the actual invasion of Iraq and the drive to Baghdad would be swift, and their feedback also showed the American public perceived the reporting as more honest and less manipulated by the government. Journalists were happy because they could verify information by way of eyewitness reporting instead of relying on secondhand briefings interpreted by military public affairs officers. There were some critics in the press, however, who felt that the close relationships that developed between the embedded journalists and the soldiers might detract from normal journalistic objectivity. Others in the media perceived some of these critiques as jealousies coming from journalists who were not selected for frontline action.

94. THE FOUNDING OF FACEBOOK

Once the Internet found its critical mass of users in the late 19th century, a flurry of developments which would change the media—and the way we use it—arose at warp speed. Since 1998 alone the world has seen the birth of Google, the immense popularity of blogs (Google covers some 17 million of them on the Web), and the founding of two popular sites where individuals can share themselves with the world and connect with friends with whom they have lost contact over the years. One of those sites is MySpace, and the other more recent development targeted initially at college students, is Facebook. The two are similar in concept, but Facebook is unique in several respects.

For one thing, it was created in 2004 by a 19-year-old computer programming whiz and Harvard dropout named Mark Zuckerberg. Within four years, the site's popularity had grown to 60 million users with 200 million users estimated within five more years. In 2008, the company's estimated worth was $15 billion.[4] Zuckerberg created the site as a means for Harvard students to message each other online and, within four months, expanded it to 40 other colleges and universities around the country. Essentially, Facebook allows users to set up their own profile page featuring pictures and information about themselves and their interests, and privacy settings allow users to keep some people, like parents or employers, from seeing the user's site. It also serves as a worldwide people-finding system. Once you post a page on Facebook, your name goes on an online user directory. Although people not on your select list can't see your page, they can e-mail you and ask if you would like to chat with them. So it becomes both a way to connect with long-lost friends, especially in a day where there are no universal cell phone or e-mail directories, as well as a way to meet new friends, too.

In this February 5, 2007 file photo, Facebook CEO Mark Zuckerberg poses at his office in Palo Alto, California. Zuckerberg has been dubbed by some, the "toddler CEO." [AP Photo/Paul Sakuma, file]

By 2008, Facebook employed some 400 people in its Palo Alto headquarters, and the 23-year-old Zuckerberg ran the show. Dubbed by some as the "toddler CEO," Zuckerberg oversees a workplace filled with young software engineers who come early, stay late, and party even later, right in the office. In many respects, it resembles a typical office setting of a large student government association suite at a big state university.[5]

Facebook and localized versions of it have also caused some of its users problems, however, as the youthful urge for students to self-disclose about their private—and/or unbridled—sides has spelled trouble for some. Whether students have been careless about setting the site's privacy levels, or whether those settings have been ignored altogether, some students have found themselves in trouble with their colleges. In one case, a 19-year-old student at a Midwestern private college was denied the opportunity to serve as an editor for the student newspaper because he had posted pictures on Facebook of him getting drunk at a party. The page came to the attention of the student affairs office, and the university had a policy of banning students from leadership positions if they engaged in underage drinking. In another situation, on a profile page like Facebook's, a student revealed the fact he was gay. The problem was he was attending a conservative religious college in the South that would not accept gay students and, despite the fact he had a solid grade point average, he was expelled from the college.

As a social networking site, especially for younger users, Facebook is without peer, and it is turning the attention of 20-something users away from other media forms as they spend more and more time interacting with their friends, making new ones, and reconnecting with old ones around the world. It has also become a popular way for students to play games—Scrabble is big—with each other online. In some respects Facebook has become the news medium of choice for younger Americans, and people often hear about news events for the first time on the site. Because the news is filtered through so many people, the accuracy of the information often varies in degree. In 2009, a rival of Facebook offering users short-burst messages was becoming very popular. This rival is Twitter, and a linkage is offered between messages appearing on each service.

95. HURRICANE KATRINA

As the month of August drew to a close in 2005, residents of the Gulf Coast wondered if they would make it through this hurricane season without a major storm. Tragically, they would not as August 28 would bring the most devastating hurricane—in terms of economic losses—to hit the United States. It was the sixth strongest hurricane in recorded history. Some 1,800 people lost their lives and more than $81 billion in property damages were sustained. As tragic as the death count was, it did not match the Galveston Hurricane of 1900 which killed as many as 12,000 people.[6] But no one would have thought that 105 years later, such human losses could have occurred in a digital age of early-warning systems, improvements in levy construction, and sophisticated procedures of agencies like the Federal Emergency Management Association (FEMA). Nevertheless, the tragedy occurred and death tolls mounted as the winds caused Gulf surges that broke through levies and dams, flooding the city of New Orleans and other areas along the coast.

Residents of the area would come to refer to the "storm" and the "flood" as if they were separate events which, although related, they were.

As a major media story, Katrina presented more than its share of challenges. Since the City of New Orleans was flooded, entry into the area by reporters or anyone else was extremely difficult. The region's major daily newspaper, the *Times-Picayune*, lost all electrical power and had to be evacuated like every other business in New Orleans. But many committed journalists remained behind, risking their lives to get the story out with the help of area newspapers that continued to print the New Orleans daily. The memories of one reporter who stayed behind were especially vivid when he wrote:

> As Katrina took aim at New Orleans, I assumed I would remain cool and professional whatever the toll. After all, I was hurricane-hardened. I had chased several, including Andrew when it slammed Franklin, Louisiana, in 1992. But as Katrina's epic tragedy unfolded, I was gradually overwhelmed by my city's descent into apocalypse: the freight-train roar of the wind, the insidious and unstoppable rising water; the haze of unchecked fires, widespread looting, and lawlessness; the masses of desperate evacuees; and finally, death, depopulation, and military takeover. Instinct and journalistic experience carried me for that harrowing, exhausting, but intensely wired first week, when it actually seemed plausible that my home for the past 20 years would become the next Atlantis.[7]

Night after night, some television news reports showed graphic images of dead bodies still floating in the streets that chilled viewers not used to the idea that this sort of devastation—and seemingly slow government response—could be occurring in the 21st century United States. Many journalists became angry at the scene, and some brought that anger into their reporting. One such reporter was CNN's Anderson Cooper who would later tell that network's Larry King that he wanted to hold politicians accountable when what he saw in the flooded New Orleans streets belied the progress the optimism the politicians were conveying to the public.[8] In one memorable interview, Cooper interrupted Louisiana Sen. Mary Landreau as she was praising fellow legislators for their response to the tragedy. "Excuse me, Senator," Cooper interrupted, "but I just saw a body float by minutes ago," and then proceeded to say that —from what he saw—the response the senator was praising just was not occurring. "Do you get the anger that these people are feeling?" Cooper demanded. Cooper represented the kind of journalist who seemed to take the tragedy personally and even told King he "made a promise" to the people of New Orleans not to leave until the ordeal was over and help was received.[9] These journalists seemed to become the voice of those in need, and that become a point of argument among journalists who believe reporters should not take sides in stories. To journalists like Cooper, however, they were just trying to report the story as they saw it.

As a result of the graphic nightly coverage of the hurricane, the size of its devastation, and the public outcry that ensued, several Congressional and executive agency probes were targeted at the failure of the area levies, the evacuation plans that resulted in thousands of people trapped in New Orleans and unable to get out, and the slow

ANDERSON COOPER'S JOURNEY

No journalist comes to reporting in exactly the same way, although many are driven by the same four motivations of the love of reading, the love of writing, an insatiable curiosity about how the world works, and a desire to make a difference in that world. While those motivations were also at work in CNN's Anderson Cooper, his path to the world of television journalism was unique. First you'd have to start with the fact Cooper comes from the family of Vanderbilts. His mother is Gloria Vanderbilt, so Cooper's rise to fame was not the story of a guy who overcame the hardships of life from the other side of the tracks.

A Yale graduate, Cooper armed himself with a video camera and set out for the hot spots of the world as a freelancer. The hotter the better, he reasoned, because competition there would probably be less extreme.

But there was something else propelling him to these war zones, and the man who lived through his brother's suicide and his father's death at an early age, writes of it in his book, *Dispatches from the Edge.* "I wanted to be someplace where emotions were palpable, where the pain outside matched the pain I felt inside. I needed balance, equilibrium, or as close to it as I could get. I also wanted to survive, and I thought I could learn from others who had. War seemed like my only option."

In another passage, he writes, "I sometimes believe it's motion that keeps me alive as well. I hit the ground running; truck gassed up, camera rolling—'locked and loaded, ready to rock,' as a soldier in Iraq once said to me. There's nothing like that feeling. You run toward what everyone else is running from . . . All you want to do is get it, feel it, be in it. The images frame themselves sometimes, the action flows right through you . . . the more I saw, the more I needed to see."

Reporting from war zones, flood zones, and providing signature coverage from Hurricane Katrina and her aftermath in New Orleans and along the Gulf Coast, Cooper seems to have seen it all, although he would probably say there is more needing to be witnessed ahead. He began shooting trauma and tragedy while dodging bullets in places like Kosovo, and his footage got noticed by Channel One, the news program beamed into secondary schools around the country. That led to greater exposure for him, and before long the big television networks took note. Cooper first landed at ABC and later joined CNN in December, 2001, as the network's weekend anchor before moving to prime time in 2003. When Hurricane Katrina struck the Gulf Coast in August 2005, he spent more than a month covering it nightly for CNN and has returned more than 20 times to do other stories on its aftermath and recovery efforts there. It was that nightly exposure to the American television audience that earned Cooper his own nightly news show, *AC 360.*

Cooper's brand of reporting, which some critics label as "emotional journalism," has sparked controversy in the journalistic ranks, especially among traditionalists. But Cooper is a man driven by emotions; that much is obvious in his book and in the way he reports. He believes it is possible to do a balanced job of accurate reporting while still feeling for the victims of tragedy.

—Anderson Cooper. *Dispatches from the Edge.* New York: HarperCollins, 2005. pp. 7ff.

—"Anchors & Reporters: Anderson Cooper," CNN.com, http://www.cnn.com/CNN/anchors_reporters/cooper.anderson.html

CNN's Anderson Cooper, on Monday, August 28, 2006, does some taping in the doorway of a house in New Orleans's Lower Ninth Ward that was damaged by Hurricane Katrina nearly one year prior. The national and international media returned to the region for the anniversary of Hurricane Katrina, however Cooper returned to the region repeatedly. [AP Photo/Alex Brandon]

response to the victims of Katrina. Getting special attention was FEMA, which came under fire for how it reacted. That attack ended in the resignation of its director, Michael D. Brown. Receiving commendations instead of condemnations were the National Hurricane Center and the National Weather Service for the abundant lead time which their accurate forecasts provided.

96. CBS TAPS KATIE COURIC

Ever since the fledging CBS television news operation called upon Douglas Edwards to anchor its first newscast in 1948, much of the American viewing public was waiting to see how long it would take for any network to put a woman in that position all by herself. It would take almost 60 years. Apparently feeling America was not ready for a solo female news anchor on a nightly network newscast, CBS waited until 2006 to put a woman in that position. That woman was Katie Couric, known to Americans as the longtime upbeat morning host of NBC's *Today* show. Couric was not the first weeknight female network news anchor, but she was the first solo female network news anchor. In 1976 ABC had paired Barbara Walters, an earlier cohost of *Today*, with Harry Reasoner to anchor its evening network news show, and in 2006 that same network had paired Elizabeth Vargas with Bob Woodruff to anchor its *World News Tonight*. When Woodruff was critically injured by a bomb in Iraq shortly after the new pair began, Vargas anchored the newscast alone for a short time before deciding to return to her signature show of *20/20*.

Other women like Connie Chung, Diane Sawyer, and Jane Pauley had filled in on network newscasts, but it was not until the spring of 2006 that a network finally announced it would turn over its weekday evening news show to a solo woman anchor the following September. The announcement that this anchor would be Katie Couric was a surprise, although many industry analysts felt it made sense because of her immense TV popularity. Couric had spent the past 15 years as cohost of the *Today* show where her forté was not serious news reporting or incisive news interviews. Instead she was given the task of livening up the show which, more often than not, focused on interviewing celebrities who were hawking their new movies; singers and pop music groups performing on the show; diet doctors and assorted health and nutrition specialists, and spearheading the lighthearted banter with cohosts Matt Lauer, Al Roker, and Ann Curry. Adjectives used to describe Couric by the press included "perky," "upbeat," and even "giggly" and "bouncy." Hardly the essential traits that a network evening news anchor should exhibit, critics charged. They were uncannily similar to the critiques leveled against putting Barbara Walters on the news desk at ABC in 1976.

Also like Walters before her, Couric did have news reporting experience. She had served as a reporter at two local television stations in Miami and Washington, D.C., and had spent two years as NBC's deputy Pentagon correspondent before joining the *Today* show in 1991. She also did several specials for the network news department wherein she interviewed key newsmakers from around the world. But there was no

Katie Couric, with NBC Today *show cohost Matt Lauer, raises a glass of champagne in a toast with cast and crew members at the end of her final show, Wednesday, May 31, 2006. At the end of three hours of farewell tributes, Katie Couric raised the glass and said, "To everyone in TV land, thanks so much." In the second row are, from left, weathermen Willard Scott and Al Roker, and film critic Gene Shalit. [AP Photo/Richard Drew]*

question her popularity came from her *Today* show persona. NBC didn't seem eager to acknowledge Couric's new persona and help her out as she jumped ship to CBS, if their final live televised send-off for her in June of 2006 was any indication. For that event, *Today* devoted the entire program to wishing Katie well, teasing her and her signature personality traits for viewers. At one point in the morning love-fest, the producers had the cast of the hit Broadway show, *Jersey Boys*, perform the old Four Seasons hit, *Bye Bye Baby*, to the lyrics of Bye Bye Katie while the star laughed, giggled, teared up, received hugs from her mates and later drank champagne toasts.

Venerable news anchors like CBS's Walter Cronkite and Dan Rather were guarded in their optimism about Couric's chances to take the CBS evening newscast to a dominant position in the ratings. In a story published in the *New York Daily News*, Rather asserted Couric was a "nice person" but said "the mistake was to try to bring the 'Today' show ethos to the 'Evening News,' and to dumb it down, tart it up in hopes of attracting a younger audience." The comment was labeled "sexist" by CBS management.[10] Cronkite said he supported Couric but told Fox News, "I think she's as good as ever, and better than the show she's on." He added however, he didn't think the broadcast had improved since she took over as anchor.[11]

Television critics charged that tapping Couric over other more experienced female journalists was just another indication that network news was emphasizing entertainment value over journalistic experience.

But CBS management defended their choice in Couric. CBS Corporate chief executive Leslie Moonves said, "She's been on the air for nine months. Let's give her a break." He said he "absolutely" had confidence in Couric and explained it was vitally important to reach younger audiences.[12]

Many industry analysts noted that Couric had developed a huge following of viewers at NBC, and the only question was whether she could translate her persona to the more serious one required on the news desk and, if she could, whether her loyal followers would appreciate that new persona. The evidence didn't look good the first year, and numerous stories pointed out how CBS was losing ground in the race for ratings against NBC and ABC. *The Huffington Post* quoted the Nielsen Co. on April 29, 2008, that *CBS Evening News* ratings had hit a new low of 5.39 million total viewers for the previous week, finishing third behind *NBC Nightly News* with Brian Williams (8.01 million viewers), and ABC's *World News Tonight* (7.79 million).[13] However, Couric's tough interview with Alaska Gov. Sarah Palin later in 2008 proved to many critics that she had the right stuff as a network anchor.

97. THE ABRAMOFF SCANDAL

Decades have passed since the Watergate scandal, considered by most journalists to be the high-water mark of investigative reporting by American journalists. Other scandals have come and gone, most notably the Bill Clinton–Monica Lewinsky affair, but many of these chosen for media coverage have been more titillating than consequential. The exposé of the impact-boosting process by the big tobacco companies in the 1990s was a notable exception. Still, many journalists have wondered if an audience remains for significant, complex investigative stories and—given that question—whether the owners of media companies have the stomach to pursue such high-risk stories. Enter the Jack Abramoff scandal in Washington, D.C., that was still being unraveled as this book was published, although Abramoff himself was already serving a five-and-a-half-year sentence in prison.

The Abramoff scandal would test the mettle and resolve of major media news organizations to chase a story of unbelievable corruption in Washington, D.C. It would include lobbyists, nongovernmental organizations, shady businessmen, vulnerable religious groups, and even a Republican House majority leader in Congress. Because the story was so complex and continued to unfold month after month and year after year, it did not fit neatly into the standard beginning-middle-end format that news organizations feel is needed for today's audience.

Essentially the scandal concerned former Capitol Hill lobbyist Jack Abramoff and the deals he made with businessmen in the Northern Mariana Islands, a U.S. commonwealth,

In this January 3, 2006 file photo, Jack Abramoff leaves Federal Court in Washington. [AP Photo/ Gerald Herbert, File]

to keep the federal government off their back and enable them to continue running factory sweatshops with deplorable conditions without paying U.S. federal minimum wages. To do that, Abramoff enlisted and received the support of Congressman Tom DeLay, then speaker of the House of Representatives, who reportedly pledged to keep a Senate-passed bill to clean up the sweatshop conditions off the legislative calendar of the House.[14]

But this was only one prong of Abramoff's scams. The other concerned his representing Louisiana Indian tribes who were running successful casino operations and wanted to protect themselves from any pending casino competition from the neighboring State of Texas. To help ensure Texas would not pass legislation allowing Indian casinos in its state, Abramoff enlisted the support of a young conservative evangelical lobbyist named Richard Reed, who mounted a large moral crusade against gambling enlisting Texas evangelicals and churches. For his efforts, Reed was promised a cut of Abramoff's millions of dollars in payments from the tribes in Louisiana.[15]

In January 2006, Abramoff pleaded guilty to three felony counts and was sentenced to five-and-a-half years in prison. *The Washington Post* reported the moment this way:

> Jack Abramoff, the once-powerful lobbyist at the center of a wide-ranging public corruption investigation, pleaded guilty yesterday to fraud, tax evasion and conspiracy to bribe public officials in a deal that requires him to provide evidence about members of Congress.
>
> The plea deal could have enormous legal and political consequences for the lawmakers on whom Abramoff lavished luxury trips, skybox fundraisers, campaign contributions, jobs for their spouses, and meals at Signatures, the lobbyist's upscale restaurant.
>
> In court papers, prosecutors refer to only one congressman: Rep. Robert W. Ney (R-Ohio). But Abramoff, who built a political alliance with House Republicans, including former majority leader Tom DeLay of Texas, agreed to provide information and testimony about half a dozen House and Senate members, officials familiar with the inquiry said. He also is to provide evidence about congressional staffers, Interior Department workers and other executive branch officials, and other lobbyists.[16]

Many wonder if the Abramoff scandal wasn't just the tip of the iceberg. Is this how government really works? Instead of government of the people, by the people, and for the people, are we living in a system of government of the lobbyists, by the lobbyists, and for their clients? A passage from the well-respected PBS program, *Bill Moyers Journal* explains the breadth of lobbying in the nation's capitol:

> There is no doubt that the numbers are big. The number of registered lobbyists in Washington has doubled to more than 34,750 since 2000. Total lobbying spending in 2005 was $2.2 billion—in 1998 $1.44 billion. At least 850 trips with a total cost well over $4 million were paid for by nonprofit organizations with one or more registered lobbyists on their boards. And it's not just the system at the federal level—there were an average of five lobbyists and $130,000 in expenditures per state legislator in 2004.[17]

And the influence of lobbyists like Abramoff doesn't end with politicians. It also includes efforts—sometimes successful—to recruit journalists into writing about issues favoring the lobbyists' clients. *The Columbia Journalism Review* noted the following about Abramoff's efforts to recruit journalists to write favorable stories and op-ed pieces:

> As the expanding and increasingly smarmy Jack Abramoff scandal investigation makes clear, lobbyists are just as hungry as federal agencies to plant messages with anyone who has a platform. According to *BusinessWeek*, one Doug Bandow, a Cato Institute fellow and syndicated columnist for Copley News Service, was pulling in "$2,000 per column to address specific topics of interest to Abramoff's clients. Bandow's standing as a columnist and think-tank analyst provided a seemingly independent validation of the arguments the Abramoff team were

using to try to sway Congressional action." *BW* took a look at some of Bandow's columns, finding that he regularly "wrote favorably about Abramoff's Indian tribal clients," and, as has become standard operating procedure for this kind of thing, he never disclosed that he was on Abramoff's payroll. Bandow isn't the only one outed by *Business Week*. Peter Ferrara, a senior policy adviser at the conservative Institute for Policy Innovation, also cashed Abramoff's checks for writing op-ed pieces praising the lobbyist's clients.[18]

Will investigative journalism make a resurgence, à la the days of Watergate, or will it give in to the dictates of the marketplace and the media organization's marketing department in going after glossier stories, easier to understand, yet less significant for the reader or viewer? Perhaps the handling the Abramoff scandal, too much for much of the nation's mainstream media to handle as late as 2008, will be the indicator of all this.

98. THE YOUTUBING OF AMERICA

On February 15, 2005, three men still in their early 20s started an Internet company out of a garage by registering its domain. Less than two years later, they decided to sell that company. It went for $1.65 billion. The startup company was called YouTube, and in its short existence, it has had a drastic impact on the way Americans—especially young Americans—are living their lives. The three founders of YouTube are Steve Chen, Chad Hurley, and Jawed Karim, and what they created seems simple, yet astounding.
Time magazine has noted the following about YouTube:

> YouTube became a phenomenon in 2006 for many reasons, but one in particular: it was both easy and edgy, a rare combination. You can watch videos on the site without downloading any software or even registering. YouTube is to video browsing what a Wal-Mart Supercenter is to shopping: everything is there, and all you have to do is walk in the door."[19]

Communication scholars may debate whether YouTube is a medium of mass communication, interpersonal communication, or whether it falls somewhere in between and has created its own defining realm. One thing is certain, however: the masses are using it. Although originally discovered by the young, all demographics have warmed up to the concept of being able to see just about any video on any subject—virtually a video version of Google, which is the company that bought it by the way—at any time. Among the newer users catching on to YouTube's applications are college professors and even secondary school teachers who find ready video examples of many current people and events as well as examples of people and events from history. Teaching a class in Intro to Mass Communication and need some clips of early-day television pioneers and the TV shows they were famous for? Just dial up YouTube. Teaching a class in Music History and need some music videos of Johnny Cash or Placido Domingo? They're on YouTube.

Writer John Cloud has noted, "The unmediated free-for-all encouraged the valuable notion that the site was grass-roots, community-run and—to use an overworked term—'viral.' These are partial fictions, of course. YouTube controls the 'Featured Videos' on its home page, which can dramatically popularize a posting that otherwise might fade. Also, the video in the top-right section of the home page is an advertisement, even though it doesn't always look like one. There's no porn on the site—overtly sexual material is flagged by users and removed by YouTube, usually very quickly. But there is an endless supply of kinda weird, kinda cool, kinda inspiring stuff there, which means you can waste hours on Chad and Steve's site."[20]

Accounts among the three differ as to the exact way YouTube came into existence, but it wouldn't have begun had Hurley not have met Chen and Karim while the three of them were working at the new PayPal e-firm in in 2002. The three would toss around ideas of a startup company, and YouTube is the one that stuck. In a version that Hurley and Chen agree to, they got the idea in the winter of 2005 during a time they were having problems in sharing videos online which they had taken at a San Francisco party.

Karim disagrees and says the party never happened, and that the video-sharing idea was his. In any event, the three are listed on the YouTube site as its cofounders, and all seem to agree they each had roles to play in hatching the plan or putting it into effect. And implementing the service would take several months before becoming a reality. Originally what came forth was a video version of an existing date-rating site called *HOT or NOT*. It gave way to another idea of helping people share online auction videos. Then an interesting thing happened that went beyond the vision of the three: They realized that users were posting all kinds of videos on their YouTube site. In effect, the users were creating their own killer applications, and it was much more broad-based than the narrower uses the trio of developers had in mind.

For one thing, some users were linking to YouTube from their own MySpace pages. MySpace was already in existence and was doing well, but there still seemed to be room for YouTube, judging from the use it was getting from MySpace users. So, in a way, MySpace accelerated the growth of YouTube, much like Facebook's effect on the new Twitter. All Chen, Hurley, and Karim had to do was to stand back and watch YouTube users define the site for themselves. Within months it was a popular site and the likes of Time Warner were interested in it. Advertisers also caught on to its popularity, and the future seemed bright. How bright and how diversified is the use of YouTube? That future is still being written. Rest assured, however, politicians have caught on to the site's popularity, as have voters. Just count the huge number of user hits for campaign videos of any of the 2008 candidates making gaffs while video cameras were rolling.

99. THE 2008 PRESIDENTIAL CAMPAIGN

Every presidential campaign is important to America and is also a milestone in which much is learned by the media for coverage of future elections. There are always innovations in coverage, technical and stylistic, and there are always mistakes that journalists vow not to make in the next election. One could make a case, however, that the most significant presidential election in recent memory was the 2008 election that pitted two very different kinds of candidates, each of whom represented two very different eras in American history. And one of them would become America's first African American commander-in-chief.

YOUTUBE/CNN ELECTION DEBATES

In 1960, network television broadcast its first-ever debates between the Democratic and Republican nominees for president in the famed Kennedy–Nixon debates. Almost five decades later, in 2007, a leading cable news network and a popular online site launched another innovation in coverage of political campaigns when they teamed up to present debates among the various contenders for the two party nominations. The cable network was CNN and the online site was YouTube. It would be the first-ever joining of television and online platforms in the presentation of presidential debates.

In a larger sense, this would signal the joining of the age of media convergence with the modern era of political campaigning and it would provide—at least symbolically—more of an opportunity for average Americans to have a say in the election process. Under this new merged-media format, the questions would come not from elite television and print journalists but from everyday Americans who would ask the questions themselves on national television.

YouTube and CNN announced their plans for cosponsored Republican and Democratic presidential debates in June 2007. The goal was to transport the standard televised debates into the online digital arena. Video content from the debates would be made available for online sharing and distribution, and the questions for the candidates would come via videos submitted to CNN by users of YouTube.

The first of the debates was the Democratic debate among eight hopefuls for the nomination on July 23, 2007 in Charleston, South Carolina. It was hosted by Anderson Cooper and, of course, aired on CNN. A Republican debate took place on November 28 in St. Petersburg, Florida, among the eight contenders for the GOP nomination. YouTube set up a home page for the CNN partnership and invited its users to submit personal videos of themselves asking questions of the various candidates. CNN then selected the videos to be aired on the televised event, and candidates responded to those questions. The pool to draw from was huge, and Cooper noted at the GOP debate that CNN had some 5,000 video questions to draw from as they narrowed those down to a usable number of some 20 questions.

The debates drew large viewership, but it was uncertain if the format was one that will stick in future televised debates. Even in 2008, when the time came for the debates between the eventual party nominees, Barack Obama and John McCain, the debate formats reverted to more traditional forms, although a "town hall" format was interspersed where live audience members asked questions of the candidates.

The YouTube/CNN format was not without controversy. About the Republican Debate, one blogger charged on the *Mashable* blog that "nearly 30 percent of all questions asked were from planted questioners. That is to say, the various Democratic Presidential campaigns put out questions to the Republican candidates, and instead of picking questions from the constituency of the Republican base, CNN decided to wave through folks into the debate who would never vote for any of the candidates in an effort to shape their image in what they hoped would be an embarrassing way."

—"YouTube-CNN Republican Debate Reflects Poorly on New Media," by Mark "Rizzn" Hopkins. *Mashable*, http://mashable.com/2007/11/30/youtube-cnn-republican-debate-reflects-poorly-on-new-media/.

MOCK NEWS SHOWS

In 2006, comedian Robin Williams portrayed a pseudo-news commentator named Tom Dobbs whose stock in trade was the humorous parody of politicians and elected officials. In the movie, *Man of the Year*, Dobbs decides to take his shtick to a new level and run for president. Through a computer glitch in the new electronic system of counting votes, he appears to win. His loyal following of television viewers is delighted, albeit much of the country is shocked. The movie, however far-fetched, poses an interesting question: Is this new breed of comedians-cum-journalists so popular that one of them could actually be elected president?

Today's most obvious manifestation of quasi-news shows like Tom Dobbs' program are the so-called mock newscasts of *The Daily Show with Jon Stewart, Politically Incorrect with Bill Maher,* and the popular show featuring comedian Stephen Colbert called *The Colbert Report.* If audience ratings are any indication, these shows and their comedian hosts which often spoof the news—along with adding their own brand of serious commentary—have become more known than the anchors on the nightly network newscasts. And some polls show they have become more credible and have greater influence than their traditional news counterparts.

Variety has noted about these celebrities, "Who knew that one day Stewart and Stephen Colbert would ask more substantive questions of politicians than Charlie Gibson or George Stephanopoulos? Colbert is also the comedian who showed more guts than any real TV reporter when, face to face at the 2006 White House Correspondents' Dinner, he gold George W. Bush: 'I stand by this man. I stand by this man because he stands *for* things. Not only for things, he stand *on* things. Things like aircraft carriers and rubble and recently flooded city squares. And that sends a strong message, that no matter what happens to America, she will always rebound—with the most powerfully staged photo ops in the world.' "

Some observers have noted that Colbert and Stewart use their humor to help others understand the absurdity in American politics, government, and in our daily lives. Sometimes eccentricity can work toward making people pay attention, as did the fictional and mad television news anchor, Howard Beale, in the classic 1976 film, *Network.* While both Stewart and Colbert are extremely intelligent and certainly don't share the debilitating madness that gripped Beale, the effect of their work is the same: America is hearing its own rage articulated, and we are listening.

The influence of these newer venues of news and commentary was the subject of a 2004 study by William P. Eveland. This study shows that "non-traditional political communication forms (including the late-night shows with Jay Leno and David Letterman) are finally producing consistent positive effects equivalent to traditional media such as television news and newspapers. Moreover there is some evidence that these positive effects may be amplified among the less educated, helping to close the knowledge gap."

The study notes that the 2004 presidential election campaign used more of these non-traditional communication forms and that the influence of these programs was just as strong as their more traditional communication counterparts such as network and local news programming.

—"TV: Mock news shows poles tough love," by Robert Hofler, www.variety.com.

—"The Benchwarmers Hit a Home Run: Non-Traditional Political Communication Effects in 2004," by William P. Eveland, Jr. Ohio State University, in a paper presented to the Association for Education in Journalism and Mass Communication annual convention, San Francisco, California, August 2006, p. 2.

The Republican John McCain came from the Vietnam era where he distinguished himself in combat and as a prisoner of war. He drew his image largely from the archetype of military heroes before him who had run for president, such as John Kerry, Dwight D. Eisenhower, and Theodore Roosevelt, and of the many military veterans who have run for other top political offices. But Sen. McCain also seemed a stranger to the digital age which has come to define the current era in American history. Acknowledging that he felt a bit uncomfortable about even using e-mail, the 70-year-old McCain appeared to be an anachronism to anyone under the age of 40 while on the campaign trail.

The Democrat Barack Obama presented a stark contrast. First of all, if elected, he would become the first African American (self-defined as he came from biracial parents) candidate for president of the United States. Secondly, he was 46 years old when he began his campaign, and he seemed very attuned to the digital age of America. His campaign made massive use of online media, both on Obama's web site and through an exhaustive e-mail campaign with individual supporters and undecideds. His television persona was terrific and, while the contrast there between him and McCain was not as stark as John F. Kennedy and Richard M. Nixon had been in 1960, it was still obvious to most observers that Obama understood how to make television work for him. In the end, of course, his savvy paid off and he won.

First, America was treated to a year-long battle between the two top Democratic rivals for that party's nomination, Obama and Sen. Hillary Clinton, as a run-up to the final campaign between Obama and McCain. That battle was even more dramatic than the final presidential campaign itself. Clinton was, of course, the first female candidate

President-elect Barack Obama, left, his wife Michelle Obama, right, and two daughters, Malia, and Sasha, center left, wave to the crowd at the election night rally in Chicago, Tuesday, November 4, 2008. [AP Photo/Jae C. Hong]

for president with a strong chance to win, and she also seemed comfortable with the new media rules of the 2008 campaign. In fact, she made her initial formal announcement to run for the presidency on her Web site.

In terms of media influence, the 2008 presidential campaign was the first one in which online media became so vitally important. So much of America had tuned out of traditional print and even television newscasts by the 21st century and had flocked instead to the online world. The best candidates of the 2008 election understood this and knew, if they wanted to reach these voters, they would have to embrace the Internet and let it work for their success. Television itself was running news and public affairs segments on the importance of the Web in political races. ABC's *Nightline* focused on the Web as a new venue for political mudslinging on November 2, 2006. Martin Bashir explained that four days before the national midterm congressional elections, the Internet had become a vital force for mudslinging and political stunts. YouTube, Myspace, and Facebook were the favored sites for featuring these satires, candidate slipups, and political attacks. Any candidate or detractor could post whatever videos they liked, showing such things as candidates falling asleep at important meetings or Sen. John Kerry's verbal slip on October 31, 2006, suggesting that those who fought in Iraq were there because they didn't get a good enough education. Another site discussed was Wikipedia, where anyone could contribute to encyclopedic-like definitions of people, issues, groups, or causes. If a candidate wants to contribute to the profile of an opponent, and maybe refer to an "addiction" that this individual has, it can be done because sources are not always cited, and those that are, are sometimes questionable.

For these and many other reasons, the 2008 presidential campaign made an indelible footprint in the history of the media and of America itself.

100. FROM ANALOG TO DIGITAL TV

On February 17, 2009, all full-power broadcast television stations in the United States stopped broadcasting on analog airwaves and started broadcasting only in digital. The move was mandated to allow television stations to offer improved picture and sound quality as well as additional channels. Digital Television (or DTV) also allows multiple programming choices (multicasting) and offers interactive options for television viewers.[21]

This was a culminating event for the American evolution of digital television from the days in the early 1990s when High Definition Television was developed. For more than a decade, analog and digital television receivers (television sets) were sold side-by-side in electronics and department stores, although the price of digital sets remained too high for a long time to be practical for many American families. But the 2009 switch to all-digital transmission meant that all newly made TV sets must include digital tuners, by law. Viewers using older, analog receivers—and who were not connected to cable or satellite transmitters—had to purchase converter boxes, which changed their sets' analog tuners to digital tuners.

Congress mandated the conversion to all-digital broadcasting because it would free up frequencies for public safety communications such as police, fire, and emergency rescue, as well as for advanced commercial wireless services for consumers. Additionally, the multicasting feature of DTV allows for broadcasting several channels within the same spectrum of one analog channel. Congress had mandated midnight, December 31, 2006, as the date for the digital change to occur, but that date was pushed back to allow television stations and home viewers more time to prepare financially for the change.

To those viewers (more than 50 million) who were still receiving their television programming via broadcast signals using home television antennae, the digital shift has brought an end to a television age. The new age actually began in the 1980s when the Japanese introduced high definition television sets that delivered higher-quality, crisper images and better color than any other sets on the world market. In response to this introduction by foreign manufacturers, a group of American companies formed a "Grand Alliance" that jumped past the Japanese technology by developing digital HDTV. As MSNBC columnist Michael Rogers wrote, "Thus, early on, HDTV invoked not just pretty pictures, but national pride and economic development. (But) one drawback to the U.S. version of HDTV was that to make it work, all broadcast television (not just high-definition) would have to convert to digital, meaning that every American television set manufactured since 1946 would be rendered obsolete."[22] To make the conversion easier for everyone, Congress allowed all local televisions stations to have additional channel space to keep broadcasting their analog signals while they ramped up their technology to transmit digital channels. As part of the deal, the stations would then give up their old analog channels following the digital transition. Another part of the deal for the long lead time that the FCC gave for the transition to occur (the transition order came in 1996), was that consumers could take their time in buying digital TV sets. That portion of the deal didn't work as well, however. Digital sets were still highly priced and out of reach of many American consumers. So extra years were added to allow the prices to come down. For consumers who still can't afford to buy digital television sets, the converter boxes offer a minimal-cost alternative that will still allow them to receive programming by converting their analog tuners to digital.

NOTES

1. Katharine E. Finkelstein. "40 Hours in Hell," *American Journalism Review*, November 2001, pp. 30–31.

2. Lori Robertson. "Anchoring the Nation," *American Journalism Review*, November 2001, pp. 40–41.

3. John Vivian. *The Media of Mass Communications*, 7th ed. Boston: Pearson, 2006, pp. 262–263.

4. Mark Zuckerberg in an interview with Leslie Stahl on "Facebook" segment, *60 Minutes*, January 1, 2008, CBS-TV.

5. Ibid.

6. "Hurricane Katrina," www.katrina.noaa.gov.

7. Michael Perlstein. "Covering Katrina: On Taking It Personally," *Reed Magazine*, Winter 2006.

8. "Anderson Cooper, " *Larry King Live*, June 6, 2006.

9. Ibid.

10. "CBS Exec.: Dan Rather's Couric Comments 'Sexist,'" Newsmax.com, June 12, 2007, retrieved on http://archive.newsmax.com.

11. "Walter Cronkite: Katie Couric Is Better Than Her Show," retrieved on foxnews.com, Friday, September 7, 2007.

12. "CBS Exec." Newsmax.com.

13. "CBS Evening News Ratings Hit New Low," *Huffington Post*, April 29, 2008, as retrieved on www.huffingtonpost.com.

14. "Capitol Crimes," *Bill Moyers Journal*, August 1, 2008, as accessed on www.pbs.org/moyers/journal/archives.

15. Ibid.

16. Susan Schmidt and James V. Grimaldi. "Abramoff Pleads Guilty to 3 Counts," *The Washington Post*, January 4, 2006, A01.

17. "Capital Crimes," *Bill Moyers Journal*.

18. "They're Coming Out of the Woodwork," *Columbia Journalism Review*, December 16, 2005, as retrieved on www.cjr.org.

19. John Cloud. "The Gurus of YouTube," *Time Magazine*, December 16, 2006, as accessed on www.time.com.

20. Ibid.

21. "DTV Is Coming," FCC Consumer Facts, as retrieved on http://www.fcc.gov/cgb/consumerfacts/digitaltv.html.

22. Michael Rogers. "The End of Analog TV," as retrieved on September 27, 2009, on www.nytimes.com.

Part V

Stretching the List of 100: Ten Notable Additional Moments

Many other developments have occurred that have had significant influence on America and the media, and several of these could be rightly substituted for moments in the preceding list of 100. Some of these other moments are discussed in this section and include a prize fight that was much more than that, a momentous Supreme Court case affecting American libel law, the assassination of the best-known leader of the civil rights movement, an early venture into online publishing, the creation of the first music file-sharing system, the launching of the first of the important and influential Web logs or "blogs" that opened the door for what has become known as "citizen journalism," and a latter-day pitched fight for the independence of PBS.

1. JOE LOUIS KO'S MAX SCHMELING

Sometimes a media event, which would normally be significant by itself, becomes even more so because of the intersection of the event and the time in which it occurs. Such was the case on the evening of June 22, 1938, when Joe Louis, former heavyweight champion of the world who lost a highly publicized fight to Germany's Max Schmeling, returned to the ring and reversed the outcome by pounding Schmeling to the mat. To the world, however, it was more than a fight; it was a symbol of German Aryanism being pummeled by a black American. Schmeling had developed a reputation of being a willing model for Hitler, a man who had met for lunch with the dictator and several times with the chief Nazi propagandist, Joseph Goebbels.[1] Later, the story of Schmeling would emerge as a more complex one as it became known the fighter had saved the lives of two German Jews in 1938 and would evidence humanitarianism in other ways during his life. But all that was known of Schmeling at the time was that

195

A DAY OF INFAMY

The morning of December 7, 1941, was a day that shook America as Japan unleashed its surprise attack on Pearl Harbor, dealing a crippling blow to U.S. Naval forces just as America was primed to enter the war in Europe against Germany. It was radio that broke the news first to Americans.

The Naval Historical Center notes that trouble between America and Japan had started in the 1930s when the two nations split over the question of China. A decade before Pearl Harbor, Japan had conquered Manchuria, which had been a part of China until that time. Japan, however, was not satisfied ending it there, and six years later started a campaign to conquer the remainder of China. Toward that end, the Japanese government joined with Nazi Germany in the Axis Alliance in 1940 and the next year had occupied Indochina. Japan's invasion of Indochina was unsettling to the American government because the U.S. had important interests in East Asia. A U.S. embargo of Japan resulted, and the Pacific stage was set for a confrontation.

The attack on Pearl came at 6 a.m. as some 180 Japanese planes were launched from six carriers. Two hours later, the damage to U.S. Naval forces was devastating. Twenty-one ships were sunk or damaged including eight battleships and three cruisers. Some 188 American aircraft were destroyed. Some 2,400 Americans died and another 1,178 were wounded. On the Japanese side, only 29 planes were destroyed. There were rays of hope for the American fleet, however. No U.S. carriers were damaged since they had been away from Pearl at the time of the attack. And the U.S. shoreside facilities at Pearl were not attacked so they remained intact.

Many Americans heard about the attack first at 2:26 p.m. on December 7 on Mutual Broadcasting's WOR, while they were listening to a professional football game between the New York Giants and the Brooklyn Dodgers. The game was interrupted with a news bulletin from United Press announcing the attack. Soon the story was dominating all media. The next day, President Roosevelt announced to the nation over radio that America was now at war with Japan.

—Naval Historical Center as retrieved on October 12, 2009, at http://www.history.navy.mil/faqs/faq66-1.htm.

—Radio Days: Pearl Harbor, as retrieved on October 12, 2009, at http://www.otr.com/r-a-i-new_pearl.shtml.

he had staged one of the biggest upsets in boxing history on June 19, 1936 when he knocked out Louis in their first meeting. American pride had taken it on the chin as did Louis, and the rematch drew great attention as news from Germany and Hitler's plans assimilated more into American veins.

Bob Considine, a well-known sports columnist of the International News Service (later to merge with the United Press Service and become United Press International), would write the story of that 1938 rematch, conveying the event in a poetic assault that may have well matched the flurry of punches Louis unleashed on Schmeling in the ring. To the average reader it was as if Considine was sitting on the next barstool in a local pub telling this account one-on-one to his best pal. His story, in part, read as follows:

Listen to this, buddy, for it comes from a guy whose palms are still wet, whose throat is still dry, and whole jaw is still agape from the utter shock of watching Joe Louis knock out Max Schmeling.

Boxer Joe Louis, left, knocks out Max Schmeling in the first round to win the heavyweight title, June 22, 1938, at Yankee Stadium in New York. [AP Photo]

It was a shocking thing, that knockout—short, sharp, merciless, complete. Louis was like this:

He was a big lean copper spring, tightened and retightened through weeks of training until he was one pregnant package of coiled venom. Schmeling hit that spring. He hit it with a whistling right-hand punch in the first minute of the fight—and the spring, tormented with tension, suddenly burst with one brazen spang of activity. Hard brown arms, propelling two unerring fists, blurred beneath the hot white candelabra of the ring lights. And Schmeling was in the path of them, a man caught and mangled in the whirring claws of a mad and feverish machine.[2]

The world of sports reporting often brings individual readers face to face, sometimes metaphorically, with their own inner battles and challenges that they must overcome to reach their goals. Reporting like Considine's, together with a parade of other great sports journalists such as Red Barber, George Plimpton, and Heywood Hale Broun, causes people who may not even be sports fans to stop, reflect upon, and borrow from those traits they see exemplified in the athletes as revealed in these stories.

2. THE CORONATION OF QUEEN ELIZABETH II

On June 2, 1953, a new dimension was added to the infant television industry when Great Britain staged coronation ceremonies for Queen Elizabeth II in Westminster Abbey in London. Some 8,000 guests were invited including prime ministers and heads of state as she took the oath of office to serve her people as queen. The ceremony was viewed live worldwide by millions as the BBC set up its largest-ever broadcast to provide live coverage on both radio and television. The event marked the beginning of pan-European cooperation in exchanging news programs and, many industry observers say, ushered in the television age. Westminster Abbey had never before authorized television cameras in the abbey. Further, it was felt by Prime Minister Winston Churchill and his cabinet that broadcasting the coronation live would place an intolerable strain on the young monarch, not to mention depriving England's privileged class of Lords of the exclusive opportunity to witness the new queen's coronation. But the young queen showed her independence when she overrode the objections and reminded her advisors she was the one being crowned, and not the cabinet, and that she was more than able to withstand the pressure of television. So while some detractors thought it wrong for people to watch such a distinguished and solemn event over a meal from their dinner table, the coverage was granted and some 20 million viewers tuned in.[3]

Live transAtlantic news coverage was still years off because of technical difficulties, different TV frequency standards in Europe and the United States, and because the industry needed to grow and mature to overcome these problems. It was, however, the first time a U.S. television network was able to bring coverage of an event in Europe to American viewers on the same day. CBS producer Don Hewitt, who would later be responsible for creating *60 Minutes*, recalled that the CBS crew developed and edited the film on the plane from London. The film was then shown on American television later that day. The coverage was warmly received by American TV audiences and set the stage for future coverage of European events, opening up a whole new portal for Americans on the world, its people, and its customs. Hewitt said CBS felt it was important for Americans to see positive events in Europe since some of the last images they had seen, just a decade before, were of Britain being bombed and Nazis parading in the streets of Germany, Poland, and Austria. "In a way, the coronation was the closing ceremony of World War II," Hewitt said.[4] The day after the coronation, the *New York Times* heralded CBS's historic coverage as the birth of international television. But CBS was not alone in airing film of the event. In fact, NBC president Reuven Frank claimed that both NBC and ABC beat CBS's coverage by a few minutes, having gotten the film via the Canadian Broadcasting Company, who received it via British Royal Air Force jets who flew it to Canada.[5]

3. *NEW YORK TIMES V. SULLIVAN*

In 1960, the *New York Times* published an advertisement with the headline, "Heed Their Rising Voices," which was part of a fundraising effort for the civil rights

Queen Elizabeth II, wearing her crown, center foreground, leads the procession through Westminster Abbey's nave after her coronation in London, England, June 2, 1953. The Queen of England is flanked by the Bishop of Durham Rev. Arthur Michael Ramsay, left, and the Bishop of Bath and Wells High Rev. Harold William Bradfield. Maids of honor follow behind, carrying the cape. [AP Photo]

A DEADLY PAPARAZZI

Celebrity fan clubs have been in existence as long as we have had celebrities. In normal conditions, these fans are welcome and encouraged by the celebrities. But in cases where fandom turns to obsession, danger lurks for the celebrities and things get scary. Hollywood has even produced its share of films on obsessed paparazzi such as *The King of Comedy* and *The Fan*, both of whom have starred actor Robert De Niro—who actually has a penchant for keeping his off-screen life private and far from prying camera lenses. Both films mirror the dark side of celebrity who too often become the target of emotionally or mentally unbalanced stalkers.

Today show contributor Mike Celzic focused on the danger in a 2008 report on celebrity stalkers noting, "The topic is in the news again, with the conviction of 37-year-old Jack Jordan of stalking and harassing actress Uma Thurman. The out-of-work lifeguard and pool cleaner faces up to a year in jail after a jury listened to Thurman's testimony that he was scaring her to death." Celzic pointed to a report by NBC's John Larson that stated, "Experts say celebrity stalkers may seem harmless, but remember Mark David Chapman began as a seemingly innocent stalker of John Lennon, and wound up his killer."

Although Chapman's name is seared infamously in the minds of all Beatles fans, he is one of only several who have caused terrifying moments for celebrities. The list includes John Hinckley, the attempted assassin of President Ronald Reagan, who believed the notoriety he received from that act would win the attention of actress Jodie Foster after he had stalked her. Another stalker was Robert John Bardo, who in 1989 killed a young television actress named Rebecca Schaeffer after stalking her.

While stalkers represent the unbalanced extremities of fandom, celebrities find most paparazzi a force to be dealt with and not always a welcome one. Stories have abounded of celebrities—from Sean Penn to Lindsay Lohan—turning on those shoving cameras in their faces, sometimes striking out physically in frustration.

America's fascination with celebrities is shared by other developed countries around the world and has, at times, contributed to deadly tragedies. Such was the case in the 1997 death of Princess Diana of Wales in a fatal car crash in Paris. Although a coroner's jury ultimately ruled the death an accident and not a conspiracy as some have believed, its verdict nevertheless mentioned the role Diana's paparazzi played in the accident. The jury found that the driver of Diana's car was intoxicated and was driving at twice the legal speed limit, but noted also it was being pursued at high speeds by paparazzi. According to a story in the *Los Angeles Times*, "the 'speed and manner of driving' of the 'following vehicles,' which most have taken to mean the paparazzi who were chasing the Mercedes at high speed, also were factors. All but one of the photographers, who are in France and are not answerable to a British coroner's summons, refused to testify." The chase vehicles contained just some of the dozens of photographers who had been stalking Diana's every move for years.

—"Celebrity stalkers pose real threat to famous," by Mike Celzic, as retrieved on December 18, 2008, www.msnbc.com.

—"Princess Diana's death no mystery, jury rules," by Kim Murphy, *Los Angeles Times*, April 8, 1008, http://articles.latimes.com/2008/apr/08/world/fg-diana8.

movement in the South. The ad contained several minor errors of fact, and Louis Sullivan, who was one of three city commissioners in Montgomery, Alabama, sued the newspaper for libel, asserting that the ad referred to him since he was an overseer of the Montgomery Police Department—which was mentioned critically in the ad as failing in their duties to protect civil rights workers and blacks in general. The case went to District Court where Sullivan was awarded damages in the amount of a half-million dollars. The *New York Times* subsequently appealed the case, and it went all the way to the Supreme Court.

The Court heard arguments and delivered a unanimous decision on the case in 1964, reversing the lower court decision and establishing a lasting precedent allowing journalists to make errors in fact when writing about "public officials" as long as there was no malicious intent involved in preparation of those stories. The Court felt this was an important latitude to allow in a democracy where the press must have the right to examine elected officials.[6]

Justice William Brennan wrote that the "profound national commitment to the principle that debate on public issues should be uninhibited, robust, and wide-open" caused the ad to become a valuable lesson in free speech. He said the value outweighed any harm that falsities could cause to Sullivan's reputation. In short, government officials should have enough toughness to withstand public criticism. The Court felt that affirming libel suits in stories involving public officials would have a chilling effect on any future reporting that might be done on the government. As a result, the watchdog function of the government could be weakened severely. Therefore, a "public official" could not recover damages for a libelous error in fact that relates to his or her official duties unless the official proves the statement was made with "actual malice," which the Court defined as knowledge it was false or with "reckless disregard" of the truth.[7]

The impact of *New York Times v. Sullivan* has been huge for journalism in America. Libel cases involving public officials (a term later expanded to include "public figures") are no longer decided on the question of errors in fact or even damages caused, but on the question of malice. Did the journalist know the information was wrong? Should he or she have suspected it was wrong? Did the journalist act in reckless disregard for the truth? The ruling has caused journalists to examine the veracity of information they receive and to try to use the most relevant and knowledgeable sources possible. If the story still comes up inaccurate and damaging, the offending news organization may have to pay compensatory damages, but the heavy punitive damages will not usually be applied if the court decides there is an absence of malice on the part of the journalist(s) involved in preparing the story.

4. THE ASSASSINATION OF MARTIN LUTHER KING, JR.

"MEMPHIS, Friday, April 5—The Rev. Dr. Martin Luther King, Jr., who preached nonviolence and racial brotherhood, was fatally shot here last night by a distant gunman who then raced away and escaped. Four thousand National Guard troops were ordered into Memphis by Gov. Buford Ellington after the 39-year-old Nobel Prize-winning civil rights leader died."[8]

So read the lead of an Earl Caldwell story on the front page of the *New York Times* on April 5, 1968. Like the assassination of President John F. Kennedy which had happened some five-and-a-half years earlier, this story shocked the nation and stunned the many followers of the beloved and sometimes controversial civil rights leader. King was in Memphis to help the city's garbage collection workers with their strike. Friends say he had a sense of foreboding about the trip, and a premonition that he had become so controversial and was hated so much by some whites that his life would probably not be a long one. Still, when his death came, it was a shock to the nation and especially to his followers and admirers. Although he did not hold the office that Kennedy held, King's power—especially among his millions of followers—seemed just as strong. And his death left a similar void in their lives and their cause that Kennedy's death left in America.

In terms of media impact, the King assassination caused the southern media to pay more attention to the racial divide and hatred which had clearly not abated in the South, although cities like Memphis were doing a pretty good job of turning it into a covert issue. As a result of the assassination, many more southern whites joined the movement to create an equal climate for whites and blacks in America, and it inspired blacks to carry on the fight that had been started by Dr. King. And on a national scale, the news media's coverage of civil rights kicked into a higher level for many months following his assassination.

Martin Luther King, Jr., second from right, and Southern Christian Leadership Conference aides Hosea Williams, Jesse Jackson, from left, and Ralph Abernathy return to the Lorraine Motel in Memphis to strategize for the second Sanitation Worker's march led by King in this April 3, 1968 file photo. King was shot dead on the balcony April 4, 1968. [AP Photo/File]

A small-time thief named James Earl Ray was arrested soon after the slaying and charged with King's death. He was convicted and sentenced to life in prison. Controversy and debate swirled around the question of Ray's guilt, and he recanted his earlier confession that he had committed the crime. He said he had been forced to make the confession under the threat of a death penalty if he did not confess. He claimed he had purchased the rifle for a man he knew only as "Raoul." Years later, the King family supported the retesting of Ray's rifle to see if it did, in fact, produce the bullet that killed Dr. King. The test proved inconclusive. Ray died in prison of liver disease in 1998.

5. VIEWTRON: RIGHT IDEA, WRONG TIME

Online publishing, and in a larger vein the Internet itself, had several would-be parents, and one of the more promising ones in the late 1970s and early 1980s was a concept called *videotex*. This was the term used to refer to a user-friendly, interactive electronic news and information service that consumers could subscribe to and access over specially designated terminals, their home television sets, or the young personal computers of the day. But the time was the early 1980s, there weren't many personal computers around at that time, and the special video terminals were expensive. Nevertheless, the day of interactive media appeared at hand to several media companies, and the videotex system was seen as having several applications including information retrieval from many databases, communication services like bulletin boards and electronic mail, and personal business transactions such as making airline reservations or conducting banking on the computer.

It all sounded like a good idea, and of course, today we would say, "Hey, isn't that the Internet?" Right, but keep in mind that Internet service providers (ISPs) were still in the formation stages during the 1980s, and the Internet didn't begin reaching popular use until the mid- or late 1990s. A 1991 report, in fact, stated there were only 1.7 million homes capable of using Videotex.[9] And most of the services offered were text-based, since the memory capacity of personal computers was ridiculously small even by the mid 1990s, so downloading graphic displays was only a dream in the decade prior.

And, since the World Wide Web had yet to be created, the content providers were few in number. In the pre-Internet days of the videotex experiments, there were just four national associations that joined users of videotex services

One of the key videotex experiments carried out in North America was done by the Knight-Ridder media company in 1983. As with other similar systems being tried in Europe, Knight-Ridder's videotex system (dubbed *Viewtron*) featured information that did not scroll down or up a screen but rather was presented as different electronic "pages" which users could access by depressing buttons on a remote-control keypad. The videotex concept was also referred to as *viewdata* and was originated in Great Britain in the early 1970s. The world's first fully operational, public videotex service opened in London in 1979 and was called *Prestel*, for "press television." Prestel users could access the system via a modem connected to their telephone lines.[10]

Knight-Ridder picked up the challenge to present videotex to Americans. The company is one of the largest newspaper companies in North America, and it saw videotex as a way of extending its services to its readers. Following tests in 1980–1981 in Coral Gables, Florida, Knight-Ridder began in 1983 the first full-service commercial videotex service operation in the United States. Basically it was the kind of service analogous to an electronic newspaper or magazine—complete with graphics—which was delivered over home television screens, designated video terminals, or PCs. Knight-Ridder created a subsidiary, Viewdata Corporation of America (VCA), to develop and operate the new service. Its product was Viewtron, and was actually a multifaceted and ambitious service, offering the full text of the *Miami Herald*, the Associated Press, some 750 topical service areas, keyword capabilities, attractive graphics, and video games.

Altogether, Viewtron began in 1983 to utilize the services of about 50 information providers and a half-dozen "gateways," or switching points between service originators and users, into still more services and IPs.[11] It was very much like an infant—and restricted—Internet.

A big problem was that accessing these various services was expensive for the general consumer. For example, Viewtron required the home purchase of a specially designated terminal developed by AT&T and called the Sceptre. Originally these terminals sold for $900 but were discounted to $600 for users of the Viewtron experiment. In 1982 this terminal was the only way into the system of services, and that proved to be a major problem for the experiment's success.

In addition to the terminals' cost, a monthly fee of $21 was charged for the basic videotex service. Southern Bell, which installed a special Local Area Data Transport network—charged subscribers a $1 per hour access fee. So if consumers went too deep into the menu of services, the meter charge climbed dramatically.

By the end of 1985 the future looked bleak for Viewtron. Tens of millions of dollars were going into the venture, and the bottom line was leaning heavily into the red. In 1986, VCA shut down Viewtron after spending some $45 million on the experiment. In sum, the PC infrastructure, the ISPs, and the learning curve were not in place when technology burst upon a confused and unprepared marketplace. But the infrastructure and market would soon catch up and give us what we know today as the Internet.

6. DROPPING IN ON A FAMINE

"All across Northern Ethiopia, famine is along each road and at the gates of every town. By the hundreds of thousands, peasants are fleeing the worst drought in memory." So began the November 1, 1984, Canadian Broadcasting Company's television report of Brian Stewart, a CBC journalist reporting on the horrific hunger event. Stewart had no way of knowing it then, but reports like his unleashed worldwide coverage of this famine and resulted in millions of dollars of international aid for this northern African region.

Stewart was among the early reporters covering the crisis that was unveiled first by a BBC reporter who virtually stumbled into the event. Michael Buerk had described the famine as "a Biblical famine in the 20th Century" and "the closest thing to hell on earth" in his earlier report to British television viewers. Before it was all over, some eight million people succumbed to the drought and famine. But without the worldwide media coverage the event drew, that number would likely have been even higher. While international news is always a hard sell to American audiences, except in times of an international threat to the United States, this coverage was an exception and showed the power of television imagery in evoking a sympathetic international response. Among the first to deliver aid to Ethiopia was Great Britain itself, as the Royal Air Force began airdrops of food to the starving Africans below. They were joined by Germany, America, Canada, Poland, Russia, and several other countries. One of the biggest money-makers for famine victims came from the United States in 1985 when entertainers Michael Jackson and Lionel Ritchie wrote the song, "We Are the World," which was recorded by an A-list group of singers and musicians who called themselves "USA for Africa" (United Support of Artists for Africa). The effort was inspired by Great Britain's "Band Aid" project, and the song reached the top of the hit charts in the United States and in many other countries around the world. Following release of the song, Bob Geldof organized the televised "Live Aid" concert in Philadelphia in July of 1985 which increased the fund-raising efforts for the famine victims. That followed on the heels of the "We Are the World" telecast.

The external support to Ethiopia from international communities was highly significant, given the Ethiopian government's inability to provide relief for its own people. Problems in government-funded aid were made even more complex by the near-total

Fans jam Philadelphia's JFK Stadium during the Live Aid concert Saturday, July 13, 1985. Two simultaneous events in Philadelphia and London were broadcast around the world and raised $100 million in relief money. [AP Photo/George Widman]

failure of crops within Ethiopia and the fighting with Ethiopia's province of Eritrea, which interfered with the delivery of the aid. One pair of editors observed, "The government's inability or unwillingness to deal with the 1984–85 famine provoked universal condemnation by the international community. Even many supporters of the Ethiopian regime opposed its policy of withholding food shipments to rebel areas. The combined effects of famine and internal war had by then put the nation's economy into a state of collapse."[12] The government's main response to the situation was to forcibly resettle more than a half-million peasants in the north to areas in the South. Some reports from international aid workers said tens of thousands of refugees died on the forced march north.

7. EXPOSING ERRING TELEVANGELISTS

If the news media played its part in elevating an evangelist named Billy Graham to the world stage in the 1950s, journalists also played a major role in publicizing the personal ethical failures of other televangelists. Among the high-profile evangelists exposed by the media in 1986 alone were Oral Roberts, Jimmy Swaggart, and Jim Bakker. Two decades later, Ted Haggard and Richard Roberts would be added to this list. Although several media "moments" were involved in these revelations, they are similar enough to group them under one of this book's 100 moments that changed the media. In going after popular preachers, the media showed itself to be unafraid of helping to expose the erring evangelists.

We'll start this collective "moment" with Oral Roberts, the Tulsa evangelist who made his fame as an early televangelist in the 1950s and 1960s and who amassed enough donations to build a university that he named after himself: Oral Roberts University. In 1986 Roberts was still on the air and delivered a highly emotional message to his television followers that unless he raised $8 million by that March, God would "call him home." Roberts said the money was needed to find a cure for cancer at his City of Faith Hospital, which he said God had commissioned him to build in 1981.[13] The Tulsa facility was a hospital which merged prayer with medicine and gave credit to God for the healing that took place there. With many Roberts followers fearing the evangelist would die—possibly by his own hand if they were reading him right —if the money weren't raised, the money began pouring in and the $8 million goal was exceeded by $1 million. The hospital still failed three years later, however, and was closed. The publicity surrounding what critics perceived as an unethical stunt to raise money for a failing project cast a stain on Roberts' reputation that ultimately did his organization more harm than good.[14]

In the same year Oral Roberts was taking money from his followers with threats of his own demise, Virginia-based televangelist Jim Bakker was facing the media spotlight for other kinds of indiscretions. The initial attacks on Bakker came not from the media but from a competing televangelist, Louisiana's Jimmy Swaggart, the cousin of singer Jerry Lee Lewis. Swaggart began calling attention to evidence of infidelity by Bakker, who was married to another televangelist, Tammy Faye Bakker.

The plot thickened when another evangelist who Swaggart attacked, Marvin Gorman, hired a private detective who found the married Swaggart having his own affair with a prostitute.[15]

All of these allegations and indiscretions found ample media air time as these self-proclaimed messengers of God were found to be as carnal as the flocks they were preaching to. The news value of men of God preaching one thing and living the life they chided others for, was impossible to pass up. One teary confession after another began to come forth from Swaggart and Bakker. Swaggart's ministry pressured him to step down from his pulpit, and he did. On television he told viewers through his tears that, "I have sinned against you, my Lord, and I would ask that your precious blood would wash and cleanse every stain until it is in the seas of God's forgiveness." Three years later, Swaggart was found with another prostitute when he was stopped by a California Highway patrol officer in Indio, California for driving on the wrong side of the road.[16]

As for Bakker, not only was he caught in a web of infidelity, but he was also charged with financial fraud regarding funds given to him in good faith by the many donors of his Heritage USA in Fort Mill, South Carolina. He was convicted and sentenced to prison. The indelible television image of Bakker was of him become hysteric as he was in handcuffs and being led from the courthouse to jail.

Some two decades after the scandals involving Roberts, Swaggart, and Bakker, the president of the National Association of Evangelicals was forced to resign for his own indiscretions. Ted Haggard, the 50-year-old pastor of the New Life Church in Colorado Springs, was accused of visiting a male prostitute and of taking crystal methamphetamine. Like Swaggart almost twenty years earlier, Haggard admitted he had sinned and also resigned as pastor of his large church. The Associated Press reported on November 5, 2006 that Haggard said he was a " 'deceiver and liar' who had given in to his dark side" and "confessed to sexual immorality Sunday in a letter read from the pulpit of the megachurch he founded." Haggard wrote, "the accusations made against me are not all true but enough of them are that I was appropriately removed from my church leadership position."[17]

Some political observers believe that, since this highly publicized case occurred shortly before the 2006 midterm congressional elections, it may have been one of several reasons for losses that were tallied by several conservative congressional candidates around the country. The fact that Haggard, accused of having a homosexual tryst himself, had been a vocal opponent of same-sex marriage, made that issue more muddled in a state that was voting on the issue at the time.

8. THE *DRUDGE REPORT*

One of the most recent important innovations in nontraditional news media is the impact that Web logs, or "blogs," have had on the way people receive and process information about the world. By giving individuals the same kind of platform that huge online media companies enjoy, blogs have created a kind of "citizen journalism" and broadened the definition greatly of who or what a reporter is. The Internet has brought the traditional op-ed piece of the newspaper editorial page to the online world via the blog, and it has added some new dimensions to such commentary. For one, blogs have interactive capability that newspapers can only dream of. For another, blogs can be continually updated and enlarged by the writer at will. Blogs started catching users' eyes as early as the mid-1990s, although their popularity has soared in more recent years. Among the first of the significant blogs on the Web was one created by a Tacoma, Maryland, store clerk named Matt Drudge.

The Report actually had begun as e-mails containing gossip to friends and then a wider usernet in 1996. His gossip began over things he heard while working as a clerk in a CBS studio gift shop in Hollywood. But the *Drudge Report* was to open the door on Web logs and the influence "bloggers" would have on the political process in the United States. It was on the *Drudge Report*, for example, that America first heard that Jack Kemp would be Sen. Bob Dole's running mate for president in the 1996 campaign, and, most famously, it was there the country, on January 17, 1998, first heard about President Bill Clinton's relationship with Monica Lewinsky after *Newsweek* reportedly declined to publish the story before getting more facts.[18]

The *Drudge Report* is actually an aggregate of different websites from different authors, although Drudge does originate some of the material himself. As an aggregation of postings from other authors, the site is not unlike another important informational Web site which has developed a huge following on the Web, *Wikipedia*. As with all such aggregate sites, the legitimacy of the information posted is only as reliable as its sources. But both Drudge and the editors of Wikipedia appear to work hard in rooting out inaccuracies from their sites.

Drudge has built his site into one of significant influence as well as controversy. *The Washington Post* Editor Leonard Downie, Jr., told the Online News Association at its 2006 annual convention that "Our largest driver of traffic is Matt Drudge."[19] For all of its influence, the *Drudge Report* has an unsophisticated graphic appeal, choosing instead to cram its site with small, 10-point Courier New font headlines and lists blogger links, stacked one upon the other, broken up every so often with small photos, graphics, and ads. The site definitely emphasizes function over form, but the success of some three million hits a month is not likely to cause it to change. The success of the *Drudge Report* spurred other bloggers into creating their own sites and, by the end of 2004, blogs had become an essential element of online culture.

9. THE FOUNDING OF NAPSTER

A lot of changes have occurred in the recorded music industry over the years, but maybe none has been so profound as that produced by an 18-year-old college dropout in Boston who set up a system for music-lovers to share their songs with each other online. The student was Shawn Fanning, and he changed the music industry forever with a file-sharing program he called "Napster." The idea of allowing online users to share and swap music files was simple, and it was really nothing more than a high-tech version of the age-old practice of swapping actual CDs and—before that—vinyl albums. But the impact was huge, because now it wasn't just one individual swapping his or her album with a friend, but millions of computer users swapping songs with millions of other users through Fanning's centralized file server which was Napster. That had the potential of negating the reason people buy CDs in the first place, and *that* sent shivers up the spine of the music industry.

Reaction came soon from the Recording Industry Association of America and several bands, including Metallica. In 2000, A&M records and several other recording companies filed a lawsuit against Napster which alleged tributary copyright infringement. Translated, that means Fanning was charged not just with violating the copyright law itself but also of enabling—indeed encouraging—others to do it as well. For its part, Napster argued that the actual music files were never in the company's possession; they were only being transferred from user to user. Therefore, Napster attorneys argued, the company never violated anyone's copyright. Also, if Napster consumers aren't guilty of copyright infringement, then how could Napster be since the transfers went "peer to peer"?[20] The larger issue, of course, involved how to protect copyright in an Internet age, and that issue will take much time to resolve.

Napster lost its case at the lower-court level, appealed it, and the three-judge panel in the 9th U.S. Circuit Court of Appeals affirmed the lower-court ruling. Napster, the court said, must stop its millions of users from downloading copyrighted files.[21] Napster was unable to do that, and it shut down the service in July 2001, declaring bankruptcy the next year. Napster reappeared and continues today as one of several file-sharing services which users pay to use. In 2008 Napster was bought by Best Buy, the American electronics retailer for $121 million.[22]

The door that Napster opened to the music download business, however, is one that will probably never be closed. Today several file-sharing services exist, including the hugely popular I-Tunes, part of the Apple computer empire.

10. THE FIGHT FOR PBS

One major story that has impacted a sometimes-forgotten media organization occurred in 2005 and changed the course that the Public Broadcasting System (PBS) was on. This was the fight between a Bush-appointed chairman of the Corporation for Public Broadcasting Board of Directors and those defenders of PBS who wanted it to remain free of political control.

PBS has long been a network of political controversy, and past presidents such as Richard Nixon have tried to exert influence on what they have often seen as a liberal bias to the news and public affairs shows on PBS. The conservative administration of George W. Bush ratcheted that attack up a notch in appointing Kenneth Y. Tomlinson to the CPB Board of Directors. Tomlinson was described by PBS stalwart newsman Bill Moyers as a "right-wing ideologue who occupied the very office that had been charged with protecting public broadcasting from political interference."[23]

At stake in the ideological battle between Tomlinson and PBS was the politically independent nature of the PBS operation. The conservative People for the American

Way referred to Tomlinson as "a martyr in the Right's long-standing battle against public broadcasting."[24] That same organization reported in 2007 that, "Claiming to have concerns about the 'objectivity and balance' of PBS, Tomlinson has used his position as head of the Corporation for Public Broadcasting to enact an agenda designed to ensure that public broadcasting favorably reflect the Republican agenda, such as hiring a White House staffer to draft guidelines for a new PBS ombudsman to monitor programs for bias."[25] Specifically, Tomlinson's crusade set its sights on Moyers and a Friday night investigative reporting show he produced and hosted. Tomlinson believed Moyers to be "anti-Bush," "anti-business," and "anti-Tom DeLay," and Tomlinson wanted Moyers censored. He secretly hired a consultant to monitor the show, "Now with Bill Moyers." The consultant was to look for specific comments Moyers might make that would prove Tomlinson's theory that the newsman was biased against Republicans.

Created by Congress in 1967, the Corporation for Public Broadcasting (CPB), was set up as a private, nonprofit corporation to be the steward of the federal government's investment in public broadcasting. The CPB's own Web site explains its nature as follows:

> The Corporation is not a government agency. It promotes public telecommunications services (television, radio, and online) for the American people. CPB invests in more than 1,000 local radio and television stations (and) their services, their programs, and their ideas . . . The fundamental purpose of public telecommunications is to provide programs and services which inform, enlighten and enrich the public . . . From its advent almost four decades ago, the CPB has had a legal mandate to ensure "strict adherence to objectivity and balance in all programs or series of programs of a controversial nature." This principle is part of the bedrock of public broadcasting in America, a country built upon a foundation of lively and open political and social discourse.[26]

In a 2005 speech to the National Conference for Media Reform, Moyers blasted Tomlinson and Bush's attack, which he said was led by Bush advisor Karl Rove, on PBS and specifically directed at Moyers' show. Reflecting on that talk, Moyers wrote in his 2008 book, *Moyers on Democracy*, the following:

> You might have thought the Bush administration would have been more than satisfied. Here was Fox News functioning as the Republican Ministry of Truth, and Rush Limbaugh and a host of wannabes constituting an OPEC of right-wing agitprop and the Beltway press according the White House a measure of deference surpassed only by that paid the Kremlin by Izvestia: Karl Rove could look at a media map of America and boast of it as occupied territory. Why bother about the sliver of the spectrum held by PBS, and especially about a single hour allocated once a week, on Friday nights, to a lone public affairs broadcast that would surely show up as a mere pinprick—no larger than, say, Guam—on Rove's wall map? Yet not a sparrow took wing in the media aerie that the Bush White House didn't want to politicize. My broadcast became the target . . . [27]

Defenders of PBS rose in Congress and, in the end, Tomlinson resigned from the CPB Board of Directors on November 3, 2005. His resignation came a day before the inspector general of the Corporation handed out a blistering report that criticized Tomlinson's leadership of CPB and asserted that he had violated agency procedures, federal laws, and the Director's Code of Ethics. The Associated Press reported, "The former chairman of the Corporation for Public Broadcasting broke federal law by interfering with PBS programming and appearing to use political tests in hiring the corporation's new president, internal investigators said Tuesday. Kenneth Y. Tomlinson, a Republican, also sought to withhold funding from PBS unless the taxpayer-supported network brought in more conservative voices to balance its programming, said the report by CPB inspector general Kenneth A. Konz."[28]

The fight for the soul of public broadcasting did not end with the Tomlinson episode, but the resolution of this incident would become a bulwark in the foundation of political independence for the Corporation for Public Broadcasting and its disseminating information network of PBS and NPR stations across America.

NOTES

1. "Remember Max Schmeling: The Story of a Hero," as retrieved on November 20, 2008, http://www.auschwitz.de/schmeling.html.

2. Louis L. Snyder and Richard B. Morris. *A Treasury of Great Reporting*. New York: Simon & Schuster, 1962, pp. 531–532.

3. "Queen Elizabeth," as retrieved on November 21, 2008, http://news.bbc.co.uk/onthisday/hi/dates/stories/june2/newsid_26540000/265401.stm.

4. http://ieeexplore.ieee.org/Xplore.

5. "1953 Coronation," National Public Radio, as retrieved on November 22, 2008, www.npr.org.

6. "New York Times v. Sullivan," analysis retrieved on http://faculty-web.at.northwestern.edu/commstud/freespeech/cont/cases/nytsullivan.html.

7. Ibid.

8. Earl Caldwell. "Martin Luther King Is Slain in Memphis," *New York Times*, April 5, 1968, A1.

9. Wallys Conhaim. "Videotex: Growing Public Awareness," White Paper Report prepared for the Newspaper Association of America, Reston, VA, 1991, V.

10. Jerome Aumente. *New Electronic Pathways*. Newbury Park, CA: Sage, 1980, p. 15.

11. Ibid.

12. Thomas P. Ofcansky and La Verie Berry, editors. *Ethiopia: A Country Study*. Washington: GPO for the Library of Congress, 1991, as retrieved on November 23, 2008, http://countrystudies.us/ethiopia/35htm.

13. "Oral Roberts Seeking Millions for Holy Mission against Cancer," *The Washington Post*, January 22, 1983.

14. "Oral Roberts' Ministry Hits a 'Low Spot'," *Dallas Morning News*, January 5, 1986.

15. "Transcript: Interview with Jessica Hahn," *Larry King Live*, CNN, July 14, 2005.

16. "Swaggart Says He Has Sinned; Will Step Down," *The New York Times*, February 22, 1998.

17. "Haggard Admits 'Sexual Immortality,' Apologizes." The Associated Press as retrieved on November 27, 2008, on www.msnbc.com.

18. "Scandalous Scoop Breaks Online," January 25, 1998, as retrieved on November 27, 2008, www.BBCnews.org.

19. David S. Hirschman. "Washington Post Editor Downie: Everyone in Our Newsroom Wants to Be a Blogger," *Editor & Publisher*, October 6, 2006.

20. "The Napster Controversy: Napster: Then and Now," as retrieved on November 28, 2008, on http://im1.jou.ufl.edu/projects/Spring01/Burkhalter/Napster%20history.html.

21. "Why Napster Was Shut Down," as retrieved on http://im1.jou.ufl.edu/projects/Fall04/Davison/napster.html.

22. Joseph Weisenthal. "The Next Chapter: Best Buy to Acquire Napster for $121 million," PaidContent.org, as retrieved on http://www.paidcontent.org/entry/419-breaking-best-buy-to-acquire-napster-for-121-million/htm.

23. Bill Moyers. *Moyers on Democracy*. New York: Doubleday, 2008, p. 265.

24. "Tomlinson, Bush-Appointed Crusader against PBS 'Bias,' Steps Down," January 10, 2007, as retrieved on November 29, 2008 on www.rightwingwatch.org.

25. Ibid.

26. "What Is the Corporation for Public Broadcasting?" and "CPB's Commitment to Objectivity and Balance," as retrieved on www.cpb.org/aboutcpb.

27. Moyers. *Moyers on Democracy*, p. 265.

28. "Report: Former CPB Chair Violated Law," Associated Press, November 15, 2005, retrieved on November 29, 2008, www.msnbc.msn.com.

Selected Bibliography

Anderson, Ken. *Television Fraud: The History and Implications of the Quiz Show Scandals*. Westport, Conn: Greenwood, 1978.

Barnouw, Erik. *The Golden Web*. New York: Oxford University Press, 1968.

Baum, Matthew A. *Soft News Goes to War: Public Opinion and American Foreign Policy in the New Media Age*. Princeton, N.J.: Princeton University, 2003.

Bennett, W. Lance. *Taken by Storm: The Media, Public Opinion, and U.S. Foreign Policy in the Gulf War*. Chicago: University of Chicago, 1994.

Bly, Theresa. *Impact of Public Perception on US National Policy: A Study of Media Influence in Military and Government Decision Making*. Washington, D.C.: Storming Media, 2002.

Boorstin, Daniel J. *The Image: A Guide to Pseudo-Events in America*. New York: Atheneum, 1985.

Burns, Eric. *Infamous Scribblers: The Founding Fathers and the Rowdy Beginnings of American Journalism*. New York: Public Affairs, 2006.

Carson, Clayborne, David Garrow, Bill Kovach, and Carol Polsgrove (advisors). *Reporting Civil Rights: Parts One and Two*. New York: Literary Classics of America, 2003

Cottle, Simon. *News, Public Relations, and Power*. Thousand Oaks, Calif: Sage, 2003.

Emery, Michael, and Edwin Emery, and Nancy L. Roberts. *The Press and America: An Interpretive History of the Mass Media*. 9th ed. Boston: Allyn & Bacon, 2000.

Finley, Ruth E. *The Lady of Godey's: Sarah Josepha Hale*. London: J.B. Lippincott, 1931.

Fleming, Fergus. *The Cuban Missile Crisis: To the Brink of World War III*. Chicago: Reed Publishing, 2001.

Funt, A. *Eavesdropping at Large: Adventures in Human Nature with Candid Mike and Candid Camera*. New York: Vanguard Press, 1952.

Gans, Herbert J. *Deciding What's News*. New York: Vantage, 1980.

213

Gibbs, Nancy, and Michael Duffy. *The Preacher and the Presidents: Billy Graham in the White House.* New York: Center Street, 2007.

Goodman, Matthew. *The Sun and the Moon.* New York: Basic Books, 2008.

Hausman, Carl. *The Decision Making Process in Journalism.* Chicago, Nelson-Hall, 1987.

Head, Sydney W.; Sterling, Christopher H.,; and Schofield, Lemuel. *Broadcasting in America: A Survey of Electronic Media.* 8th ed. Boston: Houghton-Mifflin, 1998.

Hewitt, Don. *Minute by Minute.* New York: Random House, 1985.

Hower, Ralph M. *The History of an Advertising Agency: N.W. Ayer & Son at Work, 1869–1939.* Cambridge: Harvard University Press, 1939.

Jamieson, Kathleen Hall, and Paul Waldman. *The Press Effect: Politicians, Journalists, and the Stories That Shape the Political World.* London: Oxford University Press, 2003.

Kallen, Stuart A. *Benjamin Franklin.* Edina, Minn: ABDO Publishing, 2002.

Kessler, Lauren. *The Dissident Press: Alternative Journalism in American History.* Beverly Hills, Calif.: Sage, 1984.

Kimmel, Daniel. *The Fourth Network: How Fox Broke the Rules and Reinvented Television.* New York: Ivan Dee, 2004.

Lewis, Lisa A. *Gender politics and MTV: Voicing the Difference.* Philadelphia: Temple University Press, 1990.

Lippmann, Walter. *Public Opinion.* New York: Macmillan, 1922.

Lipstadt, Deborah E. *Beyond Belief: The American Press and the Coming of The Holocaust.* New York: Free Press, 1986.

Martin, Ralph G. *Cissy.* New York: Simon & Schuster, 1979.

Morris, Richard B. *The Forging of the Union: 1781–1789.* New York: Harper & Row, 1987.

Mott, Frank Luther. *The History of American Journalism.* New York: Harcourt, 1964.

O'Heffernan, Patrick. *Mass Media and American Foreign Policy.* Westport, CT: Ablex, 1991.

Perlmutter, David. *Photojournalism and Foreign Policy.* Westport, CT: Praeger, 2001.

Pollard, James. *Presidents and the Press.* Washington, D.C.: Public Affairs, 1964.

Potts, Steve. *Benjamin Franklin.* Mankato, Minn: Bridgestone Books, 1996.

Robinson, Piers. *The CNN Effect: The Myth of News Media, Foreign Policy and Intervention.* London: Routledge. 2002.

Ryan, John, and William M. Wentworth. *Media and Society: The Production of Culture in the Mass Media.* Boston: Allyn & Bacon, 1999.

Sloan, William, James G. Stovall, and James D. Startt. *The Media in America.* Worthington, Ohio: Publishing Horizons, 1998.

Snyder, Louis L., and Richard B. Morris. *A Treasury of Great Reporting.* New York: Simon & Schuster, 1962.

Sperber, A. M. *Murrow: His Life and Times.* New York: Bantam Books, 1987.

Starr, Paul. *The Creation of the Media.* New York: Basic Books, 2004.

Steffens, Lincoln. *The Shame of the Cities.* New York: Hill and Wang, 1957.

Stone, Joseph. *Prime Time and Misdemeanors: Investigating the 1950s TV Quiz Show Scandal: A D.A.'s Account*. New Brunswick, N.J.: Rutgers, 1992.

Tebbel, John. *The Media in America*. New York: John Y. Crowell, 1974.

Tyne, Gerald. *Saga of the Vaccum Tube*. New York: Ziff Publishing, 1943.

Vivian, john. *The Media of Mass Communication*. 9th ed. Needham Heights, Mass.: Allyn & Bacon, 2009.

Wilcox, Dennis L., and Glen T. Cameron, *Public Relations Strategies and Tacitcs*. 8th ed. Boston: Allyn & Bacon, 2007.

Willis, Jim. *Reporting on Risks: The Practice and Ethics of Health and Safety Communication*. Westport, Conn.: Praeger, 1997.

Willis, Jim. *The Shadow World: Life between the News Media and Reality*. Westport, CT: Praeger, 1990.

Wolfe, Tom. *The Right Stuff*. New York: Bantam Books, 2001.

Woodward, Bob, and Carl Bernstein. *All the President's Men*. New York: Simon & Schuster, 1994.

Woog, Adam. *Bill Gates*. San Diego: Lucent Books, 1999.

Index

About the Author

Jim Willis is professor and chair of the Department of Communication Studies at Azusa Pacific University, in Southern California. He is the author of 11 books on journalism and the news media and one on the history of the University of Oklahoma football. Prior to entering university teaching, Willis served as a reporter and editor for *The Oklahoman* and *The Dallas Morning News*. He holds the Ph.D. in Journalism from the University of Missouri, an M.A. in Journalism from Texas A&M University in Commerce, and a B.A. in Journalism from the University of Oklahoma. He is married, has two sons and three stepdaughters and lives in the L.A. area.